GOAT IN THE MEZE

Book 1 in the Greek Meze Series

KATERINA NIKOLAS

To my good friend, Brenda Brittan, who had the inspirational idea of turning the old Mercedes car into a taxi, and for first edits.

OTHER BOOKS
IN THE GREEK MEZE SERIES

CHAPTER 1

Quentin and Deirdre Fancy McDonalds

Quentin and Deirdre McCain were definitely in the mood for McDonalds. The early retired American couple had treated themselves for their fortieth wedding anniversary to the economy version of the great European tour. They had done London, Barcelona and Venice in a whirlwind, had their photo taken with a Beefeater and resisted the temptation to go 'full on' Parisian and eat snails in Paris. Poor Quentin had his wallet lifted by a grubby urchin in the Louvre, but luckily all their important papers and credit cards had been stuffed inside Deirdre's ample bra.

Now the couple were enjoying a leisurely drive through the Greek countryside, determined to be photographed with every ruin they passed for posterity. The charm of Greece was slowly seducing them. With nothing pressing to rush back for they were considering extending their stay on the Greek mainland and even perhaps sampling a bit of island hopping.

Oiled out with copious amounts of Greek salad and feta cheese Deirdre was in the mood for a taste of home. "I could murder a McDonalds," she said. "Maybe we'll come across

1

one on this road. Take a left Quentin," she instructed, having taken a wild guess.

The road Quentin took climbed uphill, then uphill some more. It was some time before they realised they were negotiating hazardous hairpin mountain bends. Deirdre was too busy rummaging round in her bra for the last packet of posh Altoids mints to notice. Quentin was stunned by the majestic scenery as the sun set over the sea in the distance.

"We must be nearing the top soon," said Deirdre. "There just has to be a McDonalds at the top. I read about it in the guide book."

"They don't seem to be too big on McDonalds round here," said Quentin. As they neared the top of the mountain a petrol station loomed in the half light and Quentin pulled in. Clutching the guidebook he headed inside, hoping to get directions which would satisfy Deirdre's craving for a big Mac.

Quentin felt a bit stupid when the burly Greek mechanic guffawed loudly and proclaimed "No McDonalds, McTakis. McTakis. Mia ora," helpfully holding up one finger, before adding in broken English "one hour."

He pointed into the distance, indicating they should continue on in the same direction along the now dark mountain road.

Driving off into unchartered territory, Deirdre looked up McTakis in the guide book and discovered the menu bore no relation to McDonalds. What she had thought were onion rings turned out to be circles of fried squid. As hunger pangs set in and their stomachs started to growl they hoped they would at least find a nice friendly taverna offering Greek salad.

Half an hour later their car broke down on the dark

mountain side and their great Greek adventure began.

CHAPTER 2

Adonis to the Rescue

Deirdre sucked the life out of the last Altoid as she watched Quentin furtively emerge from behind an olive tree, zipping his flies up.

"It's all right for you," she complained "but there's no way I'm going behind an olive tree in the dark with all those goats watching. I could really kill a McTakis now. How long have we been stuck here Quentin?

"Two hours. I wonder if that little bump we had on the road had something to do with the car breaking down," he replied. "Someone will have to come along sooner or later. I just hope anyone that stops can speak English."

Right on cue a shiny pick-up truck soared by, then slammed its brakes on and reversed. A Greek Adonis, the very cliché of handsome, wound his window down and said in very heavily accented English "Friends, are yous 'aving the car troubles? Is not a goodly night to be broken down an' out I think, we 'ave the wet rain soon."

As he spoke the heavens opened and torrential rain drenched the hapless Quentin who asked "Is there any chance of finding a car mechanic in these parts? We passed a garage two hours ago."

"No, no," the Greek man said, nodding his head vigorously and clucking his tongue. Is late now my friends, all klisto, 'ow yous say closed. Better I take yous to my village for the night and tomorrow we find my cousin Adonis the mechanic. Come, I take yous now to my village. Yous a safe with my, my name Adonis, everyone know me and love me. I 'ave hotel but it is closed till tourist season. My cousin Yiota she 'ave a rooms over 'er taverna, I take yous there."

The couple exchanged wary looks but couldn't see another option other than sleeping in their broken down car on the dark mountain.

Deirdre's bladder made the decision for them and the two of them piled into the front seat of the pick-up driven by the handsome smiling Greek and prepared to be whisked away to his village. As they settled into the vehicle Adonis asked if they were English or German.

"Ah Americanos," he exclaimed delightedly, shaking their hands enthusiastically. "My cousin Adonis he go to Big Apple and open 'Souvlaki Palace.' Is very goodly, yous know it, yes?"

As the couple introduced themselves, Adonis struggled to pronounce their odd names. Quentin became K-Went-In and Deirdre became Did-Rees. Little did they envisage these botched variants of their names would end up sticking.

CHAPTER 3

A Blood Soaked Bundle

As Adonis sped along at great speed Deirdre clutched her throat in terror at the reckless way he was taking the alarming hairpin bends. She was squashed between the two men and Adonis put a hand on her thigh with a reassuring squeeze and told her he was the best driver for kilometres and not to worry. His other hand was holding a coffee and a cigarette.

The smoke from his cigarette failed to disguise the pungent smell permeating the van, which appeared to come from a bloodstained blanketed bundle thrown on the back seat.

As the Americans began to fear they were in the clutches of a deranged serial killer Adonis explained he'd had the good fortune to run into a bit of 'road kill' just lying unclaimed in the road. The blanket was wrapped around a dead goat to avoid getting blood and gore all over the upholstery.

Adonis voiced his incredulity that some utter fool had obviously engaged in a bit of goat hit and run and not stayed behind to collect his prize. "Maybe if you still in the village tomorrow evening we all a eat goat together," Adonis invited.

"My cousin Yiota do great things with dead goat to make, 'ow you say, tasty."

"Lovely," Quentin managed to say, while hoping with every fibre of his being that the earlier bump they had encountered hadn't been the goat in its live form. He would hate to be an accidental goat murderer. His wish was that tomorrow the car would be repaired in a timely fashion and they would be well away from this chain smoking, wife groping, mad goat eater.

Deirdre hoped she could find a last Altoid to quell the nausea arising from the hurtling speed, the smoke and the overpowering smell of dead goat. The road turned into a steep descent and she was far too frightened to be discreet as she rummaged around in her sizeable bra hoping to find a stray mint. Noticing her fear Adonis offered Deirdre a cigarette and a swig from his hip flask of ouzo. She declined the cigarette politely but was grateful for the numbing sensation the clear fiery liquid induced.

After several more minutes lights appeared in the distance and Adonis announced they had arrived in his village. The van failed to slow as Adonis negotiated the narrow street, lined with stone houses. He eased off the accelerator enough to shout greetings to a number of men seated outside the harbour side kafenion and then pulled into a side street fragrant with salty sea air, jasmine and citrus.

Quentin was most pleasantly surprised at how totally delightful the village appeared in moonlight. Even Deirdre managed to raise a smile as she realised she was about to put two feet on firm ground and leave the dead goat behind.

CHAPTER 4

A Warm Welcome in Astakos

As Quentin and Deirdre drank in the fragrant fresh air outside the taverna their rescuer was busy gesticulating and gabbling in indecipherable Greek with an imposing middle aged woman. Suddenly Deirdre felt herself enveloped in a bear like hug from the woman whom Adonis introduced as his cousin Yiota. "I must a leave now," Adonis exclaimed, pushing the blanket wrapped goat into the hands of his cousin, "but will return in the morning to take you to my cousin Adonis the mechanic."

Yiota showed the Americans to a pleasant room above the taverna, gesticulating to the bathroom to indicate they should wash and then come downstairs to eat. Glass doors opened onto a small balcony where they could see the sea gleaming in the moonlight. The rain had stopped which cheered them no end and they were relieved not to be stranded on the mountain overnight.

They had planned to drive across the Greek mainland and take in the cultural sights of a large town with five star amenities, but decided to make the best of their overnight unscheduled stay in this charming backwater fishing village of Astakos, named for a lobster.

The bathroom was decorated with prominently displayed signs, not only in three languages, but also in pictorial form for the illiterate, instructing not to put toilet paper in the toilet but in the bin provided. Deirdre nearly fainted when she realised the only available shower had no door or curtain and was sited next to the toilet with a convenient drain in the centre of the floor.

Quentin was the first to experiment with the shower and came out clutching a soaking wet toilet roll he had neglected to remove from the direction of the shower spray. The room obviously needed pictorial instructions advising of the danger if toilet rolls were not removed before showering.

Deirdre's stomach once again growled with hunger and she decided to avoid the slippery wet bathroom until after dinner. The pair headed downstairs feeling rather apprehensive at the thought of entering the simple village taverna and put aside all their expectations of dining on McDonalds that night.

CHAPTER 5

Tripe in the Air

The taverna was a family owned business run by Takis and his wife Yiota. It was obviously a popular place as it was full to the gills even though it wasn't yet the tourist season. It was appreciated by the local fishermen as Yiota would cook their fresh catch of the day without complaining. It was a regular meeting spot for the never married and divorced men of the village whose numbers included Toothless Tasos, Gorgeous Yiorgos, Prosperous Pedros, Fat Christos and Tall Thomas, none of whom could produce a passable home cooked meal. Once the season hots up the tourists rather like the simple ambiance of the place and the chance to engage with the interesting local characters.

As Quentin and Deirdre entered the taverna the pungent smell of tripe soup, a traditional hangover cure, pervaded the room. The aroma of tripe competed with the smoke from the grill and the fog of smoke emanating from a dozen smoking fishermen. An ominous silence fell as all eyes were turned to the newcomers, but the chatter resumed as Takis rushed over to usher the pair to a table, brandishing a paper tablecloth over his arm.

No sooner were they seated than Yiota deposited a basket of bread and a jug of red wine on their table. As the wine was poured some of the local fishermen raised their own glasses in a welcome greeting. "That's the ticket, a welcoming place full of character filled locals," said Quentin, raising his own glass in a reciprocal gesture.

Another silence fell over the taverna as a tall blonde woman with a huge, obviously silicone chest, tottered in on sky high stilettos, towering over the small thin elderly gent who followed her in. Deirdre made a mental note that mouths had not gaped open in such amazement when she had made her own entrance, but she could hardly compete in the looks department with this mini-skirted leggy apparition with her long hair extensions and fur coat.

"Greece is so family orientated," mused Quentin. "How lovely it is to see an old grandfather bringing his granddaughter out to dinner."

"That's not his granddaughter," whispered the hovering Yiota. "That's the old fool Vasilis with his mail order bride Masha. He has to bring her out for dinner as she can't cook."

CHAPTER 6

Mail Order Masha and That Old Fool Vasilis

Gold digger Masha had carefully schemed and planned her exit from the impoverished and freezing Russian town of Verkhoyansk. She had various offers from foreign men lusting over her internet profile, but was driven by her hunger for money and sunshine over any considerations of love. That old fool Vasilis was not her first choice, but he was there with an offer of a village house in the sunshine and a substantial bank balance, on the night a pack of super wolves were on the prowl in Verkhoyansk.

Few things in life frightened Masha, but she had always had an obsessive terror of wolves. As the eerie howls of the prowling wolves invaded her senses, Masha's father received the call to go out on wolf patrol on a borrowed snowmobile. The opportunity to flee her strict father and the frozen fog of her penniless home prompted the heartless twenty four year-old Masha to say yes to eighty four year-old Vasilis and his proposal of marriage.

Within the month the aged widower had made an honest woman of Masha in a small wedding ceremony in Athens. As a wedding present he paid for a gaudy and overly large ostentatious diamond ring, a silicone boob job and hair extensions. He considered himself the luckiest man in the world, imagining the envy of all his friends back in Astakos.

His new mail order bride excelled in pouting, looking sexy and spending his money. As for satisfying his carnal desires she had worn him out by the end of their honeymoon. His libido failed to revive on their return to the village, satisfiying Masha perfectly as it gave her more time to concentrate on spending his money, having her nails done and topless sunbathing.

Vasilis was disappointed to discover the extent of Masha's culinary skills was burning borscht and pouring out vodka. She was however very good with a feather duster, kept the floor tiles immaculate, the mirrors polished and never allowed the toilet paper bin to overflow.

They settled into a married life of sorts although the village women never really took to Masha with her unsuitable stilettos, miniskirts, silicone breasts and high maintenance ways. Of course all the men were delighted to cast their eyes over Masha's many physical attributes, but for the sake of a quiet life they agreed with their womenfolk that Vasilis was nothing but an old fool.

CHAPTER 7

Takis Gets Chatty

T here's no fool like an old fool," Yiota said, robustly nudging Deirdre and winking at Quentin. "Three years they've been married and he still 'asn't come to his senses. Mind you she is good for business. He brings her 'ere every night and all these idiot men stopped frequenting the rival taverna of Stavroula so they ogle her."

Masha appeared oblivious to the stares of the roomful of men as she pondered her nail extensions and wondered what colour to paint them next. She was happy to tuck into tripe soup and octopus washed down with vodka as long as Vasili didn't expect her to attempt to recreate the delicious dishes in their kitchen.

Quentin and Deirdre could not be persuaded to partake of tripe soup and ordered a Greek salad and French fries. Yiota said the goat wouldn't be on the menu until the next evening as she still had to scrub the tyre marks off it.

Deirdre opted for beefteki, fancying it was like a Big Mac hamburger, while Quentin made the very adventurous deci- sion to go with octopus. Quentin agreed to swap plates with

14

Deirdre when she complained her beef burger was full of lemon and oregano, leaving her to sample the delights of octopus for the first time.

The rubbery flesh was too much for Deirdre and she surreptitiously wrapped the octopus in a napkin and stuffed it in her handbag. Luckily all eyes were fixated on Masha as she chose that exact moment to flick her hair extensions with wild abandon, arching her back and sending her ample bosom into seeming orbit.

Deirdre had picked all the olives out of the Greek salad with gusto. She was developing quite a love of this local delicacy, which Takis was quick to notice. Deciding to take a well earned break from the grill and practise his English he rushed over with a dish of olives and a bottle of Metaxa brandy, pulled out a chair and joined Quentin and Deirdre.

Deirdre asked Takis if his delightful establishment was the McTakis taverna she had read about in the guidebook, explaining she was quite missing a taste of home in the form of McDonalds. Takis scoffed in derision, proclaiming they'd find "none of that foreign muck 'ere." He and Yiota cooked only good Greek food and their taverna was called 'Mono Ellinka Trofima' meaning 'Only Greek Food'.

Feeling chatty Takis asked the couple about their family in America. He was delighted to discover they had a young grandson, saying, "I am a happy to 'ear there is a little K-Went-In to carry on your name."

"It's Quentin," Quentin automatically corrected before adding "but actually our grandson is called John, not Quentin."

"Why they call him Yiannis and not K-Went-In?" queried Takis. "You must have a fallen out with your family if they not call their son K-Went-In after you. I 'ave four sons and they all a call their sons Panioytis after me."

"But your name is Takis," piped up Deirdre, thinking Takis was losing the plot.

Takis proceeded to explain Takis is short for Panioytis and his four grandsons were proudly named Panioytis, Panioytis, Panioytis and Panioystis. His one granddaughter was named Panioyta after Yiota.

"Doesn't that get rather confusing?" asked Quentin.

CHAPTER 8

What's in a Name?

K-Wents-In and Did-Rees, I knows you foreigns get confused with Greek names as so many of us 'ave the same one, but round 'ere we use lots of nicknames." Takis said.

Pointing at a customer he said, "that there is Toothless Tasos, we call 'im that ever since he lost all 'is teeth."

Quentin, observing Tasos appeared to have plenty of teeth and was at that moment sinking them into a pork chop, said "He seems to have found his teeth now."

Takis told him, "thems is false teeth, but we still calls him 'Toothless.' The name 'as stuck."

"Over there sees that fisherman," he said pointing to a large scruffy man who looked like a walrus with obviously boot polished dyed hair. "That's Yiorgos but we call him 'Gorgeous' on account of he used to look like a Greek god, so 'andsome he was when young."

"Really, that's hard to imagine now," Deirdre commented, trying hard not to stare at the obviously 'gone to seed' fisherman."

"An' that's Tall Thomas," Takis carried on "but he'll always be tall unless he loses 'is head or legs."

"This is all most fascinating Takis," Quentin said, to which Takis replied, "that's another funny thing about Greek names, when yous talk to Greek men yous always takes the S off the end of their names."

CHAPTER 9

The Octopus Blockage

Quentin and Deirdre were having a thoroughly good time in the taverna, enjoying the company of Takis. They were more than a little intrigued to wonder what sort of life Toothless Tasos had led and if it was true that the large badly dressed lump of lard pointed out to them as Yiorgos had indeed ever been 'gorgeous'.

Deirdre excused herself to make a trip to the bathroom, leaving Takis and Quentin to enjoy their three star Metaxa brandy. Her handbag was beginning to stink rather obviously so she took the opportunity to flush the octopus down the toilet. However she neglected to remove the octopus from its paper napkin wrapping and as she flushed she realised she'd caused a blockage in the system by ignoring the pictorial warning not to flush paper down the toilet.

Standing in the puddle of flooded toilet water awash with bits of floating octopus, Deirdre was unsure of the niceties of explaining the situation away. She decided the best thing to do was ignore it and call it a night, hoping no one would realise she was the guilty party. She had not failed to notice the mail order Russian bride Masha had been eating octopus too and may get the blame for the blockage. Dragging Quentin by the arm the pair made a hasty retreat to their upper quarters, pleading exhaustion.

Once they had left they were the talk of the taverna as the remaining customers speculated how long it would take the mechanic Adonis to fix their car. Bets were placed the couple would be stuck in Astakos for a least a fortnight, but they appeared pleasant and harmless so would be made to feel welcome. It was always good to have new blood in the village and the local businesses all benefited from the extra spending power.

Picking up her mop with a scowl and a weary sigh, Yiota headed into the toilet to deal with the blockage, wondering how long it would take the Americans to adjust to the 'no paper' rule.

CHAPTER 10

Unrequited Love in the Moonlight

As Quentin and Deirdre enjoyed a quiet moment on the balcony before bed they noticed a figure lurking below in the moonlight. The stocky man was clutching a bottle and gazing wistfully at the door of a harbour-side house, as though reluctant to knock and make his presence known.

The figure in question was none other than Toothless Tasos. The lovelorn fisherman had spent many a long night gazing at the same house and attempting to pluck up the courage to knock on the door to proffer his token bottle of olive oil as a declaration of his undying love for the goddess of his dreams, Thea. Tonight he felt courageous. After thirty years of unrequited love he could feel his passion about to explode, secure in the knowledge his new set of false teeth made him passably handsome. Tonight was the night and he definitely intended to make his feelings known.

Bracing himself to finally take the plunge and approach Thea's door he noticed the object of his admiration sauntering down the street hand in hand with another man. The other man was none other than that old reprobate Gorgeous Yiorgos. It appeared his rival in fishing was now the rival for the object of his affections.

A single tear coursed down the weather lined face of Toothless Tasos as he realised he had only himself to blame for being tardy in declaring his love to Thea. It seemed he could never find the right time to catch her between husbands. How he wished he had approached her as soon as he'd saved the money to pay for his dental work instead of waiting until the last shiny new tooth was in place.

Thea's reputation was impeccable and she would never conduct a dalliance with a man that did not have honourable intentions of marriage. She had buried three husbands already and Toothless Tasos could not really blame Gorgeous Yiorgos for courting Thea so soon after her third husband's burial, as they both knew she didn't hang around between husbands.

Toothless Tasos watched the couple part at her door in the moonlight and saw Thea accept a bottle of olive oil, a traditional courtship gesture, from Gorgeous Yiorgos. As he walked away in despair he tossed his own bottle of extra virgin over the harbour wall into the sea. He had never been lucky in love.

CHAPTER 11

Unlucky in Love

Toothless Tasos had never been lucky in love, even in the days before he was toothless. He had only ever loved one woman, the beautiful Thea, from afar, but had endured the hideous misfortune of an arranged marriage to the ghastly Stavroula. As a youth Tasos was painfully shy, finding it hard to stand up to the assertive and bossy woman he ended up shackled to.

Every day with Stavroula felt like a life sentence. The only respite he enjoyed was in the solitary hours he spent fishing. He would cast his nets from his boat and instead of returning to shore would spend hours sitting out at sea, imagining his freedom.

The pretty young thing he married seemed to gain fifty kilos on their wedding night and never stopped nagging. Stavroula was an avaricious type with never a good word to say about anyone. She wanted far more than the wages his fishing could provide. She had ambitions to build a modern new house, rather than live in the old fishing cottage Tasos had inherited.

Stavroula, to her credit, was a fine cook and kept a neat home, however her enduring greed nagged him into finding extra work for money to put towards the building work, leaving him permanently exhausted. Still he preferred being exhausted from overwork rather than from attempting to satisfy Stavroula's voracious sexual appetite. He rather suspected his bride was unfaithful, yet only felt sympathy for any unsuspecting men she could lure into her clutches.

Tasos was mentally unfaithful everyday as he fantasised of an alternate life with the goddess of his dreams Thea, a woman he was too shy to even speak to.

Inevitably Thea was wed and Tasos' breaking heart could endure no more. He devised a cunning plan that would allow him to escape Stavroula, yet fulfil her greed for money. He would leave his beloved village of Astakos, the fishing life he adored and any chance he had of catching a glimpse of his love goddess Thea, and take a job far across the sea in Australia. He promised to send Stavroula most of his wages so she could go full speed ahead with her new home building project.

Tasos settled into a new life in Australia, earning a good wage which he sent to Stavroula. He spent his spare time fishing but could never forget the object of his true love, Thea. Every two years he took an extended visit home. Stavroula's new house was completed and now she demanded more money for all her tacky furnishings and her plan to open a taverna. On one of his visits back his heart broke all over again as he and Stavroula attended the nuptials of Thea and her second husband, shortly after she buried the first one.

Back in Australia Tasos had word on the gossip vine that Stavroula was definitely carrying on with a travelling salesman from the north. He sighed with relief at the prospect of getting her off his hands once and for all and put his long devised cunning plan into action. It only took one willing accomplice to send word to Stavroula of his tragic demise at sea as he fiendishly faked his own death, leaving Stavroula a merry widow. He resigned himself to never returning to Astakos but considered it was a price well worth paying to be eternally free of his marital obligations and the financial hold Stavroula would never relinquish through divorce.

CHAPTER 12

Not a Ghost

On the moonlit night when Toothless Tasos tossed his bottle of organic olive oil over the harbour wall he had been back in Astakos nearly a decade, living in his old fishing cottage, leading a very quiet life, fishing and pining over Thea.

When word had reached him in Australia that unbeknownst to her Stavroula had bigamously remarried and moved up north to the village of Pouthena, named for nowhere, with her travelling salesman, Tasos had thought it safe to return to the village if he kept a low profile.

Four years after his return to Astakos Stavroula also returned, telling everyone she had left her second husband Kostas. The rumour mill went into overdrive as word spread like wildfire that her second husband had actually disappeared.

There was a nasty moment when the pair first ran into one another, but with dark secrets of her own to conceal Stavroula went about her business of opening a taverna and left Toothless Tasos well alone after discovering he wasn't actually a ghost.

CHAPTER 13

Coffee with Adonis

The next morning Quentin and Deirdre had only just showered when they heard the toot toot of Adonis's pick-up horn below their balcony. They hurried down to meet him but Adonis was in no rush as he needed his morning coffee. Herding them into Stavroula's taverna he ordered three coffees, explaining his use of the rival shop by saying his cousin Yiota didn't open till lunchtime.

Adonis told them his cousin, Adonis the mechanic, had already towed their broken down car to his garage. He couldn't start the repairs immediately as he had to finish re-pairing the postman's car or no one would have their letters delivered at speed. Petros the postman was reduced to deliv-ering the mail by donkey whilst his car was off the road. He'd been forced to borrow the donkey from that old fool Vasilis and he wasn't sure the donkey was entirely sober as old Vasi-lis liked to share a drop of ouzo with the beast.

Adonis told them not to worry as Yiota had reserved the room for Quentin and Deirdre for the rest of the week so the pair could enjoy the village at leisure and he would join them for tasty goat that evening.

"I think yous killed the goat K-Went-In," Adonis said. "Adonis he say your car 'ave dead goat and blood all over the tyres."

"It's Quentin," Quentin corrected, going a rather white shade of pale, worrying if he could possibly be arrested by the Greek police for killing the goat.

"Is okay," Adonis reassured him "We eat the evidence tonight."

Toothless Tasos' bigamous supposed widow Stavroula arrived with their coffees and Adonis introduced Quentin and Deirdre as "my good friends from America K-Went-In and Did-Rees. They ave the car troubles."

Turning to Quentin he whispered not to mention the goat, explaining, "Stavroula's a jealous busy body. If she know my cousin Yiota 'ave the road kill on her menu she'll cause trouble."

Stavroula flounced off towards her kitchen, kicking the taverna cat Boukali on the way, annoyed that she couldn't understand the English words being spoken. Stopping by the table of Gorgeous Yiorgos who was having his morning coffee laced with a tot of brandy, she told him to try and eavesdrop on Adonis' conversation and report back to her. Gorgeous Yiorgos raised a shaggy eyebrow, well used to Stavroula's bossy ways.

Petros the postman took that moment to arrive on his borrowed donkey, throwing some letters through the open doorway onto a table. As he attempted to reverse the donkey down the taverna steps it left a steaming deposit on the doorstep. Stavroula rushed out from her kitchen screaming "Malaka," and "fool," at Petros, while throwing a large cooking pot at his head.

Petros fell clumsily from the donkey, telling Adonis to make sure his lazy good for nothing cousin Adonis the mechanic got a move on repairing his car as he couldn't get on with this donkey much longer and was tempted to turn it into a stew.

CHAPTER 14

Stavroula Stirs Snails

S tavroula was in a foul mood as she returned to the food she was preparing in the kitchen. She had heard rumours Yiota at the rival taverna was cooking 'road kill' goat tonight which meant there would be a tidy profit to be made from free food. Stavroula wondered if she could pass off the cat Boukali as chicken, but then remembered she had a nice pot full of free snails to cook up she had collected at the weekend. She would concoct a big pot of delicious snail and tomato stew for this evenings offering.

Business could be better and she hoped it would pick up a lot once the tourist season started. She had lost a lot of regular male customers when that old fool Vasilis had married his mail order bride and started taking her to Yiota's for dinner every evening. Stavroula decided she would make friends with Masha in the hopes of attracting her custom and luring her regulars back from the opposition. She smiled at her own clever scheming, bashing cooking pots together noisily as she considered the tribulations she had endured before finally opening her own taverna.

Stavroula recollected the joyous relief she felt on hearing of the death of her first husband Toothless Tasos. Tasos was more of a mouse than a man and she was very glad to keep him at arm's length in Australia while she lived off his money. She used his wages to build a modern house in the village and considered herself a cut above those still living in quaint traditional dwellings.

When travelling salesman Kostas had arrived in Astakos selling his wares she was quick off the mark to sample them personally in her bedroom. Kostas was building up a good business and she considered him a better bet than Tasos in keeping her in the style in which she wished to become accustomed. The announcement of Tasos' disappearance at sea left the coast clear for her to run off with Kostas without giving up half of everything in a messy divorce. Renting out the modern house for a tidy profit she followed Kostas up north where she soon persuaded him to make an honest woman of her.

Stavroula had a smile on her face as she added a generous helping of fresh oregano to the snails in the pot and gave them a vigorous stir.

CHAPTER 15

The Deadly Consequence of Wanting a Divorce

L ike Toothless Tasos before him it didn't take Kostas long to regret tying the knot with Stavroula. She gained another fifty kilos on their wedding night and her avaricious side soon revealed itself as she constantly nagged him to bring home more money. She had the money from her rental house and other undeclared sources of income she was reluctant to talk about, but it was never enough.

Kostas soon discovered Stavroula's almost morbid fear of banks as he caught her squirreling away the money he brought home in cooking pots, under the mattress and in a deep hole under the chicken coop. Like Tasos he rather enjoyed a quiet life but Stavroula's constant nagging drove him to spend more and more time on the road. Kostas had the gift of the gab so requisite in a travelling salesman and as he spent more time away from home his business grew to become very lucrative.

Stavroula always welcomed Kostas home with an excellent home cooked meal and a good time in the bedroom. However her idea of romantic post coital chatter focused on how much money he was earning and how they could increase their growing wealth. Her constant demands wore him down and she sent him back out on the road to earn more money before he'd barely had time to take his boots off.

Inevitably Kostas decided they must divorce though he had trepidations about raising the subject with Stavroula as she could be prone to violence when angered. The first time he brought up the "D word" Stavroula clouted him over the head with a cooking pot, chasing him out of the house before he had time to put his vest on.

Stavroula soon had enough of Kostas raising the "D word" as though it was a perfectly reasonable topic of conversation. She had no intention of giving up half of his worldly goods. His ever increasing income had allowed them to build a brand spanking new house she had filled with her beloved tacky ornaments, but rather than give in to Kostas' demands for a divorce Stavroula devised a cunning plot of her own and with never a hint of conscience set about carrying it out.

One evening Kostas returned home from a weary week on the road, exhausted from selling. He was in no mood for an argument with Stavroula over divorce and just wished for a quiet evening. As Stavroula heard his car pull up she went into full seduction mode, draping her ample figure in a 'come hither' sexy lace negligee. Generously dousing herself with cheap perfume she greeted Kostas at the door with a flurry of sloppy kisses and a big pot of her special homemade chicken soup, liberally laced with the strongest, most deadly, weed killer.

Smiling sweetly she made bedroom eyes and poured Kostas glass after glass of ouzo to disguise the noxious taste of the soup. Stavroula had always been able to make Kostas feel amorous. Standing up to carry her off to the bedroom

Kostas swayed woozily and then collapsed in a dead heap on the floor.

Throwing her raincoat over her negligee Stavroula dragged the lifeless body of Kostas through the back door. She rolled him into the wide trough beneath the chicken coop she'd spent all afternoon preparing, picked up the shovel and threw heaps of soil on top of his frozen, in lechery, face and body. That would teach him to want a divorce and take half of everything that was now hers through murder.

She had a long night ahead as she drove his car away. After pushing it over a mountain top into an overgrown deep ravine she began the long walk home. The next day she would say he was off on the road and then act very worried when he never returned.

CHAPTER 16

Let Dead and Fake Dead Husbands Lie

It didn't take long for Stavroula to grow bored of all the questions asking where Kostas had gone to. She feigned great sadness as she falsely claimed "the malaka has left me." As she'd dealt with all the finances since their wedding the brand spanking new house was in her name only and she decided to sell it; making a tidy profit she could use to open a taverna. The last thing she did before she left the up 'north village' of Pouthena, named for nowhere, was to give the chicken coop a new cement floor.

Stavroula had always hankered after opening a taverna in Astakos as it was becoming popular with tourists, so she returned to her village. The taverna was soon up and running. It was frequented by seasonal tourists who appreciated good Greek home cooking and she soon had a regular evening clientele of local men, until that old fool Vasilis went and married mail order Masha.

Never one to be on her own Stavroula quickly took Slick Socrates, a local lawyer, as her lover. He was the first man she had ever loved with a passion and for some unfathomable reason he loved her too. Socrates put his foot down and refused to let her boss, declaring himself to be the man of the house. Stavroula loved the manly way he stood up to her and the way he shared her ambitions.

The only fly in the ointment was his roving eye, but she was confident that even if Socrates strayed he would always return to her. Not a day went by with Socrates proposing marriage to Stavroula. Eventually she confided in him that her husband Kostas was cemented beneath the chicken coup and she could not marry him without producing a divorce paper from the now dead Kostas.

The first time Stavroula encountered her supposedly dead husband Tasos in the village she was dumbstruck. Tasos was riding his bicycle and wobbled precariously as Stavroula lobbed the onions in her shopping bag hard at him. She was tempted to kill him on the spot but her wide girth prevented her from running as fast as his bicycle, so he made a hasty escape.

Socrates was already waiting at home with some news of his own for Stavroula. As she pleaded with him to sue the lying Tasos for faking his own death Socrates advised her it wasn't really a good idea to draw undue attention to her now bigamous status. She may have been the injured party over Tasos but questions were being asked about the apparent disappearance of Kostas.

Kostas' meddling sister Katerina had returned to the mainland from one of the islands and was nagging the police to investigate his whereabouts. They decided it was best to let dead and fake dead husbands lie rather than draw attention to her murderous ways. Stavroula and Socrates resigned themselves to living in unwedded bliss.

CHAPTER 17

Beauty Parlour Time

S tavroula decided to try and drum up some more trade for the evening and rushed over to the table of Adonis, Quentin and Deirdre with a fake smile of conviviality on her face. Asking Adonis to translate she told the American pair they were very welcome to come and sample her delicious snails later. Suddenly the lure of dead goat appeared inviting in comparison as Deirdre had a lifelong aversion to eating anything slimy that left a mucus trail.

Pleading a prior engagement excused them without the need to express their revulsion at the prospect of snails. Feeling rebuffed Stavroula stormed back to her kitchen where she banged a few pots and then telephoned Socrates and told him to find out what he could about the Americans and if the rumours about Yiota's dead goat were true.

With much 'yassouing' the American pair arranged to meet Adonis later for a goat dinner at the rival taverna. It was a lovely day so they decided to explore the village as they had nothing else to do. Stepping over the donkey deposit on the doorstep they wound their way at a leisurely pace along the harbour-side street, admiring the gentle bobbing of the colourful fishing boats at anchor atop the crystal clear blue water.

They exchanged a pleasant greeting with Toothless Tasos who was sitting outside the harbour-side kafenion playing tavli with Fat Christos. Both fishermen suddenly came to attention, sitting up straight, sucking in their stomachs and adjusting their hair with greasy fingers as they spotted Masha the mail order Russian bride tottering along on her stilettos. With a flick of her long blonde hair extensions she disappeared into the beauty parlour to have her nails done, oblivious to their ogling.

As their most frequent customer Masha was greeted very warmly in the beauty parlour. Taking her seat she complained that old fool Vasilis was missing his donkey since he lent it to Petros the postman. Without his regular drinking partner for company Vasilis had taken to constantly sparring with his old neighbour Sotiris. He was once again threatening to take Sotiris to court over a thirty year dispute over an olive tree whose ownership they both claimed. The disputed tree sat slap on the boundaries of both their land and they had, until now, amicably resolved their argument by each collecting olives from one half of the tree.

Now that Vasilis was feeling belligerent without the company of his donkey, simply named Onos, he had hotly accused Sotiris of taking more than his fair share of olives during the last harvest. He wanted Masha to call into the offices of the lawyer Socrates to start proceedings to sue Sotiris, but she decided to spend the lawyer's fee on getting her nails done instead.

The other women in the beauty parlour listened politely to Masha, while secretly judging her as little better than a trollop. They tolerated her while not really welcoming her into their circle, feeling threatened by her flashy looks and vampish ways. Still Vasilis had always been well respected even if they did now consider he had lost his marbles by taking a bride more than sixty years his junior. Everyone was surprised the marriage had lasted so long. It was now three years since Vasilis had brought mail order Masha home to the village.

CHAPTER 18

Disappearing 'Frillies'

Beauty parlour talk soon turned to the ongoing scandal concerning the disappearance of women's underwear from the village washing lines. Either someone was supplementing their own collection with stolen push-up bras and frilly knickers or there was a deviant pervert on the loose with an unnatural interest in their smalls. In truth only the smalls that are quite ample in proportion are disappearing and the thinner women are spared the indignity of their underwear going astray.

It was no laughing matter as expensive silk lingerie items embellished with the finest lace and perky black and red bows were involved. The women were at first suspicious of the women who only hung large plain serviceable bras and bloomers on their lines, considering perhaps the thief was a jealous type who coveted their more luxuriant underwear.

Masha was a repeat victim of this crime and her bedroom drawers were rapidly being depleted of their finest silk thongs. It was difficult to think of another woman with breasts big enough to fill her bra cups though. The scandal had been going on for some time and they were no nearer to identifying the culprit. They would have called in the services of the Pancratius the village policeman, but he was signed off sick with a bad case of pancreatitis.

Having spied Masha entering the beauty shop Stavroula decided to follow her in and try to befriend her. Stavroula was immediately ruled out by the other women present as the underwear thief as she was notorious for always going braless with her ample breasts jiggling way down past her stomach.

Stavroula was immensely pleased when Masha professed her adoration of delicious snails and promised to try and persuade Vasilis to give up on goat and frequent Stavroula's taverna that evening. Of course she would need to put Socrates in his place and warn him off fixating his roving eyes on this potential new customer with her long blood red finger nails.

Wiggling her fingers in the air to ensure her newly painted nails were dry, Masha declared she was off to top up her tan with a spot of topless sunbathing.

CHAPTER 19

Hideous Old Lady Dresses

I wonder if they sell postcards in here," Deirdre said, dragging Quentin into the local hardware shop. Amidst the eclectic mix of ladders, plant pots, paint, gas bottles and chainsaws, the local hardware shop had a new item on offer which was the talk of the village. Quaintly hanging behind the counter on full display was a blue and black patterned dress as sported by many elderly Greek ladies, most usually complemented by a pair of black pop socks. It is a most unusual item for a hardware shop, most frequently frequented by the male population, to stock.

There is method in Bald Yannis, the shop owner's madness. He was inspired to purchase two hundred of the old lady dresses in memory of his grandmother who sported the unlikely fashion on a daily basis. Indeed, her wardrobe boasted a seemingly endless supply of the identical dresses as evidenced by the great number flapping on the washing line in unison, scaring off the birds.

Bald Yannis was so flushed with success by the sale of his dresses he was thinking of venturing into bras and pop socks.

Yet amazingly not a single woman has purchased a dress from his store. The sales have all been made to the local village men who, transfixed with delight at the sight of the single dress hanging in all its glory, are reminded of their own grandmothers and practically weep in nostalgia.

The village men have been queuing up to buy dresses for their good lady wives and their mothers. The village women are daily receiving presents from their men folk without the excuse of a 'name day' in sight. As they rushed to rip the brown wrapping paper from the unexpected gifts, many of the village ladies felt their hearts sink.

In addition to being shapeless, drab and unflattering, the old fashioned dresses are made from a thick heavy material guaranteed to make the flesh boil and sweat in the Greek summer heat. Yet what Greek woman could deign to insult her godlike male off-spring by voicing her objections to wearing his thoughtful gift with pride? What good Greek wife could show her ingratitude to such a thoughtful husband, even as she covets the latest fashions from Athens? The village ladies dutifully don the dresses which add ten years to their appearance, huddling in small groups to spit and curse at how useless their men folk are.

"Oh, take a look at that hideous dress," Deirdre instructed Quentin as they both clapped eyes on this out of place item. Bald Yannis, who was sitting at his cash register polishing a chainsaw overheard and understood her, and decided then and there to overcharge her if she made any purchases.

"Do you sell postcards?" Deirdre asked him. Bald Yannis decided to amuse himself and pretend to speak only a few words of English. "Postcards," Deirdre enunciated loudly as Bald Yannis held up the shop cat and said "fat cat not for sale." "Not post cat, post cards" Quentin joined in. "Good cat" replied Bald Yannis holding the cat aloft "very tasty."

"Thank you very much, I think we'll leave it for today," Deirdre said, heading towards the door.

"Are you sure I can't tempt you with that hideous dress?" Bald Yannis asked in perfect English, choking on his own laugher.

"That man is stark raving mad," Deirdre declared when they were safely outside. "And did you notice that he had a lace strap sticking out of the top of his tee shirt? It was very obvious against his hairy chest."

"I think that's enough excitement for now." Quentin said, suggesting they retire to their room above the taverna for a siesta.

CHAPTER 20

Slick Socrates Insults Stavroula

Feeling most refreshed after their siesta Quentin and Deirdre decided to pop back to Stavroula's taverna for a late afternoon coffee. Delighted to see the returning customers, Stavroula ushered them to her best table. A rather dapper man in a bow tie and braces was sharing a table with Gorgeous Yiorgos. Stavroula was most eager to introduce the Americans to her live-in-lover lawyer Socrates. However as neither Socrates nor Stavroula could speak more than a handful of words of English the conversation soon dried up.

Socrates told Stavroula he had heard on the village gossip vine that old Mr Antonopoulos up in the mountain village of Katsika, named for a goat, is missing one of his prize goats. "If someone has stolen or killed that goat then Mr Antonopoulos plans to sue them," said Socrates.

"That old malaka should put up proper fences," opined Stavroula, before suddenly catching on this could be the elusive goat possibly in the clutches of her rival Yiota's kitchen.

"Why don't you call in to Yiota's taverna tonight," she suggested to Socrates "and see if there's anything fishy going on." She had yet to tell Socrates mail order Masha and that old fool Vasilis were expected for dinner and would rather keep Socrates well out of the way of the other woman. There was no need to put temptation in the way of his roving eye.

"I hear Adonis is hoping to sell a house to those Americans," Socrates said.

"But they are only 'ere a few days while their car is repaired" Stavroula told him. "As if that will stop Adonis and his machinations" Socrates mused "they'll be here much longer than that if Adonis gets his way. He's desperate to get some property sold before the taxes fall due and we all know what suckers foreigners can be when Adonis turns on the charm."

"By the way my love bunny, I have a gift for you," Socrates suddenly remembered, fishing out a brown paper bag and presenting it to Stavroula.

"You spoil me," Stavroula said, ripping open the bag to discover with horror one of the hideous old lady dresses sold by Bald Yannis at the hardware shop. "Why did you buy me this grotesque skinny woman's dress?" Stavroula cried in disgust.

Stavroula couldn't be bothered to go all the way to the kitchen to get a pot to hit Socrates round the head with so she settled for bashing him with her shoe, to the great amusement of Quentin and Deirdre. "Don't expect me to wear that foul sweat making old rag," screamed Stavroula, "it's only fit for lining the chicken coop with."

Socrates remembered the dire fate of Kostas in the chicken coop and apologised profusely for insulting his beloved, promising to buy her something special from the jewellery shop instead.

CHAPTER 21

The Papas Plays Footsie

S
tavroula blushed a bright shade of red as the local
Pappas entered the taverna carrying a briefcase. She
was embarrassed he may have seen her bashing Socrates about the head as she always tried to make a good impression around the local priest. If the Pappas knew Socrates
had been calling at his house to visit his wife Petula he would
have encouraged Stavroula to hit him some more.

Taking a seat the Pappas ordered a large whiskey. He was
feeling out of sorts, overheated and had money worries. His
long black clerical dress and chimney pot hat were too hot for
this weather and it wasn't even summer yet. Some idiot malaka had put a condom in the church collection box and his
wife Petula was demanding driving lessons. He nodded politely at Quentin and Deirdre, thinking to himself what a
handsome woman the American lady was.

He cheered up at the thought perhaps he could persuade
Stavroula to purchase some of the discounted fake silver cutlery he had in his briefcase. With a flourish the Pappas displayed his silverware. This greatly amused Quentin and

Deirdre who never expected a man of the church to be flogging cutlery from a briefcase.

Stavroula felt obliged to support the Pappas and bargained him down from his original price for six fake silver teaspoons. Meanwhile Gorgeous Yiorgos made a hasty exit from the taverna, overcome with guilt that he had been meeting the Pappas's wife Petula while the Pappas had been conducting his services. He hoped that the lovely Thea didn't get word of his dalliance with Petula and get the wrong idea before he had a chance to explain about the driving lessons.

Slick Socrates had also been calling on Petula, not to woo her but because he felt sorry for her. He was painfully aware though that if Stavroula ever found out his life wouldn't be worth living.

Noticing the American woman kept glancing at his briefcase the Pappas took a seat next to her, all the better to impress her with his fake wares. At first Deirdre thought nothing of it as the Pappas' foot brushed up against her leg. Edging her leg away discreetly she recoiled in horror when his persistent foot followed. Grabbing Quentin by the arm she made a quick exit, exclaiming "I do believe that horrible little priest with the briefcase was trying to touch me up with his foot from underneath his dress."

CHAPTER 22

How Tasos Lost his Teeth

As Quentin and Deirdre headed back to their room above the taverna they crossed paths with a rather miserable looking Toothless Tasos. He was still feeling lovelorn from the previous night and was really regretting he had waited for all his new teeth before attempting to court the goddess Thea.

Toothless Tasos arrived at his fishing cottage which boasted few home improvements since he first inherited it many years ago. A large cooking pot was strategically placed to catch any drips from the leaking roof. His few pathetic attempts at home decoration were limited to several wall mounted stuffed fish noses he had decapitated from his best swordfish catches. They left a lingering aroma of dead fish in the air.

A solitary deckchair was sited beneath the large wall-mounted television in the living room, but Tasos' electrical knowledge was so abysmal he had never been able to get a clear picture. Still he spent many an hour in his deckchair watching Greek soap operas. His secret addiction was watching re-runs of 'Seven Deadly Mothers-in-Law'.

Toothless Tasos threw himself into the deckchair to contemplate life. He often dwelled on the night he had lost his teeth, blaming the encounter with a belligerent seal for sealing his fate. He had been drifting at sea after pulling in his nets in an effort to avoid the nagging company of Stavroula. He cursed the stupidity that prevented him returning to shore with his catch rather than falling asleep in the boat.

Tasos had been dead to the world when a sharp jolt shook his boat, waking him from his deep sleep in time to see an enormous seal stealing the fish he had caught. Imagining Stavroula's wrath if he returned home with no fish to sell he engaged in a ridiculous fist fight with the seal and came off worse. The seal knocked him hard into the rudder, loosening his teeth which fell out with a sickening crunch. Before he had a chance to retrieve them the seal swallowed them.

The cost of his move to Australia which soon followed left him short of the necessary funds for the dental work needed. He remained toothless and over time he got used to eating pureed souvlaki and gyros. It was only when he returned to Astakos he was able to start saving up for false teeth as he no longer had to finance Stavroula's grasping ways.

Tasos had just had the last new tooth fitted when he heard the news that once again Thea was a widow. He thought his happiness was complete as he attended the funeral. Not only was he rid of Stavroula, but the lovely Thea was now a free woman. It was however a completely inappropriate moment to display his new treasures in a beaming smile directed at Thea over the coffin of her dead husband and he understood his faux pas immediately.

He decided to give it another two weeks before approaching the widow. Sadly it appeared it was now too late and he kicked himself for smiling at the funeral. Ironically it was the first time he had smiled in years.

CHAPTER 23

Goat on the Menu

Those church bells don't half make a terrible din," complained Deirdre, looking for something suitable to wear for the goat feast ahead.

"I can't persuade you to attend a quick service then?" Quentin said with a twinkle in his eye as the fresh sea air of Astakos was agreeing with him very nicely. "Goodness no I've had quite enough of that ghastly little Pappas and his wandering foot for one day," Deirdre replied.

Over at the church the Pappas was delighted to discover someone had left a fish in the collection box. He would take the fish home for Petula to cook. It was a definite improvement over the condom someone had left earlier. He had angered the village women by giving it to the children to play with as he mistakenly thought it was a balloon.

The evening service had failed to attract anyone yet again. The Pappas hadn't had a good turn out since the funeral for Thea's third husband. He secretly hoped there would be another coffin in pride of place very soon so he could welcome a full congregation. The Pappas decided to take a quick swig of Holy wine and then close up early. As he reached for the bottle he realised it was almost empty. Throwing the fish in his briefcase the Pappas headed to Yiota's taverna to purchase another bottle to replenish the church stock of wine.

Quentin and Deirdre were already seated in the taverna waiting for Adonis to join them when the Pappas entered. Noticing he only stopped long enough to buy a bottle of wine Deirdre voiced her suspicions aloud that perhaps the Pappas had a drinking problem. "Oh look Quentin that strange priest has got a fish in his briefcase," she said, as the Pappas opened his bag to accommodate the bottle. "I think we should avoid his church unless it is of special historical interest."

The Pappas cursed under his breath as he passed Adonis entering as he was leaving. The two men were not friends as Adonis thought the Pappas treated his wife Petula, who just happened to be Adonis' cousin, badly, always refusing to pay for her driving lessons. He further suspected the Pappas of being a bit free with his fists when in his cups, which was often.

Adonis was delighted to see his new American friends and joined them saying "Yiota telephoned to say she 'as done the tasty things to the goat so I 'opes yous are very 'ungry my friends."

"Well it certainly sounds better than Stavroula's snails," Quentin quipped.

Yiota had spent all morning scrubbing the tyre marks off the goat then rubbing it with copious amounts of oregano and lemon before handing it over to Takis to put on the spit. It was cooked to perfection and Yiota emerged from the kitchen carrying huge platters of the succulent meat to every table.

The tempting prospect of spit cooked goat had attracted many customers to the taverna. Gorgeous Yiorgos was arguing loudly about fishing methods with Fat Christos and another fisherman known as Prosperous Pedros. Gorgeous Yiorgos rubbed his hands with glee at the sight of the succulent goat, but Prosperous Pedros declined his plate, announcing he was a vegetarian. "Oh not this nonsense again," said Yiota, "you know as well as I do Pedro that goat is a vegetable."

CHAPTER 24

Of Course Goat is a Vegetable

Prosperous Pedros was a 'sometime' vegetarian. His rejection of meat was a recent thing that was a constant source of amusement throughout the village. He was a fine looking man who took himself seriously and favoured the simple life over worldly possessions. Noticing the beginnings of a gut that had the potential to grow into the style of the ten-month pregnant belly sported by many of the village men of a certain age, Pedros was determined to give up anything that could potentially turn him fat.

Most of the village men of a certain age carried way too much blubber for their health. Their wobbling overhanging bellies were a ghastly sight in the summer when they stripped off their shirts. Prosperous Pedros noticed things had got much worse since there was so much publicity about the health benefits of the Mediterranean Greek diet. It seemed the men had decided to pick all their favourite Greek dishes with no thought to their calorific or fat content and eat extra portions of everything, washing it all down with the line "this is the healthiest diet in the world, even the BBC says so."

Pedros realised it was true the Greek diet of olives, olive oil and fresh vegetables was indeed very healthy, but the healthy label could not really be applied to massive portions of souvlaki, gyros and cheese pies. He would rather give up meat and turn vegetarian than go on a diet or exercise.

Vegetarianism was an alien concept in the kitchens of Astakos. While it is true the village diet was rich in fresh fish, fruit and vegetables the villagers rejected the notion of vegetarianism as not normal. If anyone ordered a meatless meal they were encouraged to have some meat on it while being assured the dish would still be vegetarian.

As Prosperous Pedros was partial to chicken he allowed the villagers, after much heated debate, to persuade him that chicken was technically a vegetable. When he was in the mood for lamb one night Yiota managed to persuade his impressionably warped mind that lamb was also a vegetable. No one could persuade him though that souvlaki was a vegetable as he often watched Fat Christos devour six portions of the skewered meat and then loosen, with greasy fingers, the buttons that strained against his stomach.

"Of course goat is a vegetable," Yiota told Prosperous Pedros "it's from the same family as lamb. Any self respecting vegetarian would be happy to eat goat and this one is particularly tasty."

Prosperous Pedros pondered the dilemma he faced. The goat looked very tempting but he wasn't convinced it was really a vegetable and he had been looking forward to a nice plate of wild green horta with a drizzle of fresh lemon instead.

Yiota drew the American pair into the ensuing debate, asking them to confirm that in America a goat was a vegetable. "Goat isn't a vegetable," declared Deirdre with confidence, "vegetables grow in the ground and need watering, they don't gambol around on hillsides looking cute."

Yiota wasn't convinced by this argument; pointing out if it was true then chickens would not be vegetables. "Well they aren't," said Quentin to the amusement of the whole taverna that had collectively convinced themselves chickens were most definitely vegetables.

Prosperous Pedros' dilemma was resolved by Yiota who told him to eat the goat quickly as it was evidence of road kill which must be hidden before the lawyer Socrates arrived. She had just had a phone call to say Socrates was on his way to snoop around on the instructions of Stavroula and find out if the goat was the missing one belonging to Mr Antonopoulos from the mountain village of Katsika.

Pedros agreed they would argue about the origins of goat as meat or vegetable another time and tucked into his plateful of goat with obvious relish.

By the time Socrates made his entrance every table in the taverna had only empty plates and all the evidence had been eaten. "You were very lucky to get away with goat murder my good friend K-Went-In," said Adonis, absolving himself of all responsibility for driving away with the road kill. "Socrates could have made a bigly fortune suing you."

Realising he'd had a lucky escape Quentin ordered another jug of wine to be sent over to Prosperous Pedros as a thank you for disposing of the last bit of goatly evidence.

CHAPTER 25

Socrates is Sent Out Snooping

It seemed to Socrates that Stavroula was in almost indecent haste to send him away from the taverna and out on his snooping over the possibility of abducted goat mission. She didn't even serve him up a plate of snail stew which was one of his favourites, so desperate was she to remove him from the premises before mail order Masha and that old fool Vasilis turned up. Usually Stavroula disapproved vocally of Socrates frequenting the rival taverna, even though he and Takis were great friends of old.

Spotting the hardware shop was still open Socrates decided to call in and demand his money back for the hideous old lady dress he had purchased there and which Stavroula hated. He realised he may have to get all 'lawyerly' with Bald Yannis, the hardware shop owner, as each man shared a mutual antipathy towards the other. Bald Yannis had a reputation for being a bit mad and openly insulting his customers. At least Stavroula only referred to her customers as malakas behind their backs and not to their faces.

Bald Yannis was sitting behind his cash register, furtively

thumbing through the pages of a women's underwear catalogue, as Socrates entered. Hurriedly shoving it under the counter, Bald Yannis picked up a chainsaw in a threatening manner at the sight of Socrates fingering his irritating komboloi worry beads, something Bald Yannis considered a great affectation.

"Yassou Yanni," Socrates said. "I want my money back for this hideous dress as it too small for Stavroula."

"Po po," tutted Bald Yannis in reply, "that's the largest size I stock. Stavroula must be a bit of a heifer if she can't squeeze into it." Pointing to a prominently displayed sign on the wall which read 'No refunds and no credit: the war is over,' Bald Yannis said "use your 'lawyerly' skills to read that and put it in your pipe and smoke it, malaka. No money back for that perfectly lovely dress." With that he pulled the chain on the chainsaw while laughing manically.

Making a quick exit Socrates threatened "you've not heard the last of this," shamefacedly tripping over the hardware shop cat on his way.

Hearing the church bells ringing in the distance Socrates decided to make an impromptu visit to Petula, the Pappas's wife. She would be sure to appreciate the thoughtful gift of an old lady dress as the priest was very tight with his money and considered new clothes an excessive luxury.

Petula was busy pickling stifado onions when Socrates arrived unannounced at her kitchen door. Her heart sank at the sight of this unwanted visitor, worried he may notice the painful black eye she was doing her best to conceal. She was far too polite to show her true feelings so invited him in and poured him a glass of ouzo, saying "the Pappas will be home any minute you know and won't be best pleased to find you here drinking his ouzo."

"But my cherub, I have brought you a gift," said Socrates, presenting the dress to her with a flourish. Petula melted a little inside at the considerate gesture. It was so long since the Pappas had given her anything apart from the back of his fist. The dress delighted her , being so lovely and just her size. The Pappas never noticed what she wore and wouldn't realise she had received something new so it seemed safe to accept the thoughtful gift.

Socrates had of course noticed Petula's black eye but spared her embarrassment by not mentioning it. He suspected the Pappas had been a bit free with his fists. Not wanting to land her in more hot water he knocked back his ouzo and stood up to leave, feeling sorry for Petula and the miserable life the Pappas made her endure.

It was time someone stood up to the Pappas, but if the Pappas knew that people knew he knocked Petula around he may well make her life even more difficult. It was a delicate situation which Socrates dwelled on as he made his departure, turning his footsteps in the direction of 'Mono Ellinika Trofima.'

CHAPTER 26

A Festive Mood in the Taverna

Still fretting over Petula's black eye Socrates arrived at the rival taverna and was greeted with delight by his good friend Takis. He confessed Stavroula has thrown him out by the ear, not wanting him tempted by the voluptuous silicone charms of mail order Masha. Takis was most surprised to hear Stavroula was the jealous type, but then again Socrates had quite a reputation as a ladies' man.

Yiota acted completely surprised when Socrates asked for a plate of goat, telling him "goat's out of season," and offering him the night's special of a scrumptious dish spinach and black eyed beans. "Yous can 'ave some keftedes on the side if the spinach dish is too vegetarian for yous liking."

Socrates was quite relieved that his good friend Takis was not after all involved in the mysterious case of the disappearing goat as he didn't enjoy taking his good friends to court. As a bonus Yiota's keftedes were definitely worth giving up snails for.

Takis confided in Socrates the American visitors had laughingly expected him to cook up some foreign McDonalds muck. Socrates knew this little gem of gossip would make Stavroula happy as she would be willing to cook McDonalds, whatever it was, to lure the Americans to her taverna.

Meanwhile Adonis was making plans to take Quentin and Deirdre out to show them the sights the next day. He planned to woo the pair with his charms during a scenic drive and then surprise them with a viewing of a local house he was trying to sell for a large commission. The fact they had no intentions of buying a house in the village was a moot point as he could be incredibly persuasive, as other impressionable foreigners had discovered.

A silence fell over the taverna when Masha the mail order bride entered, followed by that old food Vasilis. All the men had missed Masha's presence that evening and were most delighted she had made an appearance at this late hour, even if she did usually ignore them. Stomachs were sucked in and mouths gaped open as Masha removed her fur coat to reveal a tarty little number, leaving little to the imagination.

Masha ordered a large glass of vodka while complaining to Yiota she had made a mistake by dining at Stavroula's taverna. She suspected the bossy woman has poisoned them with stale snails as the dish had been quite offensively malodorous. Yiota was most flattered to be told by Masha that she was a far superior cook to Stavroula.

Vasilis was very happy to have the chance to bend Socrates' ear about the latest olive tree feud with his old neighbour Sotiris. Socrates promised to pay a personal visit to the olive tree the next morning and would bring his tape measure along to ascertain the exact dimensions of the disputed border. Masha felt no guilt at all she had already spent the lawyer's fee on her blood red nail extensions.

Socrates had a quiet word with Adonis, relaying his concern he had spotted Adonis' cousin Petula with a bit of a shiner of a black eye. He discreetly didn't mention he had called at the house. "If that malaka the Pappas has been beating my cousin a curse on his 'ouse," said Adonis, promising to call round and get to the bottom of it all.

"He can't even stay sober through his services anymore," Adonis said, reflecting the Pappas often appeared to be drunk and bad tempered, a dangerous combination in his opinion.

The mood in the taverna was festive as everyone apart from Socrates, Masha and Vasilis had dined very well on the tasty road kill goat. Drinks were flowing freely and the conversation was lively as everyone shouted across the tables. Quentin and Deirdre were feeling remarkably at home, enjoying every moment of the most excellent company and looking forward to a trip out with Adonis the following day.

Prosperous Pedros stood up to go, pondering on the likelihood of running into the Pappas lurking by the harbour. He was convinced the sight of the Pappas was a bad omen for the night's catch even though the moonless night sky was a good sign for fishing. Everyone was sad to see popular Prosperous Pedros take his leave. "He go to the fishing now," explained Adonis. "He fish at the midnight as he 'ave no woman to go home to."

CHAPTER 27

The Pappas' Fishing Curse

Prosperous Pedros, the 'sometime' vegetarian, had suffered a dismal time fishing recently. On top of the full moon which stops the fish from biting he'd had the misfortune to entangle his lines in Toothless Tasos' nets, leading to many wasted hours laboriously untangling his lines. His catch was so poor it was a waste of time putting the boat out to sea, not to mention the cost of the diesel and bait. Now his luck had precipitously changed and he was catching far more fish than any of his fishing rivals.

Apparently this change of fortune is all down to him passing the Pappas in the harbour as he returned from a poor night's fishing. He convinced himself the sight of the Pappas was a good omen as immediately his luck changed.

On the flip side Prosperous Pedros ended up superstitiously convinced if he passes the Pappas in the harbour after a good night's fishing his good fortune will be immediately reversed, a syndrome he has named the 'Pappas' fishing curse'. He must now be extremely careful there are no priests hanging around before legging it back to dry land with his bounty of fish.

A good catch is all about bragging rights for Prosperous Pedros. Although he splits his time between olive farming in the winter and fishing after springtime he does it for pleasure rather than for any need to increase his bank balance. His wise father made some excellent investments in land and property after the war, which fell into Pedros' lap as a sizeable inheritance.

Despite his wealth Pedros is not at all flashy, preferring to live a simple life in a little stone cottage with an outside bathroom. His old pick-up truck is precariously held together with tape and his fishing boat is an old weatherworn wooden type rather than the modern plastic variety. He likes to spend his days studying the many historical books his father collected and he has an unnatural fear of leaving the confines of the village.

He is only comfortable around those he knows well, accounting for his habit of spending every single evening in the same taverna. His idea of social hell is to have to drive over the mountains into town and conduct any business in stores with strange staff.

On his last visit to town four years ago he was mortified at the thought of entering a clothes shop and dealing with a strange woman. He finally plucked up the courage to call out his needs from the entrance, returning home with two new pullovers and some work trousers he hadn't tried on. Ever resourceful he is contemplating taking up knitting so as to avoid a repeat visit when his pullovers become threadbare and need replacing.

Prosperous Pedros uses the excuse of the old crone of his widowed mother to avoid leaving the village. He keeps her in a separate house in the neighbouring village of Rapanaki, named for a radish, calling in dutifully every evening to check on her needs. His mother Fotini is a nagging shrew with not an ounce of natural motherly love for her dutiful son. She is a tiny woman rattling round in a large house she rarely leaves, constantly expecting her son to be at her beck and call. Her nasty nature has permanently alienated the good folks of the village whose patience has worn thin from her endless insults.

Prosperous Pedros gets worn down by her demanding phone calls as she telephones at the oddest of hours, instructing him to come round and change a light bulb or oil a squeaky door. She continually expects him to call in the village shop to purchase chocolates and sweets to satisfy her voraciously sweet tooth, and to collect her numerous prescriptions from the pharmacy.

He attempts to limit his visits to once a day, calling in on his way to the taverna in the evening. Although he has repeatedly told her not to cook for him she always has a meal prepared that she expects him to eat. He dutifully consumes it before leaving to eat another one at the taverna.

He finds the convivial company there relaxes him after the daily ordeal of dealing with his formidable mother. It is no wonder he has remained single all his life as he was a first hand witness to the way his mother's nagging made his docile father's life a living hell.

CHAPTER 28

The Outside Bathroom

When Prosperous Pedros' father first purchased the tiny stone fishing cottage by the sea, which Prosperous Pedros now lives in, he envisioned it as a bolthole to escape from his demanding wife. He filled it with his musty history books and enjoyed many a solitary hour living in the past.

One of the great ironies of modern Greek history is the military junta, who came to power in 1967, and were generally despised as a cruel dictatorship, did introduce one thing to rural Greece which was a welcome change. The junta decreed every home had the right to have a bathroom. This may strike some as a contradictory communist notion for a military power to come up with. The truth is quite a few people were suspect of this generous offer, because not only were the junta decreeing bathroom rights for all, they were paying for them too.

Now when a house has never had a bathroom the natural thing for the rural peasant of that time was to build an outdoor bathroom. Some built them onto the sides of their houses with outside access and many old village houses still feature this style.

Others didn't quite understand the concept so well and simply installed a modern toilet in the garden with a wooden surround. Prosperous Pedros' father originally planned to have his new outside loo adjoining the cottage but the neighbour's wife complained it would spoil the view from her kitchen window.

Not wanting to become embroiled in a lifelong feud with the neighbour, a common Greek occurrence, Pedros' father complied and moved the position of the toilet a good few hundred meters away, ensuring a muddy tramp across water-logged ground in winter to reach the facilities.

Most excellent work was done within the small confines of the four walls. An uneven concrete floor was laid but never tiled, nails were inserted into the walls for handily hanging clothes on while showering, and a hosepipe was connected to a water barrel on the roof, allowing cold showers. No light was installed as electricity hadn't reached the rural out-reaches then.

Despite having the financial means to improve the bath-room situation Prosperous Pedros was quite content to leave things as they were. He tramped across the garden to shower with the cold water hosepipe and carried a new fangled torch if he needed a light.

Ten years ago the unexpected happened and Prosperous Pedros met a woman and fell madly in love. His friends convinced him no matter however much the woman loved him no modern woman in her right mind was going to be satisfied with an outside toilet with a hosepipe as a place to do her ablutions. The very idea was absurd.

In the first flush of love Prosperous Pedros rushed out

and purchased a modern spray head shower attached to a water cistern, which he balanced on the toilet roof in lieu of the barrel. He even connected the shower to the electric system to heat the water. There was no getting round the fact the shower was still practically on top of the toilet, as space was at a premium.

Instead of his thoughtful efforts being received with gratitude the woman was not amused. Pedros expected her to cross the soggy land in public view, stand on a wet and ant ridden concrete floor, disrobe and hang her clothes on the by now rusted nails, to shower. A howling draught came under the door along with the insects.

Her disappointment was evident and it was clear she would settle for nothing less than an inside bathroom, rather than one on public display. Having known nothing better himself Pedros considered her ungrateful.

The final straw was reached when one day the woman had no choice but to partake of the toilet facility and entered only to burst in upon a pig. It was too much. No woman should be expected to share her bathroom facilities with a pig, when the goat and wandering cows had been bad enough. She had no choice but to leave him.

She soon met another man who could offer her the luxury of an inside bathroom. One day after showering in the new man's bathroom she slipped on the wet tiles, banged her head on the marble washbasin and bled to death on the bathroom floor. As Prosperous Pedros expected to remain single he never bothered installing an indoor bathroom.

CHAPTER 29

Olives Aren't Eatable from the Tree

I t's so nice of you to take us out for a scenic drive," Deirdre said to Adonis as they enjoyed a morning coffee in Stavroula's taverna before setting off on their journey.

"This is what the good friends do," Adonis replied. "When I visit your country you take me all round Big Apple."

"We don't live in New York," said Quentin "we come from Idaho."

"Is all fine," said Adonis, "you can take me round yous potatoes."

Stavroula appeared table side, asking Adonis to tell the American pair she was preparing a special meal of homemade McDonalds for them that evening. Socrates had told her they were craving this strange foreign food and she had instructed him to find out what it was so she could use her culinary skills to replicate it.

"What a treat to look forward to," Deirdre said, though in truth she wasn't craving it as much anymore and was really developing a taste for the delicious Greek food. Last night's goat had been first rate, tasting just like the finest lamb.

"Let us be on our way," Adonis said, leading the way out to his pick-up truck. Roaring off through the village they narrowly avoided knocking Petros the postman off his borrowed donkey.

Driving along the coastal road Deirdre caught a glimpse of Prosperous Pedros crossing his garden wrapped in nothing but a towel. "Ah that Pedros he live in the past like a peasant with the outdoor bathroom," said Adonis. "I 'ave very modern 'otel, but is closed now as I 'ave the builder in nailing up shower curtains in the bathrooms. We open soon and if yous still 'ere you can move in instead of staying over Yiota's, no?"

"No," agreed Quentin "the car will be fixed soon and then we will be off on the rest of our Grand European tour. Mind you we do like it here very much, the pace of life is so relaxing and everyone is very friendly and welcoming."

"Well apart from Bald Yannis at the hardware store," said Deirdre "I think he tried to sell us a cat to cook."

"Bald Yannis is bigly malaka," agreed Adonis, pointing out things of interest they were passing. The sea lined one side of the road and the other side was dotted with row upon row of olive trees below the undulating hills. His habit of taking his hands of the steering wheel to make the sign of the cross as they passed every roadside shrine unnerved Deirdre, but he squeezed her thigh and told her not to worry while offering her a sip from his hip flask.

"Come I a show you one of my fields. These olive trees are so old they is almost Greek ruins," Adonis laughed as he pointed out the difference between the trees which produced olives for olive oil and olives for eating. "Before the olive 'arvest these trees are a laden with fruits, but now they is empty."

Deirdre took one of the few olives left on a tree and tried

it as she loved olives. Her face puckered up in disgust at the bitter taste and Adonis told her "Did-Rees no eat olives straight from tree, they need a lot of work to make 'em eatable. Come my friends we 'ave time to take tour of old olive press before we stop for eating lunch."

CHAPTER 30

Bartering the Doctor's Bill

As Adonis, Quentin and Deirdre were off on their jollies it was business as usual back in Astakos. At Stavroula's taverna Gorgeous Yiorgos tried to explain what a McDonalds was as he had seen one of those fast food junk food shops on a trip to Athens. Stavroula bribed him with the offer of a free brandy laced coffee to head off on his moped to the nearest supermarket to see if he could find anything resembling processed junk food. He returned with a packet of frozen octopus which was of no utter use at all.

Stavroula confided her dilemma to her neighbour old Mrs Kolokotronis who said she had just the thing in her own freezer, a special treat she kept for when her young grandson visited from Athens. Stavroula was quite ecstatic with relief as she exchanged the frozen octopus with Mrs Kolokotronis' mystery parcel, asking Gorgeous Yiorgos to translate the English printed cooking instructions.

The pharmacist Vangelis came in for a quick gossip as everyone liked to discuss the ailments of his customers. Vangelis had never quite grasped the idea of 'confidential' and happily gave away the secrets of the various symptoms the locals were suffering from. Everyone soon knew the old fool Vasilis had been in with a prescription for Viagra and that Bald Yannis from the hardware shop was trying out a new hair growing remedy to try and fix his baldness. He even revealed the American woman Did-Rees had been in for a packet of travel sickness pills before she would get back in the car with Adonis.

Fat Christos waved as he walked past clutching a large bag of spinach pies from the bakery. He was on his way to a doctor's appointment as he was suffering from a nasty case of recurring indigestion. Fat Christos was the rather reluctant suitor of Tassia. He had been courting her for the last fourteen years, but was in no hurry to marry as he still lived at home with his indulgent mother, Stavroula's neighbour Mrs Kolokotronis, even though he had just celebrated his fiftieth birthday.

Tassia was no oil painting, nor had she mastered the domestic goddess routine. She had rather a reputation for keeping a dirty house. She owned her own house following the death of her father and she stood to inherit her uncle's supermarket, which was her main attraction to Fat Christos.

Fat Christos was quite lazy and liked being looked after by his mother who was pathetically indulgent of her only boy's every wish. She still chose all his clothes and made appointments for his regular haircuts at the beauty parlour. He had never needed to learn how to sweep and mop a floor, make a bed, cook a meal or do his own laundry. In return the income from his fishing supplemented her meagre pension. The only way he could afford to marry Tassia was if she kept him, but he was doubtful she would look after him as well as his mother did.

Entering the doctor's waiting room Fat Christos greeted Bald Yannis who was scratching a rather revolting red rash on his bald head. He'd had a nasty allergic reaction to the specially patented bald remedy sold to him by Vangelis the chemist. Bald Yannis was hoping the doctor would accept a credit note to his hardware store in lieu of a cash payment for his treatment, while Fat Christos hoped to settle his own bill with the freshly caught octopus he had secreted about his person.

CHAPTER 31

The Lemoni Spiti

After a lovely drive through the Greek countryside and a quick tour of an old olive mill Adonis pulled into the small fishing village of Gavros, named for anchovies, for a late lunch. "Before the road he come the only way to get here from Astakos was by boat or donkey," Adonis mused. "It would have taken all day, but see 'ow quickly my pick-up got us 'ere."

"It is such a beautiful spot," said Deirdre, tucking into olives, a freshly made white bean fasolada soup and fried anchovies. "It seems a very quaint custom to name all the villages after fish or vegetables."

"Don't forget animals," Quentin added, remembering that the road kill goat had disappeared from the village of Katsiki.

"We also 'ave the onion, cabbage, leek and lettuce villages nearby," Adonis told them. "I think they 'ave 'ow you say the character. In your country you just call everything new, with your New York, New Jersey, New England. 'Ere in Greece everything is old and ruined. After lunch I take you to very special ruin yous will love."

Quentin and Deirdre loved pottering about in Greek ruins and ancient sites. They hoped the ruin Adonis promised would be an amphitheatre or a temple of historical interest.

Two hours later they were most surprised when they pulled up outside an old village house with an overgrown garden in Rapanaki, the neighbouring village to Astakos.

"See this beautiful ruin," beamed Adonis "it 'as everything you need with a three bedrooms, kitchen and even the inside bathroom. Over the wall you 'ave a nice quiet old lady Fotini, in fact she is mother to Prosperous Pedros. She won't a keep you up all night with noisy wild parties. Garden is bigly and 'as lots of lemon trees, but you could chainsaw 'em down and put in a swimming pool. This 'ouse is a bargain, what you call a steal."

"But we don't want to buy a house," Quentin said.

"Nonsense," Adonis replied "everyone loves to 'ave Greek 'ouse to call 'ome. This 'ouse very special and called 'Lemoni Spiti.' With a bit of imagination this 'ouse be most impressive."

A thin old lady clad from head to foot in black was perched precariously atop a three-legged wooden olive tree ladder, peering over the wall with a scowl on her face. She hissed at Adonis "what you doing here you malaka Adoni?"

"I am a showing K-Went-In and Did-Rees from America this 'ouse," Adonis told her "maybe they will be yous new neighbours."

Fotini dashed indoors with remarkable speed to telephone her son Prosperous Pedros, telling him to come and remove the foreign intruders. She cursed and spat in annoyance when he did not answer his phone.

"Well we may as well take a look as we're here," Quentin

said, quite captivated by the beautiful mountain views with the sea in the distance. The stone work was old but showed signs of excellent craftsmanship. They picked their way through overgrown nettles to reach the back door which opened into a dilapidated kitchen full of stray kittens.

"See yous 'ave yous very own fireplace in the kitchen and all these cats mean there won't be any mouses." The thick layer of dust made Deirdre cough and she noticed even the stray cats were looking a bit dusty.

"Come see the balconies and bedrooms," Adonis invited. Quentin thought it was rather magnificent he could stand on the balcony and pick an orange from the tree beneath.

"That is a ridiculously low price," Quentin whistled when Adonis told him how much cash the owners wanted for it. Adonis agreed, thinking the commission he could earn would be as nearly as much as the price of this ruin.

"And I borrow you my builders to make all sound," he offered "they do very good things with shower curtains."

Deirdre hoped Quentin was just being polite and was not seriously considering buying this run down ruin of a house in a foreign country. She reminded Quentin they had to get back as Stavroula had promised to cook them McDonalds tonight.

Driving away Adonis spied the old lady next door making obscene gestures from her window in his rear view mirror.

CHAPTER 32

Stomach Stapling or Death

Bald Yannis was lurking in the back of his hardware shop, hoping no one would catch him illegally siphoning off gas from the full gas bottles he had for sale into empty bottles. If any malaka came in with a lighted cigarette Bald Yannis risked being blown up. He was in a bad mood as the useless doctor had lectured him on being too vain with his hair restoration attempts and had prescribed him some greasy ointment which smelt strongly of vinegar.

Fat Christos entered the hardware shop only to hear Bald Yannis screaming at him to wait as he was busy. Fat Christos had also received a lecture from the village doctor who pointed out the very obvious fact that Christos was now unhealthily obese. He had even gone so far as to confiscate Fat Christos' bag of spinach pies. The doctor told him in no uncertain terms he must lose weight at once or he could drop down dead of a fatal heart attack at any moment.

The doctor told him if he could lose twenty kilos through diet and exercise he may consider the much easier surgical option of stomach stapling to help Fat Christos lose even more

80

weight. He wouldn't even contemplate the surgical option until he shifted the first twenty kilos though. The prospect was a gloomy one to Fat Christos whose idea of exercise was walking to the bakery to buy more pies.

Fat Christos decided he would try to lose twenty kilos and then have his stomach stapled, as he wanted to live a long life and realised he had let himself go. The price of the operation was a large brown envelope he could not easily afford and the doctor refused to accept the promise of octopus or lobster instead of cash. Of course he realised he would save a small fortune by not buying any pies and souvlaki, but the bribe to the doctor was still a large sum.

His thoughts turned to Tassia and her impending inheritance, as her uncle the supermarket owner was fast approaching ninety. If he married Tassia she would be sure to pay the brown envelope bribe to the doctor once he got his hands on her land and olive trees. Once her old uncle pegged it they would be very rich. The thought of being both thin and rich inspired Fat Christos to step up his game in the courtship stakes and convince Tassia his intentions were finally serious.

"Hurry up there Yanni," Fat Christos called "I'm in a rush you know." Bald Yannis appeared from the back of the shop, frantically scratching his spotty scalp and muttering malaka under his breath.

"I want a ladies dress and a nice plant pot. Better make that ceramic and not plastic," Fat Christos requested, planning to fill the pot with a plant and present it to Tassia along with the dress. Usually he would turn up with sweet cakes from the bakery when wooing Tassia but he was resolved to put all temptation out of harm's way. "Make that a heavy pot," he added, deciding he would use the pot as a form of weight lifting as he took the long route to Tassia's on foot.

"Is that gas I can smell?" he asked, watching Bald Yannis hastily disappear to the back of the shop.

CHAPTER 33

A Wedding Proposal

Tassia paid a lot of the money to the dentist to have her teeth straightened but despite her efforts Fat Christos remained her only suitor.

An honest and pleasant woman with deep brown eyes and a fair complexion, Tassia had spent most of her child bearing years looking after her cantankerous father. She had no idea the selfish old man had chased away any potential suitors apart from Fat Christos. The old man had reluctantly welcomed Fat Christos as he kept him supplied with free octopus. Now with the old man buried Tassia was desperate to be married as she longed for a baby. Time was still on her side as she was a good ten years younger than her only beau.

It was true she had a reputation for keeping a dirty house but her tight fisted father had deprived her of all the essentials of modern housework, refusing to invest in a vacuum cleaner, washing machine or indoor oven. He expected her to scrub floors and wash clothes by hand, while baking bread in the outdoor wood oven.

She had no idea until after he was dead that he was worth

lots of money. When she discovered his bags of buried coins she cursed his memory and went straight out to buy an indoor cooker, a washing machine, refrigerator, deep freezer and vacuum cleaner. Her true love was the garden though and she only really felt happy as she tended her vegetables and flowers while dreaming of babies.

As she watered her exquisite rose bushes she wondered if Fat Christos was really serious about her. Without a ring on her finger she worried she would miss out on the bliss of her own baby. She was surprised to see Fat Christos arrive bearing a ceramic plant pot brimming with a fragrant basil plant. Usually he only brought her sweet cakes, and then ate most of them himself.

"Things must change my dearest Tassia," Fat Christos announced, handing her the plant. "I have decided to diet and lose all this blubber so I will look more 'andsome standing beside you in my wedding suit. That's if yous will 'ave me Tassia," he added, belatedly going down on one knee in a muddy puddle.

Tassia could not fail to notice her suitor made no declaration of love as she weighed up his unromantic proposal. "Oh I almost forgot I have another gift for you," said Fat Christos, handing over the hideous old lady dress.

Tassia considered the dress a most thoughtful gesture and her heart warmed towards her suitor. She decided to be honest and told him she was willing to marry him if he promised they could have a baby right away. "Of course my dearest, whatever your heart desires," Fat Christos agreed, feeling satisfied things were going to plan and Tassia would soon fill a brown envelope with the cash bribe for his life saving stomach stapling surgery.

"I would take yous to the taverna to celebrate our engagement but I've already started my diet and won't be eating," said Fat Christos.

"We aren't really engaged yet as yous forgot to put a ring on my finger," Tassia mentioned.

"My dearest I apologise profusely, I am so hungry I cant's think straight and forgot all about a ring. I promise to return tomorrow with a sparkling diamond and we will make our engagement official and set a wedding date."

"You can take me to the taverna to celebrate tomorrow," Tassia said as she rarely went out in the evenings "and I will wear my lovely new dress and my new diamond ring."

With those determined words Fat Christos realised Tassia may not be quite as malleable as he'd hoped. He said goodbye as he needed to go home and break the news of his impending wedding to his mother. He could only imagine how heartbroken she would be at the thought of him leaving home. He expected she would be completely devastated, distraught and inconsolable.

CHAPTER 34

Stavroula Cooks McDonalds

Quentin and Deirdre popped into 'Mono Ellinka Trofima' taverna to promise Yiota they would return for a nightcap after dining on McDonalds at Stavroulas. The tables were just filling up and the most delicious aromas of garlic and herbs filled the air.

"I'm sorry yous will miss my little shoes tonight," said Yiota, confusing the Americans who had yet to sample the traditional dish of papoutsakia. "I save yous some for tomorrow if yous like the stuffed aubergines."

The Americans took a table in Stavroulas, looking forward to the real taste of American cooking Stavroula had promised them. Waiting for their food to arrive they looked longingly at the platters of lamb chops that were leaving the kitchen and the plates of orange infused sausages, a local delicacy.

Meanwhile in the kitchen Stavroula stared in horror at the frozen plastic coated lumps of chicken she had taken from the box Mrs Kolokotronis provided. She was clueless as to how to make them look edible.

Scratching her head in amazement that anyone would prefer to eat these sad little pellets rather than good Greek cooking she sent Socrates out to assure the Americans the taste of fine dining would be on its way shortly. Socrates encouraged them to eat lots of bread with olive oil as he'd had the misfortune to take a look at the unappetizing food they would soon be receiving.

Eventually Stavroula emerged from the kitchen brandishing a covered platter she deposited on the Americans table. Whipping the silver lid off with a flourish she presented them with a dozen green speckled fried chicken nuggets swimming in a sea of olive oil, saying "McDonalds."

She had liberally doused the nuggets with fresh oregano to make them appear more tempting. "How lovely," the pair announced in unison, thinking this was the most awful meal they had ever seen in Greece.

"They don't look very thrilled," Stavroula whispered to Socrates "but it does look really 'orrrid."

"Don't worry my love dove," Socrates assured her "I hear in the United States they even eat the cheese out of an aerosol can, so their taste buds must be dead."

Vangelis the chemist was dining on lamb chops and offered to share them with the Americans when he saw how ghastly their meal looked. Vangelis had travelled to England and knew all about McDonalds. He tried to explain to Stavroula although chicken nuggets were on the children's menu in the foreign fast food place these two adults had been expecting something like a hamburger.

"Well I could have cooked them beeftkei if they'd said," she complained, feeling unappreciated after all the trouble she had gone to.

Stavroula was distracted by her neighbour old Mrs Kolokotronis entering the taverna in great excitement. Deirdre took advantage of the moment to wrap the greasy chicken nuggets in a napkin and stuff them in her handbag. She would find a bin on the way back to their room, having learnt her lesson about the dangers of flushing napkin wrapped unwanted food down the toilet.

"Such wonderful news," Mrs Kolokotronis announced "my son Christos is to be married to Tassia and will finally leave home. How I have longed for the day when the big lazy lump would move out but I truly believed it would never come. Stavroula, come take a drink with me to celebrate. After fifty years I am finally to be rid of him."

"Ah but your new daughter-in-law keeps a dirty house," Stavroula reminded her sourly, still in a bad mood over the chicken nuggets.

CHAPTER 35

Late Evening Gossip

Quentin and Deirdre called into 'Mono Ellinka Tro-fima' for a nightcap, confiding to Yiota that Stavroula's attempts at American food had been a disaster. Deirdre had saved one chicken nugget to show Yiota who voiced her opinion "fast food will never catch on in this part of the world where people appreciate slow food."

Yiota failed to see the irony in this comment as she carried a plate of gyros, considered to be Greek fast food, to Tall Thomas. It couldn't really be called 'fast food' at the slow speed it took Takis to produce it and Tall Thomas had been waiting impatiently for nearly an hour for his order.

Gorgeous Yiorgos was at a loose end as his good friend Fat Christos had failed to turn up this evening. Spotting Quentin and Deirdre he decided to join them and fill them in all the latest village gossip. "Yassou K-Went-In and Did-Reesm" he said "'ave yous seen the noxious rash all over Bald Yannis' head?"

Everyone was most amused to hear about Bald Yannis' rash and everyone agreed it served him right for being so

89

vain.

Gorgeous Yiorgos warned Deirdre to be very careful where she dried her smalls as the elusive underwear thief was still at large. Deirdre was most shocked to hear of this as she had no idea the village was in the midst of such a major crime wave. Her mind flashed back to the lacey strap she had spotted beneath Bald Yannis' tee-shirt. However, just because the obnoxious man had obviously been wearing women's underwear she had no reason at all to believe he had stolen it, so she kept her suspicions to herself.

Gorgeous Yiorgos was kept busy translating as lots of the villagers wanted to know if the American pair were going to buy the 'Lemoni Spiti' in the neighbouring village of Rapanaki. News of their visit to the old ruin had got round quickly and opinion was divided as to whether they should go ahead with the purchase.

While Gorgeous Yiorgos thought it may well fall down, Takis opined "if you borrow some builders to do it up goodly yous will make a tidy profit when you sell it."

"Or you could keep it as an 'oliday home," Toothless Tasos suggested "and keep pet goats in the garden."

Prosperous Pedros kept his opinion to himself, thinking it would definitely be to his own advantage if they bought it and his mother had some new neighbours. Perhaps Quentin would be useful at changing Fotini's light bulbs and oiling her squeaky doors, thus reducing his own burden.

"But we are only staying here until the car is repaired," Deirdre explained, worrying Quentin was being swayed by the idea of buying the run down house with the spectacular views.

Fat Christos made a late entrance. He had an announcement to make and wanted an audience. Waving away Yiota's attempts to bring him food he requested a glass of tap water with a slice of lemon. He had no intention of announcing his engagement to Tassia until she was with him the next evening but he wanted everyone to know he was serious about losing twenty kilos quickly.

Fat Christos had no inkling his mother had already broken the news of his impending marriage and was taken aback to receive everyone's hearty congratulations. Everyone wanted to raise a toast to Fat Christos but he insisted on making do with his tap water.

Sticking to the lie he had told Tassia, Fat Christos told everyone "I am on a diet to lose lots of weight and get 'ealthy so I will look 'andsomely dapper in my wedding suit."

He did not want everyone knowing the doctor had pronounced him morbidly obese, nor that he planned to have his stomach stapled. He had already started a new exercise regime by taking a late afternoon swim in the still chilly sea and not a morsel had passed his lips since the last spinach pie he had greedily scoffed in the doctor's waiting room that morning.

Fat Christos planned to get up very early and jog round the harbour before going fishing. He asked if anyone would like to join him as having a jogging partner might well provide extra motivation. Quentin offered up his company saying "I often go jogging back home in Idaho and will be delighted to join you Christo."

Sitting in the taverna surrounded by everyone eating, Fat Christos was not actually tempted to break his fast. His resolve to lose weight was sound as the doctor had actually scared him witless. Prosperous Pedros piped up Fat Christos should become a vegetarian like him and Fat Christos agreed that from now on he would give up meat and eat lots of horta and salad.

"Does that mean you'll be giving up goat or is it a vege-table?" Yiota enquired.

CHAPTER 36

A Morning Jog

Bright and early the next morning Quentin and Fat Christos met up to jog around the harbour. Quentin thoughtfully slowed his pace to allow the larger man to keep up with him, encouraging him to keep at it when he showed signs of waning. Pouring with sweat Fat Christos looked quite a sight with his wobbling stomach protruding over his too tight shorts. Every few meters he collapsed on the ground panting and groaning, before hoisting himself up to continue the torture.

As the village slowly came to life everyone they jogged past welcomed Quentin with a cheery "Kalimera K-Went-In," making him reflect what a very friendly place Astakos was and how nice it would be to part of the community if he purchased the 'Lemoni Spiti' and got the borrowed builders in. He decided he would at least persuade Deirdre to take another look at the house.

Bald Yannis cycled past them en route to his hardware shop, openly laughing very rudely at Fat Christos' struggling attempts to stay upright. Bald Yannis sported a hat on his head this morning as he was fed up with the village folk making derogatory comments about his noxious itchy rash. In his pocket he had a brochure all about the latest hair transplant operations and was considering booking an appointment once his revolting rash cleared up.

"A curse on that malaka doctor," he said to himself "there is nothing vain in wanting a full head of hair." Ironically Bald Yannis had been one of the first to laugh at the vanity of Gorgeous Yiorgos when he had started to disguise his greying hair very obviously with black boot polish.

Collapsing in a sweaty heap Fat Christos said he could not jog one more step. Quentin revived him by pouring a bottle of water over his head and informing him they had made excellent progress by jogging a total of three kilometres. Fat Christos announced he was off home to jump on the scales and eat a breakfast of healthy carrots before going fishing.

"Yous and Did-Rees must join me on boat tomorrow," he invited, having appreciated the motivational support of his jogging partner.

Fat Christos was disturbed to find his mother measuring up for new furniture in his bedroom. "When are you moving out my boy? Soon I hope," Mrs Kolokotronis questioned him, adding "I think this room will make a lovely sewing room."

"I will set a date with Tassia later," he told her, insulted to his core that his mother was not weeping and wailing at the prospect of his imminent departure. "There is no real rush after fourteen years of courting," he said.

"That's not what Tassia said," his mother retorted. "She wants a baby soon and it is high time you gave me another grandchild. I hardly ever see your sister's son since they moved to Athens. I will have a word with the Pappas later and see when he can conduct the ceremony."

If his mother was going to turn into a nag perhaps it wouldn't be so bad moving in with Tassia after all, thought Fat Christos, reminding himself to buy an engagement ring before the evening.

His mother had a plateful of cheese pies from the bakery waiting to tempt him in the kitchen and Fat Christos suspected she could be trying to sabotage his diet. Declining the pies he grabbed a handful of carrots and headed off to the peaceful solitude of his boat.

CHAPTER 37

Mobile Refrigerated Fish Van Ahoy

As Quentin headed back to their room above the taverna he was surprised to see his wife taking coffee with Adonis in Stavroula's taverna. Deirdre had been fast asleep when he left for his jog with Fat Christos and he'd hoped to manage a quiet word with Adonis about a return visit to the 'Lemoni Spiti' out of her hearing.

"Kalimera K-Went-In," Adonis greeted him. Quentin started to respond "Actually it is Quen..." and then thought better of it as the whole village was seemingly determined to pronounce his name incorrectly.

"I 'ave the excellent news my good friend," Adonis announced "my cousin Adonis the mechanic 'as finished fixing the van of Petros the postman an' will a make start on yous car as soon as he 'ave the spare parts from Athens. Should not be more than a few days or maybe a week till the spare parts arrive."

This was the first time that Quentin and Deirdre had heard there would be a wait for spare parts. They resigned themselves to staying longer than they had planned in

Astakos, yet were secretly delighted at the prospect of spending more time in the village. They loved the slow and relaxed pace of rural Greek life and were enjoying the company of their intriguing new friends.

"We've been invited to go fishing tomorrow," Quentin told Deirdre "and this evening we will join the celebration to mark the engagement of Christos and Tassia."

"There are lots of things to keep us busy," the pair reassured Adonis, not realising he wanted to keep them around indefinitely so he could earn a large commission on the sale of the ruined 'Lemoni Spiti.'

"Oh look," Deidre pointed as that old fool Vasilis rode up to Stavroulas on his donkey.

"Ah I sees that old fool Vasilis 'as 'is donkey Onos back from Petros the postman," Adonis muttered.

Tethering the donkey outside Vasilis entered the taverna, ordering a glass of ouzo for himself and a saucer of ouzo for the donkey. Vasilis was in a remarkably good mood as having his donkey back had lifted his spirits.

"Tomorrow my lovely wife Masha has the birthday and I want to invite yous all to a surprise party at my house," Vasilis said, generously including Quentin and Deirdre in his invitation.

"How delightful," Deirdre replied, assuring him they would be there as she accepted Adonis' invitation to drive them.

Just then the peace of the morning was disturbed by lots of shouting and swearing on the street outside. Spotting Petros the postman driving by in his newly repaired car, and hoping to intercept him and retrieve a parcel he was waiting for, Tall Thomas had hastily parked his van in the 'No Parking' spot outside Stavroulas.

KATERINA NIKOLAS

The 'No Parking' spot was on a slight incline leading into the sea and in his haste Tall Thomas had neglected to secure the handbrake. Everyone was frozen in horror as the van rolled in slow motion down the incline and landed in the sea.

CHAPTER 38

All Hands to the Rope

Tall Thomas has a rare and embarrassing, for a fisherman, condition. So mortified is he at the thought of his affliction becoming public knowledge he will go to any lengths to conceal it. Indeed, considering how Astakos thrives on gossip it is quite remarkable that no one has discovered Tall Thomas endures the frightful malady of sea sickness. If anyone was to discover a fisherman suffered from sea sickness he would be a laughing stock among his fishing rivals.

The condition worsened as Tall Thomas got older. He never experienced sea sickness in his younger days, but for the last few years each journey to sea sees him hanging over the side of the boat vomiting endlessly. His incessant nausea is only abated on dry land and his condition has become so bad Tall Thomas will do anything to avoid going out to sea.

Tall Thomas lied about his fishing routine to avoid anyone catching on. He told his rivals he had fished in the morning if they were fishing at night, to avoid questions as to why his boat was not out in the water at the same time as theirs. When it became difficult to explain away his lack of a catch Tall Thomas took to driving down the coast to Gavros to buy fish from the fisherman there and then pass it off as his own and re-sell it locally.

Eventually Tall Thomas decided to give up any pretence of going to sea and established a small business as a mobile fishmonger. Now he makes a good living driving between villages and selling fish from his mobile refrigerated fish van. He buys the daily catch from the Astakos fishermen and they are relieved to no longer have to go to the bother of finding their own customers.

It was this mobile refrigerated fish van which rolled down the incline and into the sea. As everyone watched transfixed the van at first bobbed buoyantly on the water and then began to sink. The fishermen drinking coffee outside the kafenion joked to Tall Thomas he had better not expect them to re-catch the fish they had already sold him that morning.

Within moments all the men had pooled their resources to come to Tall Thomas' aid, despite their mirth and laughter. Strong ropes were retrieved from car boots and secured to the backs of pick-up trucks and Tall Thomas dived into the sea to secure the other ends to his mobile refrigerated fish van. As Gorgeous Yiorgos grabbed a rope from the hardware shop Bald Yannis followed him onto the street screeching "yous pay for that later malaka, no credit here."

Everyone came out to heave on the ropes as Adonis revved his accelerator and tried to tow the van from the sea with the strength of his pick-up truck. Prosperous Pedros, Vangelis the chemist, Quentin, Socrates the slick lawyer and Petros the postman, were side by side pulling the ropes with all their strength, while Fat Christos lent his considerable bulk to pushing Adonis' pick-up alongside Toothless Tasos.

Stavroula surprised everyone by jumping into the sea to assist Tall Thomas with tying the knots, even though her motivation was a potential discount on the future price of his fish.

After what seemed like an age the mobile refrigerated fish van was safely tugged out of the water and the soaking wet Stavroula invited everyone in for warming glasses of brandy. Adonis offered to tow the mobile refrigerated fish van to the garage of his cousin Adonis the mechanic.

Vasilis suggested Tall Thomas make use of the old banger gathering dust in his barn so he could continue with his fish selling business. A price was agreed upon for the hire of Vasilis' old car and hands were shaken all round.

Quentin was most impressed with the speed and resourcefulness of the villagers as there had been no need to call out the emergency services. "For such a quiet and quaint village there is no end to the excitement," he confided to Deirdre.

CHAPTER 39

A Rush on Old Lady Dresses

Bald Yannis was hurriedly increasing the price tickets on his lengths of strong rope before Gorgeous Yiorgos had the chance to return and pay for the one he had grabbed. Yannis had laughed like a drain at the sight of Tall Thomas' mobile refrigerated fish van rolling into the sea and was very annoyed the village men had managed to retrieve it. He would have enjoyed seeing Tall Thomas' small business suffer as he had a mean streak, plus a loathing of fish.

Bald Yannis was unsure how to react when old Mrs Kolokotronis came into his shop and asked for one of his hideous old lady dresses. He was used to insulting his male customers, but didn't dare try it on with this elderly lady. It was however the very first time he had sold a dress to an actual woman and he supposed he ought to ask her what size she would like, a service he never bothered to extend to his male buyers.

"It isn't for me, it's for the mail order bride Masha," Mrs Kolokotronis said "it's her birthday tomorrow and she must be one of the only women in the village not to have one of your hideous dresses. My son Christos already bought one for me."

Bald Yannis duly wrapped the dress in brown paper and rang up the sale in his cash register.

Next through the door was Thea, the love interest of Toothless Tasos, who had recently buried her third husband. She also made a purchase of an old lady dress, confiding in Bald Yannis it was a birthday gift for mail order Masha. By the close of business that day he sold a total of nine hideous old lady dresses, each one to a woman who intended to gift it to Masha for her birthday the next day.

Personally Bald Yannis thought the village women had taken collective leave of their senses as there was no way a beauty like Masha, with her distinctive flair for flashy fashion, would be seen dead in one of his shapeless dresses. Certainly that old fool Vasilis had never attempted to insult his mail order bride by buying one for her. Bald Yannis concluded the village women were jealous of mail order Masha's good looks and were just being shrewish.

The hardware store was not the only village shop enjoying brisk trade. When old Mr Mandelis re-opened the jewellery shop after siesta time he found a queue of desperate men on his doorstep.

Fat Christos was there to buy an engagement ring for Tassia, Socrates was after a nice necklace for Stavroula to make up for insulting her with the hideous old lady dress, and that old fool Vasilis needed an expensive piece of jewellery for Masha's birthday. All three men politely stood to one side when Petula, the Pappas' wife entered, but she rushed out when she realised the shop was not empty, saying she would return later.

Petula cautiously returned to the jewellery shop when the

three men had left with their purchases, A week earlier she'd sold Mr Mandelis her engagement ring, swearing him to secrecy. He was delighted to oblige as he despised her drunk of a husband and had no intention of setting foot in the church again until the Pappas was excommunicated.

Petula was confident in his discretion as Mr Mandelis had never been known to gossip. She desperately needed the money the sale of her ring could offer and thought it doubtful that her husband would notice her ring was missing. If he did happen to notice she planned to tell him it had slipped off her finger in the tomato patch and his pampered pet goat had eaten it before she could retrieve it. The Pappas loved his pet goat Krasi, whom he had named after his favourite tipple of wine.

Petula had underestimated the observational powers of her husband. It only took the Pappas three days to notice her ring finger was bare and he launched into an abusive tirade when she tried to accuse his darling Krasi of eating it. "Blame my goat would you for your slovenly ways," the Pappas screamed at her, punching her painfully in the face.

He demanded Petula follow the goat round the house to see if it passed the ring, having believed her lies and not suspecting she had sold it. Obviously the goat didn't pass the ring as it hadn't eaten it, so now Petula was as desperate to retrieve it from Mr Mandelis as she had been to sell it to him last week.

Petula fell to the floor in a faint when Mr Mandelis delivered the unfortunate news that he had just sold her engagement ring to Fat Christos.

Mr Mandelis had no idea what to do when Petula collapsed in a dead faint on his shop floor. He poured a large glass of brandy to revive her and spotting Gorgeous Yiorgos drinking coffee at the kafenion he called him into the shop, imploring him to drive the sickly woman home.

As the church bells were clanging Petula knew her husband was safely out of the way at the church so she invited Gorgeous Yiorgos into the house. Between pitiful sobs she explained her dilemma to Gorgeous Yiorgos who listened with a sympathetic ear.

In addition to hating her husband Petula was also deathly afraid of him. Since he'd started drinking heavily in recent years he was far too free with his fists and the only affection he ever showed was showered on his pet goat Krasi. Petula had been saving whatever money she could get her hands on in the faint hope of buying a car and leaving him. Gorgeous Yiorgos had been complicit in her plans to the extent he had been giving Petula free driving lessons behind her husband's back.

Now Petula needed Gorgeous Yiorgos' help to get her engagement ring back from his very good friend Fat Christos before he presented it to Tassia. As Gorgeous Yiorgos promised to do his best to help, Krasi the goat wandered into the kitchen and chewed up the hideous old lady dress Socrates had given to Petula.

CHAPTER 40

A Man with a Kind Heart

Gorgeous Yiorgos felt immense pity for Petula. The pair had been childhood friends and it saddened him greatly to see the way in which the once vibrant and attractive young woman had been bullied by the Pappas into a meek shadow of her former self.

Back in his youth, his legendary good looks, coupled with the body of a Greek god, had earned Yiorgos the soubriquet 'Gorgeous.' His handsome face was adorned with a stylish moustache he liked to twirl suggestively and his deep black locks made women want to run their fingers through his hair.

Age and the elements were not kind to him, leaving him with a weather beaten face and overgrown shaggy eyebrows. His black locks had turned an undistinguished shade of grey which he tried to hide with liberal applications of black boot polish, leaving it looking permanently greasy. The polish had a tendency to run in streaks down his neck at the first sign of rain. His body had fattened and coarsened, though he still had a long way to go to catch up with Fat Christos in the obesity stakes.

GOAT IN THE MEZE

These days, when Gorgeous Yiorgos looks in the mirror he only sees his handsome youthful self, believing he is the same magnet for the women as he was in the days when he was an expert in the art of 'kamaki'. In his late fifties he still practises kamaki, the Greek art of reeling women in, primarily on unsuspecting tourist women who he perceives as loose floosies flocking to Greece for a holiday romance. Sadly for him they are not too impressed with his lame chat up lines, though he never stops trying.

In winter when the tourist women are a rarity Yiorgos encases his bulky body in layers of too tight clothes and goes round in a foul temper as only the prospect of love ever keeps him cheerful. In winter Yiorgos gives up shaving and washing as there is no one to try and impress, and the pungent aroma of dead fish precedes him everywhere.

Over the years he has left a trail of broken hearts behind and had, at the last count, three ex-wives. Even though Petula and Gorgeous Yiorgos have only ever been friends the Pappas had banned his wife from having Yiorgos in the house because of his reputation as a lifelong lothario. What the Pappas fails to appreciate, as he lacks one himself, is the kind heart Gorgeous Yiorgos is blessed with.

"I will do my best to get yous ring off Fat Christos," he promised Petula, passing her a tea towel to wipe up her tears. "But this violent behaviour of your husband can be tolerated no longer. Let me think of a way to put a stop to it, my dear. Now tomorrow afternoon I can't make your driving lesson as I promised to go to mail order Masha's surprise birthday party. Why don't yous come along with me, it may cheer you up?"

"I would love too but my life wouldn't be worth living if my 'usband found out I'd been in her house. Do you know he calls her a prostitute, even though Vasilis told him she only left home to escape the rampaging wolves prowling her Russian town?"

"Po po, the Pappas never has a good word to say about anyone. He must have skipped the bit where priests are meant to be full of Christian charity," Gorgeous Yiorgos said.

"Well he does love his pet goat Krasi," Petula said in his defence. "Yous 'ad better be going Yiorgo. He'll do his nut if he finds yous 'ere," she added.

"Try not to worry," Yiorgos told her, giving her a chaste kiss on the cheek as he took his leave.

CHAPTER 41

Bald Yannis' Excruciatingly Painful Back Wax

In anticipation of her excursion to 'Mono Ellinka Tro-fima' to celebrate her engagement Tassia spent several hours in the beauty parlour having her hair coiffed and sprayed. It was the first time she'd ever spent any time really talking to mail order Masha who was having a pedicure in the next chair. She discovered Masha was delightful company and presumed the other woman only exuded a stand-offish air as the village people were so quick to judge her on her tarty looks without getting to know her.

The two women exchanged curious looks when Bald Yannis entered the beauty shop and disappeared behind a cur-tained off area. Their curiosity reached fever pitch as the air soon reverberated with the sound of his agonised screams. As he stumbled out biting down hard on a towel still clenched between his teeth, Evangelia, the beauty shop owner, ex-plained that Bald Yannis had been in for a back wax. The man was quite desperate to have hair on his head, but at the same time he hated with a vengeance the surfeit of hair that grew like untamed weeds on his back.

Tassia confided in her new friend Masha she suspected Christos was only marrying her for her money, but she didn't care as long as he got her pregnant on the wedding night.

Masha said she too wanted a baby but Vasilis was having a few problems in the bedroom department. She had sent him to the doctor who had prescribed Viagra. It pained her when everyone gossiped about it, but the gossips had no idea she needed Vasilis to be virile in order to get her pregnant. The two women parted as firm friends, looking forward to meeting up again that evening in the taverna.

Tassia felt almost beautiful as she waited for Fat Christos to arrive. She was wearing her lovely new dress, the gift from her fiancé, and her hair was neatly curled. Her happiness was complete when Christos arrived and went down on one knee, slipping a delicate diamond engagement ring onto her finger. "It is good for my exercise plan if we walk to the taverna," he said, selfishly giving no thought to the fact the rain would ruin Tassia's new hairdo.

CHAPTER 42

Merriment in the Taverna

G orgeous Yiorgos drove away from Petula's house hoping to intercept Fat Christos before he could slip Petula's engagement ring onto Tassia's finger. He cursed as he drove over a nail in the road and felt all the air escape from his front tyre. By the time he had replaced the flat tyre with the spare he was too late to intercept Fat Christos.

It was late when Gorgeous Yiorgos arrived at the taverna and the drenched Tassia was proudly showing off her shimmering new diamond to all the customers. Gorgeous Yiorgos hoped with every fibre of his being the Pappas would not choose this evening to make an entrance and spot his wife's ring on the finger of another woman.

The taverna was bustling and Tassia was struggling to cope with so much attention. She greeted mail order Masha with genuine warmth, happy to share the company of her new friend on this special evening. Tall Thomas was treating everyone to drinks in appreciation of the help he had received that morning when his mobile refrigerated fish van rolled into the sea. "'Ave a drink on me K-Went-In and Did-Rees," he invited, remembering the American had not minded getting his hands dirty in his efforts to help.

"Are you planning a big wedding?" Deirdre asked the newly engaged couple, to which Fat Christos replied "no, I tell you I will be very small soon."

Tassia declared "I would love to wear a magnificent white wedding dress embroidered with pearls."

Fat Christos mentally deducted the price of such a dress from the money he supposed Tassia was worth and told her "I'm sure my mother can knock you up a lovely dress on her sewing machine."

Fat Christos was resolutely sticking to his new diet, ordering nothing more than a salad of lettuce, onion and tomato. His conviction that his mother was trying to sabotage his diet had grown when he discovered she had left a large bar of shop bought chocolate on his pillow last night for the first time ever. He had given the chocolate to Stavroula's taverna cat but it was promptly sick in the harbour.

Everyone enjoyed a good laugh at the expense of Bald Yannis when they heard the tale of his excruciatingly painful back wax. "Maybe they will transplant the hair from his back to his vain bald head," said Vangelis the chemist who was quick to spill the secret of Bald Yannis' impending hair transplant.

"It's too late for that," Prosperous Pedros said "he's had it all waxed off."

That old fool Vasilis was in a cheery mood, most delighted to be reunited his donkey. He told the tale everyone had heard a thousand times before of how as a youngster he had walked ten kilometres uphill every Monday to attend school, carrying with him the provisions which must last until he returned from school to the village on Friday. "Every week it was the same," Vasilis explained, "a loaf of home baked bread, some olive oil and some sea salt. Yous youngsters don't know how good yous 'ave it with yous fancy foods and modern transport."

At the end of each olive harvest when his father no longer needed the donkey for work he had lent it to Vasilis so he could ride to school. His current donkey Onos was the direct descendant of that childhood donkey and he held it in great affection.

Mail order Masha empathised with the hard life of that old fool Vasilis' childhood and told him "I had to walk through the snow to school with only a loaf of bread and a bottle of vodka, hoping the wolves would not eat me."

The merriment in the taverna was abruptly interrupted when Mrs Kolokotronis rushed in, panting in distress and demanding to know if anyone had seen Socrates the slick lawyer and live-in-lover of Stavroula.

"He must be found quickly," she declared "the police have just arrested Stavroula and taken her away in handcuffs."

CHAPTER 43

The Interrogation

Mrs Kolokotronis had got the wrong end of the stick. Stavroula hadn't actually been arrested, but was merely being interrogated by two policemen from the up 'north village' of Pouthena about the disappearance of her second husband Kostas. The policemen hadn't actually dragged Stavroula away in handcuffs as Mrs Kolokotronis erroneously reported.

Instead Stavroula had turned on the charm, invited the two policemen to take a seat in her taverna and poured them two large glasses of her finest brandy. Before they even had a chance to start questioning her she was buttering them up with delicious saganaki followed by heaped platefuls of moussaka.

As soon as the policemen started to question her Stavroula broke down and started weeping. She had craftily secreted a cut onion in her breast pocket to bring on fake tears.

"He left me with never a word," she wept hysterically. "The malaka was always on the road and never at home. I suspect he had another woman. I could not bear the humiliation of his desertion so I packed up my things and came home to Astakos with a broken heart. Every day I pine for my Kostas, but what can I do? I open this taverna to keep myself busy and forget the pain. Yous want to find the malaka yous find him with another woman I bet," she said convincingly, hoping they never got a warrant to dig up the chicken coop.

The policemen apologised profusely for upsetting her but explained they had to follow up as Kostas' sister Katerina had reported him missing. "What is a poor helpless woman to do when she is deserted?" asked Stavroula. The policemen both agreed Kostas' behaviour was shocking, what man in his right mind would neglect such a wonderful cook?

As they tucked into large platefuls of Stavroula's homemade baklava they cursed Katerina who had obviously wasted their time by sending them off on a wild goose chase. Never had they interrogated a more innocent suspect than the poor deserted Stavroula.

Luckily Socrates didn't arrive back until the policemen had left, saving Stavroula the awkwardness of explaining away how such a heart broken woman had been so quick to take a live-in-lover.

CHAPTER 44

Deirdre Catches a Fish in Her Hat

Stavroula was in a terrible temper the next morning, cursing Katerina, the sister of Kostas, for giving her name and address to the police. Socrates advised her to lie low as he was painfully aware not only had she accidentally, he believed, killed and disposed of Kostas but she was also still bigamously married to Toothless Tasos. Her plan to lure her customers back from the rival taverna was not working so she decided to turn on her charm when Quentin came in for coffee after his morning jog with Fat Christos.

"Kalimera K-Went-In," she said with fake bonhomie "Pou einai Did-Rees?"

"It's Quentin," he replied while leafing through his American-Greek dictionary to look up the translation of 'pou'.

"Hurry up and finish your coffee Quentin," Deirdre ordered, walking in wearing a bright yellow sou'wester hat and a natty blue and white striped nautically themed outfit. "I can't wait to go out fishing with Christos on his boat."

A light breeze was blowing as the threesome cast off from the harbour and headed out to sea. Fat Christos was excited to show off the latest addition to his boat, declaring he had gone all computerised. Whipping off an oily tarpaulin cover he revealed the fishing boat's brand new computerised guidance system.

"Don't touch that button," he commanded as Quentin's finger hovered perilously close to an array of knobs and dials.

"Why, what is it for?" Quentin queried."

"I 'ave no idea," Fat Christos admitted.

"What about this one?" Quentin asked pointing at another button.

"I 'ave no idea," Fat Christos replied. He was painfully aware the only instructions available were printed in Chinese.

Prosperous Pedros had gone to the expense of having one of these new-fangled computer boxes installed in his boat, so naturally every other fisherman in the village had to have one too, to not be outdone. They all used the same cheap Chinese supplier and not one of them could translate the instructions and fathom out how to use it. They were even pretty clueless about what it was actually meant to do. The only thing their collective wisdom had managed to work out was that one particular button allowed them to take a close up look at the bottom of the sea bed beneath the boat on the computer screen.

All the other functions of the sophisticated new-fangled computerised guidance system were a complete mystery. Each fisherman feared if the wrong button was pressed something catastrophic would happen and perhaps their boat would explode.

They had collectively wasted a lot of money on this fancy new- fangled technology they were clueless how to operate. As long as no single fisherman could claim the advantage of knowing how to use it they were all in the same boat and declared it quite marvellous they could see if the sea bed was rock or sand.

Deirdre was enjoying the boat trip and became quite excited when Fat Christos offered to let her help to pull in the nets. As another boat came into view Fat Christos roughly shoved Quentin and Deidre onto the floor of the boat, telling them to stay out of the way.

"The sea police will give me a bigly fine if they find tourists in my boat," he explained.

"The coast is clear," Fat Christos exhaled, lending Quentin a hand to haul Deirdre out of the fishing net she had fallen into.

"Oh look Deirdre, you've caught a fish," exclaimed Quentin, pointing to a lifeless sea bass stuck in the brim of her luminous yellow hat.

As an apology for pushing her down so roughly Fat Christos gifted Deirdre the sea bass, telling her "take it to Takis' later and Yiota will cook it very tasty."

Meanwhile Quentin was hoping he could find an internet cafe somewhere and look up an operating manual written in English for Fat Christos' new-fangled computerised guidance system. He wasn't too optimistic as it struck him Astakos was stuck in a time warp and life was about twenty years behind more sophisticated places.

CHAPTER 45

Mail Order Masha's Surprise Party

Mail order Masha had no inkling that old fool Vasilis was throwing her a surprise birthday party. He had done a disappearing act with the donkey long before the first guests began to arrive, appearing en masse on her doorstep shouting "Surprise."

Masha was indeed caught by surprise as she'd been sunbathing topless and only had chance to pull on Vasilis' old towelling bathrobe as she answered the door, removing cucumber slices from her eyes. She hated being caught out looking anything but her best. Leaving her unwanted visitors to rummage round in the kitchen for some snacks, Masha disappeared to get more suitably dressed for a party.

The guests complained as they tripped over saucers of ouzo left out on the kitchen floor for the donkey. They could see no signs of the feast Vasilis had promised them and turned their noses up at the big pan of foreign red borscht, with a rather suspect scummy surface, simmering on the stove.

Masha returned dressed to the nines in a silver sequin

evening dress with a plunging neckline and a provocative high-thigh side slit, even though it was still only the middle of the afternoon. She towered over everyone in her matching silver platform shoes and in her haste to get ready had only applied false eyelashes to one eye.

Masha passed round a platter of olives and some boiled sweets she found in the cupboard saved for donkey treats. She poured everyone generous glasses of vodka and cursed Vasilis for leaving her in this predicament. "The old fool malaka not tell me of party," she said.

"That's because it's a surprise," Mrs Kolokotronis told her, passing her a brown paper parcel containing one of the hardware shop's hideous old lady dresses.

In no time at all Masha had unwrapped a total of nine hideous old lady dresses and could not muster the grace to feign delight or say thank you. "Why yous all bring me these hideous dresses," she complained "they are so ugly and shapeless and sweaty?"

Adding insult to injury Masha knew the hideous dresses hadn't even come from a proper dress shop but rather from the local hardware store, where the creepy owner Bald Yannis spent all his time thumbing through women's underwear catalogues.

The other women began to feel ashamed, secretly agreeing with Masha the dresses were everything she described and no one under the age of eighty should be obliged to wear one. They hated receiving them from their own men folk and they cursed Bald Yannis, the malaka, for putting them in temptations way. It wouldn't have hurt them to buy Masha something nice and thoughtful like a new nail polish, a box of chocolates or a bunch of flowers.

They realised Masha hadn't any warning of a house full

of guests and she had done her very best to offer them refreshments on such short notice. She went up in their estimation when they realised she kept a clean house and all the mirrors were gleaming with polish. They reached the conclusion that the old fool Vasilis had treated his young bride abominably by leaving her in this awkward situation.

"Where has that old fool Vasilis got to?" asked Gorgeous Yiorgos.

"He go off on donkey at crack of dawn and both of them are probably drunk," said Masha. "He forget all about my birthday," she wept with mascara bleeding down her face.

"But he knew it was your birthday today," Yiota assured her. "He arranged this surprise party and showed me the big expensive gold brooch shaped like a donkey, with diamonds for eyes, he bought yous."

"Po po, the useless drunk give me nothing, nothing," Masha exclaimed, telling her unwanted guests it was time they took their leave and she hoped that old fool Vasilis fell off the donkey.

Masha may not have been quite as hard on Vasilis if she knew the truth. He had woken that morning and gone off on the donkey to meet Petros the postman, leaving Masha to enjoy her beauty sleep. He loved his trophy wife and planned to surprise her with the expensive gold brooch in the shape of a donkey and then be on hand to greet the guests he had invited to the party.

Things took a drastic turn and all his good intentions were foiled when he opened the ominous looking letter Petros the postman delivered. The letter was from the Pappas, informing him Stavroula at the taverna was Vasilis' secret love child. The letter left him frozen in shock.

He could not imagine breaking the news to his young

wife Masha she was now the step-mother of Stavroula, it just didn't bear thinking about. Vasilis broke down in hysterical tears as he reached for the ouzo and drank steadily ever since.

CHAPTER 46

A Return to the Lemoni Spiti

B
y the time Adonis, Quentin and Deirdre arrived at the party all the other guests had already left. Masha was packing her suitcases in a temper, cursing that malaka old fool Vasilis and his drunken donkey.

Adonis had collected Quentin and Deirdre as promised to drive them to the party. He had however taken the long scenic route and they ended up at the Lemoni Spiti in the neighbouring village of Rapanaki where Adonis had arranged to meet Achilles the borrowed builder.

"This goodly 'ouse K-Went-In," Achilles declared "lots of room for bigly swimming pool."

"I don't think we'd need a pool as it's only a few minutes' walk to the sea," Deirdre said, before realising that was far too much encouragement for Quentin.

"Good good," agreed Achilles "it is bad waste of water to 'ave swimming pool but lots of yous foreigns like them. I build yous a chicken coop instead and yous 'ave lots of fresh eggs. 'Ow many shower curtains you want me to nail up and what colour you want I paint the shutters?" he asked as

Deirdre and Quentin started squabbling over blue and green paintwork.

"Stop," Deirdre suddenly commanded "why are we even discussing the paintwork Quentin, when we have no intention of buying this ruin of a falling down house?"

"Let me talk her round," Quentin whispered to Adonis, who brightened up at the thought of an imminent commission.

Negotiations came to a halt as they were rudely interrupted by loud screams. Fotini, the old crone next door and the mother of Prosperous Pedros, had taken a nasty tumble from the top of the three-legged wooden olive tree ladder she had been perched on in her efforts to eavesdrop.

"Adoni get over here and carry me into my 'ouse," she demanded "and get on the telephone and tell my useless son to come and take me to the 'ospital. I have broken my leg and will need a cane."

The thin old lady was sprawled scowling on the ground with her skirt in the air. As Adonis leant down to pick her up she slapped him soundly round the head, screeching "don't you go looking up my skirt yous young pervert." She jumped to her feet remarkably quickly for an old frail lady with a broken leg.

"Perhaps it isn't broke after all," said Adonis, pushing her into her house and telling her not to be so nosey.

Shaking hands with Achilles borrowed builder Adonis assured him Quentin and Deirdre would be making use of his services very soon.

"I think I 'ave charmed them and they buy this 'ouse," he said. "Anyways they will be 'ere for a while as my cousin Adonis can't find spare parts for their car. It give me more time to charm them."

CHAPTER 47

A Passionate Fling

Before he fell into a drunken stupor Vasilis cast his mind back many years, delving into long forgotten memories. It was fifty years back when he'd had a passionate fling with that flighty young thing Melina, the newlywed bride of Gregoris. The newlyweds were only on a quick visit to Gregoris' home village of Astakos at the time, having settled in Athens where Gregoris had opened a butchers shop.

Vasilis, who had been a married man at the time, was quite taken with the charms of the pretty young thing Melina who was already bored of her new and much older husband. Gregoris was an off-putting sight, always clad in a blood stained apron and smelling distinctly of offal. Even on his holidays in the village he loved to spend his time cutting up dead carcases, determined to be a perfectionist in his craft and rise to the level of a master butcher.

Vasilis and Melina enjoyed a brief and secret liaison conducted passionately in an overgrown olive grove. When Melina returned to Athens with Gregoris she became nothing more than a pleasant memory to Vasilis and by the time he next saw her, decades later, she had aged beyond recognition and there was no longer any spark between them.

Vasilis had never had any clue Melina's grown up daughter Stavroula was in fact the fruit of his own loins, as the letter from the Pappas claimed. It turned out Melina had kept her own secret counsel about the true parentage of Stavroula, only making a death bed confession to the Pappas. Stavroula herself had no clue about the true identity of her father, always believing the deceased Gregoris was the one due that title.

Now the Pappas had sent this horrendous blackmail letter to Vasilis in an attempt to extort lots of money from him. He threatened to reveal Melina's death bed confession unless Vasilis paid up a hefty sum. Vasilis cursed the Pappas and his blackmailing scheme, but the reason he was devastated to tears by the news was that he had always desperately wanted children of his own. His own first marriage had produced no off-spring and he would have lavished love on Stavroula if he had only known she was his child.

It particularly pained Vasilis to think he had never really taken the trouble to get to know Stavroula as he hadn't realised they were related. He'd never even paid her a compliment and if truth be told he considered her a bossy and unpleasant woman.

Mopping his tears with his sleeve Vasilis decided to head home and tell Masha he had discovered Stavroula was his love child. He would seek her advice on what to do next as she had a sound head above her silicone chest. Masha had been demanding a child of her own of late and he guessed that a fifty year-old step-daughter was not quite what she had in mind.

Onos the donkey found his way home with Vasilis lurching drunkenly on his back. As he reached the house he belatedly remembered it was Masha's birthday and fully expected her to greet him in a furious temper as he had forgotten all about it until now.

Masha was nowhere to be found though. The drawers in their bedroom were flung open and lots of frilly items were scattered around the room. The suitcases usually stored on the top of the wardrobe were gone, as was Masha's beloved fur coat. Vasilis came to the hasty conclusion Masha had left him.

Vasilis had actually only missed Masha by a matter of minutes. When Adonis, Quentin and Deirdre had arrived late to the party which had abruptly ended early, Masha was in a rage and throwing things around in a temper tantrum. Even the thoughtful birthday gift of a lovely coral nail polish proffered by Deirdre did not calm her down.

She demanded Adonis give her a ride to the bus stop as she ranted about the malaka old fool Vasilis forgetting her birthday and how the village women had insulted her by gifting her hideous old lady dresses. In no time at all Masha's suitcases were secured to the roof of Adonis' pick-up truck with a length of old rope and the four of them drove off to the bus stop with Masha perched cosily on Quentin's knee.

Vasilis was overwhelmed by the empty house and the thought Masha had left him. Coming on top of the Pappas' blackmail letter and the news that Stavroula was his love child he broke down again. Weeping and wailing in self pity Vasilis got into bed with a bottle of ouzo and drank himself into a comatose stupor.

CHAPTER 48

A Waster in a Dress

Bald Yannis was disgruntled that he seemed to be one of the few villagers not invited to mail order Masha' surprise birthday party. Even those peculiar American tourists Adonis rescued on the mountain seemed more popular than him and had received a party invitation, he mused.

He was pleased to see his next customer was someone even more unpopular than him. The Pappas was gaining a terrible reputation in the village of late as he always seemed to be drunk and, rumour had it, was not very nice to his wife Petula.

"Yanni, you malaka," the Pappas proclaimed "this chainsaw you sold me is useless. I want my money back unless you can fix it."

"I sold you that chainsaw twenty years ago, not last week," Bald Yannis said. "Give it me to repair if you like, but don't expect me to fix it for free."

The Pappas grudgingly handed the chainsaw over while muttering "It isn't right to charge a man of the cloth who does good work in the village."

"A no-good drunken waster in a dress more like," Yannis replied, asking "and when was the last time you did any good works? Not for years now I think. The only good you do is making fat profits for the shop that sells yous your booze." The Pappas went bright red and stormed out, shouting he would return the next day for the chainsaw and it had better be ready.

The Pappas had planned to send Petula out for a bit of illegal logging with the chainsaw, but the blade was too dull. He considered he could not possibly go out chopping wood himself as it would not be good for the dignity of his reputation if he was caught. He seemed oblivious to the fact his reputation was going down the pan fast and failed to make the connection between his own bad name and the empty pews in his church.

If that old fool Vasilis could be persuaded to hand over the blackmail money the Pappas decided he would expand into further extortion attempts. All he needed was some extra juicy deathbed confessions and he would be in a most lucrative business. He felt very smug that he had been clever enough to think up the blackmail ruse, giving no thought to the potentially destructive effect of revealing closely guarded lifelong secrets.

Cursing Bald Yannis for calling him out as a waster he stormed off to the church and decided to ring the bells early and loudly, thus disturbing anyone trying to enjoy a quiet siesta time.

Bald Yannis examined the defunct chainsaw, putting it aside to fix the next morning. He had just reached a good bit in the women's underwear catalogue, having discovered the section on push-up padded bras. His reading was interrupted by a phone call from the hair transplant clinic, confirming his appointment for the day after tomorrow.

"Most excellent," said Yannis excitedly. "I cannot wait to have the 'air on my head once again. I am sure it will make me so 'andsome that everyone will be jealous and I will be fighting off all the woman."

He decided to close the hardware shop early and went off to celebrate by purloining a few items of women's underwear hanging on the local washing lines.

CHAPTER 49

Fish with a Lemon Dress

After dropping mail order Masha off at the bus stop Adonis suggested Quentin and Deirdre join him for the evening in the taverna. He would use the time to put his persuasive powers to good use and sell them on the excellent potential of the Lemoni Spiti as a great buy.

"This will be our treat though," Deirdre insisted, pulling the large sea bass out of her handbag and telling Adonis she was going to ask Yiota to cook it.

"Don't you think you should have left that thing on ice somewhere?" Quentin asked.

"Oh really K-Went-In don't make such a fuss, I'm sure it will be fine, it hardly smells at all," Deirdre declared.

"Darling Deirdre we have been married forty years and this is the first time you ever called me K-Went-In. I think these quaint Greek village ways are beginning to influence you," Quentin said.

"Oh dear, I didn't realise. I suppose you can always start calling me Did-Rees," Deirdre laughed.

Entering 'Mono Ellinka Trofima' Deirdre sent Quentin off

in the direction of the toilets, telling him he needed a good scrub with soap as he reeked of cheap perfume from having mail order Masha sitting on his knee. As Yiota relieved Deirdre of the large sea bass she assured her "Is no problem you bring your own fish but better next time you gut it first. I no like gutting. I make a nice lemon oil dress for the fish and yous eat it with fried potatoes and salad."

"Better use lots of lemon," Takis advised her as she carried the fish into the kitchen "that thing smells a bit high. Have they never heard of refrigerators in America?"

"Maybe not," Yiota said. "Socrates told me American people don't eat feta but prefer cheese out of an aerosol can. They do have some strange foreign ways abroad."

"Ah, we show the nice K-Went-In and Did-Rees our superior Greek ways. We will convince 'em it is better over 'ere and they will buy that old falling down 'ouse and spend their money in 'ere every night," Takis said.

As they tucked into sea bass with a lemon dress Adonis told Quentin and Deirdre that very soon they must come to eat dinner at his hotel and meet his good wife Penelope. The pair declared they would love to, adding "we never even realised you were married Adoni, you kept that quiet."

"Well yous never asked," he replied. "Penelope 'ave 'ow you say the working 'oliday. I send her on course to Athens on hotel management. We go five star this year we 'ope, what with new shower curtains nailed up and new mosquito eating plugs in all rooms. Penelope tells me she 'ave learned 'ow to take bookings on that new-fangled computer thing, so the course was money well spent I am thinking."

Talk turned to the inevitable topic of the Lemoni Spiti and Adonis had lots of suggestions to make it more modern.

"Yous get rid of the kitchen to make living room more

bigly," he suggested. "Yous won't need a kitchen if yous eat 'ere every day. K-Went-In I don't a think you want to chain Did-Rees up in kitchen, no? You build a bigly fence very high then Prosperous Pedros' mother Fotini cant's peer at yous as yous sunbathe without the cloths."

"Oh I'm sure the old lady is harmless," Quentin opined, belatedly assuring Adonis neither himself nor Deirdre were into nude sunbathing.

Tall Thomas was loudly complaining the local council had installed a street light outside his fishing cottage and he couldn't sleep for the unnatural light. Toothless Tasos had suggested he use a catapult to break the light bulb in it and Tall Thomas had misunderstood and wasted hours hurling the cat up the pole. Now the cat had a headache but the light bulb still glowed.

"What a waste of our taxes," Takis agreed "we don't need any new- fangled street lights."

"I 'eard the council installed them because of the under-wear thief," Yiota explained "all the better for spotting the pervert if he goes out stealing at night."

"He needs catching does that one" Takis agreed, an-nouncing to all his customers "Yiota hardly has a single pair of knickers left."

Before Tall Thomas had time to tuck into his taramosalata he was disturbed by Prosperous Pedros calling his mobile phone. Prosperous Pedros had pulled into the harbour with a fine catch but was superstitiously worried his fishing luck would be cursed as the Pappas was furtively hanging around the harbour. Prosperous Pedros pleaded with Tall Thomas to pop down to the harbour and distract the Pappas so he could make a quick dash from the boat.

"How am I meant to distract the Pappas?" Tall Thomas

questioned.

"You could pretend you want to buy some cutlery from his briefcase?" Deirdre piped up.

Leaving his food on the table Tall Thomas exited the taverna, grumbling loudly. Talk of the Pappas had reminded Gorgeous Yiorgos of his promise to Petula and he duly asked Fat Christos if he could have a quiet word outside. The two men exited the taverna but could not come up with a solution to retrieving Petula's engagement ring without breaking Tassia's heart. Fat Christos promised to give it some thought, but short of asking Petula to always wear gloves so the Pappas would not notice the ring, he could not think of anything original.

The two men returned to their table and were soon joined by Tall Thomas and Prosperous Pedros. Tall Thomas had successfully distracted the Pappas by telling him he thought the local children were kicking condom balloons in the church and filching the Holy wine, which resulted in the Pappas running off to the church in a foul temper. This allowed Prosperous Pedros to leap to dry land without incurring the Pappas' fishing curse.

"What a load of superstitious old codswallop," Quentin whispered to Deirdre.

Everyone was most impressed by the resolve Fat Christos was demonstrating by sticking rigidly to his diet, dining once again on nothing but salad and water. "No sign of mail order Masha and that old fool Vasilis tonight" Vangelis the chemist noted.

"She go," Adonis said to everyone's surprise. "I give 'er ride to bus stop. I think she go back to Russia as she take many 'eavy suitcases."

"Do you think she has left that old fool Vasilis?" Yiota

questioned.

"It look like so," Adonis replied. "She won't like cold snow back in Russia I think and will miss the unseasonal heat wave we 'ave 'ere tomorrow."

Deirdre declared the fish was most delicious and Yiota had cooked it to perfection. She asked what was in the delectable lemon dressing but Yiota refused to reveal her secret ingredient, joking it was petrol. The fishermen were most impressed when Fat Christos told them "Did-Rees she catch that fish in 'er 'at."

Prosperous Pedros noticed he had fifteen missed calls on his mobile phone and declared his mother would send him to an early grave with her constant nagging. Winking at Prosperous Pedros, Adonis told Quentin and Deirdre once you got to know her Fotini was a charming old woman and would make a most delightful neighbour. Prosperous Pedros tried not to choke on his plate of vegetarian chicken at such a preposterous lie.

The evening finished nicely with Quentin treating everyone to glasses of brandy and toasting their good health.

CHAPTER 50

An Unseasonable Heat Wave

The unseasonal heat wave struck with a vengeance the next morning. The brilliant sunshine highlighted the scenic beauty of Astakos and drew attention to the vibrantly colourful delights of the blooming wild flowers.

Quentin was so depleted by the soaring heat Fat Christos left him lagging behind in a sweaty heap as they endured their daily jog. "Is thirty five degrees today," Fat Christos told Quentin who, doing a quick conversion, worked out that was ninety five in his Fahrenheit language, far hotter than anything he was used to back in Idaho.

Quentin decided to pop into the hardware shop and buy a portable fan for Deirdre. She was suffering from the effects of the heat and a dodgy tummy possibly brought on by eating the fish she had failed to refrigerate. Bald Yannis was sitting at his cash register, feverishly mopping his brow with what appeared to be a pair of frilly lace panties. He hurriedly shoved them in his pocket as Quentin approached, rotating his arms in the air to mimic the workings of a fan.

"Just tell me what you want in English," Bald Yannis said,

puffing his chest out with self importance. "I don't have all day to stand around watching you flapping round killing imaginary flies. I've important things to be getting on with yous know."

Quentin's request for a fan was met by a lot of muttering malakas from the back room as Bald Yannis went through his stash of boxes. He emerged with a fan, reminding Quentin to tell his wife not to stick her fingers in the blade.

"She isn't stupid you know," Quentin told him.

"That's what Mrs Patoulis said right before the fan I sold her sliced off three of her fingers," Bald Yannis retorted with a supercilious grin on his face. Thinking of the sliced off fingers made Bald Yannis appreciate the pleasures his job occasionally brought him. The recent sales he had made accounted for two lost fingers to chainsaws, a mutilated thumb from a hammer and a near fatal electrocution from a rewired plug. He ought to demand the local doctor paid him a commission, he reflected.

Quentin was happy to leave the cluttered and fusty hardware shop. Carrying the large box containing the fan he tripped over Boukali, Stavroula's taverna cat, fast asleep in the sunshine. Deirdre was most pleased to receive the cooling fan. She assured Quentin she would be fine on her own relaxing with a bucket handy in case she was sick again and he should go off and enjoy himself.

"But don't let Adonis sell you that ruined house," she instructed.

Bald Yannis was due at the clinic the next day to have his hair transplant operation so he needed to find someone to mind the store in his absence. It was difficult to think of anyone he hadn't insulted who would be willing to stand in at short notice. After much scratching of his head he decided to call Moronic Mitsos and see if he was back in the village.

Mitsos had acquired the nickname 'moronic' as he fell for every con going, which was a bit worrying really considering he had been the chief of the local police before his early retirement. Criminals could run rings around the very gullible Moronic Mitsos. In the last few years before his retirement he had been shipped off to work in the politician protection detail in Athens, leaving younger and sharper minds to deal with any criminal elements.

Bald Yannis remembered Moronic Mitsos and his wife had been visiting one of their sons, a policeman on one of the Greek islands. He hoped he was back from his family visit and could be induced to watch the shop.

As luck would have it Moronic Mitsos had returned just the day before from the island and was desperate for an opportunity to get away from his wife.

"Nag nag nag all day long," he complained to Bald Yannis when they met up. "I'll be glad to escape to your shop for a bit of peace and quiet. I would gladly have left her on the island but she insisted on returning as she wants to supervise the decorators we are getting in. She fell for my bad back story so I don't have to go up the ladder and do the decorating, but I will of course end up paying for it all out of my generous police pension."

Moronic Mitsos never missed an opportunity to boast about his generous police pension. His supposedly dangerous duties as an armed protector of politicians had netted him a tidy sum.

"Have you found me a woman off the internet yet?" Moronic Mitsos asked Bald Yannis.

"All in good time. There is quite a selection for yous to peruse when I return from my visit to my cousin," Bald

Yannis said, baldy lying about his intended whereabouts. He had no intention of telling anyone he was really off for a hair transplant and all the glossy brochures from the clinic assured him the results would be so natural no one would notice. It would simply escape them he had ever been hairless, the completely deluded Bald Yannis hoped.

When he returned from the clinic there would be plenty of time to make a laughing stock of Moronic Mitsos who so far had fallen hook, line and sinker for Bald Yannis' internet dating scam.

CHAPTER 51

Goat in the Sunroof

After retrieving his chainsaw from Bald Yannis the Pappas handed it to over to Petula with instructions to go out and chainsaw some wood for their winter supply, telling her not to let anyone see her as it would reflect badly on his dignity. He was still in the most awful temper about the loss of the engagement ring and demanded Petula give his pet goat Krasi special treats to encourage the creature to pass it. Petula freely cursed the Pappas as she chain sawed, it was far too hot for this heavy work and if her husband had been any kind of man he would have done the job himself. She blamed her father for insisting she marry a man in a dress, though no other Pappas of her acquaintance shared the same nasty streak as the man she was stuck with.

Returning to the house for a glass of water Petula was disturbed to find the goat Krasi had been sick all over the bedspread. She could not persuade the Pappas the goat belonged outdoors and he insisted on giving the animal free reign in the house. Wondering what had made the goat sick she followed the pool of water which led to the bathroom and realised once again the goat had been drinking out of the toilet, which that very morning she had liberally doused with bleach.

Sighing wearily Petula telephoned Gorgeous Yiorgos to see if he was free to drive her to the vets with the sickly goat. Luckily the vet was able to pump the goat's stomach and promised there would be no lasting damage.

Petula was relieved the goat was not about to croak it as the Pappas was quite unnaturally attached to it. Oftentimes he would fall into a drunken sleep on the sofa, cradling a bottle of actual krasi in one arm and cuddling the goat Krasi in the other. She would much rather he cuddled the goat than her. The nights he slept with the goat on the sofa rather than snoring beside her in their double bed was a treat Petula relished.

Gorgeous Yiorgos suggested a driving lesson when they left the vets and they enjoyed a pleasant drive with the goat sticking its head out of the sunroof. "You must take the driving test soon Petula," Gorgeous Yiorgos advised "you are really a very good driver now. We just need some more work on your nine point turn to get it down to a three point."

Quentin was greatly amused to spot a goat's head sticking out of a car's sunroof as Petula passed Adonis' car on the road. Quentin had been easily persuaded to once again return to the neighbouring village of Rapanaki and another viewing of the ruined 'Lemoni Spiti.'

"Has your cousin Adonis the mechanic got the spare parts for the car yet?" he asked.

"My cousin Adonis he busy make dry the refrigerated mobile fish van of Tall Thomas. What to do K-Went-In? Tall Thomas he take old banger from that old fool Vasilis to sell fish from but it missing refrigerator. Patience my friend, all in good time my cousin will fix yous car I promise."

Achilles the borrowed builder was once again waiting as they arrived at the 'Lemoni Spiti.' Climbing down from his ladder to greet them Achilles declared "you 'ave 'ardly any 'oles in your roof K-Went-In. I thinks Did-Rees be 'appy it not rain in."

"How many holes exactly is hardly any?" Quentin asked.

"No yous worry, I fix," Achilles answered, evading the question. "Now no rain as sunny. You want I knock this wall down?" he asked as they ambled inside.

"I wouldn't think so as it appears to be a supporting wall," Quentin replied, beginning to wonder about the building credentials of the borrowed builder.

"Yous must make decision to buy 'ouse as others with the bigly monies 'ave eyes on it," Adonis said. "I like yous buy as we goodly friends."

Quentin wondered if this was just a crafty selling technique by Adonis or if someone else really was interested in the property. The only eyes he knew for sure were fixed on it at that very moment was those of the old crone Fotini, perching on her three-legged olive tree ladder, spitting and cursing at them over the wall.

"I will speak with Did-Rees," Quentin promised "but I must say I am rather taken with this house and can imagine many pleasant years living in it."

CHAPTER 52

Secret Addictions

Back in the village Toothless Tasos had an exhausting afternoon drinking coffee outside the kafenion and losing at tavli to Vangelis the chemist. Not realising how late it was he dashed off at great speed to catch the latest gripping episode of his favourite soap opera 'Seven Deadly Mothers-in-Law' when the voice of his dreams addressed him.

"Taso, I wonder if you could help me with a little problem," the object of his affections Thea said, grabbing at his arm in the street. "My television is on the blink and I wondered if yous could fix it as I cannot bear to miss the latest gripping instalment of my favourite soap opera 'Seven Deadly Mothers-in-Law?'"

"It is due to start any moment I think. I wouldn't know as I don't watch soap operas," Toothless Tasos said, thinking he would lose face if it became public knowledge he had a secret soap opera addiction. "There's no time to fix yous television before it starts but yous is most welcome to come to my 'ouse and watch it there."

"That is so kind of yous, just give me five minutes to pop home and feed the cat and I will be right with yous," Thea said, oblivious to the romantic dreams swirling around Toothless Tasos' head.

Toothless Tasos dashed home to tidy up, kicking the bucket from the living room outdoors and throwing an old cushion onto the single deckchair. Rummaging round in the kitchen he was mightily relieved to find a dusty bottle of shop bought wine lurking in the back of the cupboard and reached it out to impress Thea. He'd only just finished his housewifely duties, giving a last quick polish to the stuffed swordfish heads on the wall, when Thea arrived.

Offering Thea the only deckchair, Toothless Tasos hovered nervously. Thea was immediately engrossed in her favourite soap opera while Toothless Tasos feigned a complete lack of interest in it. Remembering the wine he went to find some glasses, but the lack of a corkscrew thwarted his plan to offer Thea liquid refreshment.

"I should have bought an impressive bottle of shop bought wine with a screw top," he muttered to himself as Thea shushed him.

Toothless Tasos was in raptures at having the love of his life in his house and gazed at her adoringly, desperately trying to think of something interesting to say. When he finally came up with a bit of juicy village gossip Thea shushed him again as she did not want to miss a moment of her show. When the soap opera finished Toothless Tasos plucked up all his courage and asked Thea to join him for dinner. He was disappointed when she told him she already had plans for the evening.

"Are you seeing Gorgeous Yiorgos?" he asked

"No, why would I be doing that?" Thea replied. "I promised to help old Mrs Kolokotronis sew Tassia's wedding dress. I can probably fit in dinner with you tomorrow evening," she suggested, realising it would keep him more interested if she played a little bit hard to get.

Unbeknown to Toothless Tasos, Thea was actually in the market for a new husband now she had buried her third one. The village pickings were slim though. Toothless Tasos was a contender for her hand she had not previously considered. He was so shy around her it was almost painful.

Gorgeous Yiorgos appeared quite eager for her attention but Fat Christos had put himself out of the running by proposing to Tassia. Prosperous Pedros was quite handsome she thought, but his outside bathroom was most off-putting and she had no intention of living like a peasant. She did consider Vangelis the chemist had possible romantic potential but he had yet to show any interest in her. As for Bald Yannis she couldn't imagine ever being so desperate that she would consider him.

Satisfied she now had a date lined up with Gorgeous Yiorgos at the weekend and one with Toothless Tasos tomorrow, Thea thought to herself she could soon land herself a fourth husband.

Thea actually needed a fourth husband quite desperately as her debts were piling up to an embarrassing level. In addition to her addiction to soap operas she also had another secret addiction which was landing her in hot water. Thea was a compulsive impulse purchaser, completely hooked on buying tat from the addictive home shopping channel. Her house was filling up with unwanted junk constantly arriving by post but she simply could not curb her spending.

CHAPTER 53

Laughing Too Loudly

Due to the unseasonable sweltering heat wave Takis and Yiota had carried all the tables from inside the taverna and lined them up on the street for an evening of al-fresco dining. Feeling somewhat recovered from her bout of heat stroke and a dodgy tummy, Deirdre was happy to join Quentin there for a bite to eat.

She recounted to Quentin how thoughtful and kind Yiota had been, bringing mountain tea made from some kind of twigs up to the room to combat her nausea.

"It wasn't actually as disgusting as it looked," Deirdre said "and it certainly helped with my dicky tummy."

Quentin agreed the people of Astakos were forever making kind gestures, relieved to see his wife still retained all her fingers and had not come to any harm from using Bald Yannis' lethal fan.

Quentin told Deirdre all about his return visit to the 'Lemoni Spiti,' happy to reassure her Achilles the borrowed builder had pronounced the roof almost sound.

"Really Quentin, it isn't practical at all to consider buying a falling down house in a foreign country, even if the thought of keeping chickens and goats with a sea view does appeal to you. Our home is in Idaho."

"Yes I know our main home is in Idaho, but think how lovely it would be to have our own little holiday home here too. It's such a friendly place and we have been made so welcome. I really do love it here and it already feels like a second home. Also I am enjoying picking up new Greek words to converse with our new friends," Quentin said, pausing to say "Kalimera" to Takis.

"Even I know that means good morning rather than good evening," Deirdre told him, adding "I guess I must be picking up a few Greek words here and there too. Seriously Quentin if you have your heart set on buying that falling down house then you need to go through our finances with a fine toothcomb."

The unseasonably hot heat wave attracted many customers to 'Mono Ellinka Trofima' that evening. Tables were packed as Yiota served plates of vegetarian chicken and bowls of fish soup without fish, a particular local favourite.

The retired former police chief Moronic Mitsos joined the others, causing great amusement when he announced he would be running the hardware shop while Bald Yannis went off to visit his cousin for a short visit.

"He's had yous," Tall Thomas said. "Bald Yannis isn't off to visit his cousin, he's off to have a hair transplant. Trust yous to be the last one to find out Mitso."

The ensuing laughter was too much for Stavroula who spotting the full tables as she returned from the bakery to her own, nearly empty taverna, was overcome with angry jealousy.

"Disturbing the peace they are," she ranted down the telephone to the local police station, demanding to make an official complaint about noise pollution. Pancratius, the village policeman who was off sick with pancreatitis, was very annoyed to be dragged from his sick bed over such trivial nonsense, and yet was nevertheless duty bound to investigate.

Strolling up to Takis who was firing the grill he reported "I have had reports your customers are laughing too loudly and disturbing the peace."

"Let me guess, that old cow Stavroula has made a complaint again," Takis guessed. "It's the same old nonsense every year when we carry our tables outside. My customers don't make half as much noise as Stavroula herself when she screams at Socrates. Sit down for a bowl of fishless fish soup Pancrati and I'll step outside and tell them to keep the noise down a bit."

Pancratius took a table well away from Moronic Mitsos as he was in no mood to hear his endless stories of his glory days as the local chief of police. Moronic Mitsos could bore for Greece once he set off reminiscing about his days in the police force.

"Is it an offence to laugh too loudly in your country K-Went-In?" Takis asked. "Stavoula knows all our laws since she took up with Slick Socrates the lawyer and is forever making complaining phone calls to the police."

"I am not familiar with any such ordinance," Quentin replied.

Taverna talk soon turned to the horrendous crime wave Astakos was experiencing, namely the theft of fancy underwear from washing lines. It was the first time Moronic Mitsos had heard of this outrage and he decided to make it his business to discover the identity of the culprit. Deirdre confessed she was missing a bra she had hung over the balcony to dry.

The former chief of police assured her he would do his best to recover her smalls, saying "my dear Did-Rees, yous underwear will be safe in my hands."

"No sign of that old fool Vasilis," Prosperous Pedros noticed. "It's not like him to miss an evening in here." As the talk turned to Vasilis concerns began to be voiced no one at all had seen the old fool since Masha had left him.

"Perhaps someone should call round and make sure the old fool is still alive," Gorgeous Yiorgos said.

"Very good of you to volunteer," everyone agreed as it was settled Gorgeous Yiorgos would go the old fool's house the next morning.

CHAPTER 54

Gorgeous Yiorgos Makes a Grisly Discovery

News of Gorgeous Yiorgos' grisly discovery was the talk of the village before noon the next day. The gossip was soon confirmed by the loud clanging of the church bell announcing the sad demise of that old fool Vasilis.

Gorgeous Yiorgos was not short of an audience as he re-counted finding Vasilis sprawled out dead on his bed, clutch-ing a glossy photograph of Masha posing in a bikini, in his gnarled and stiffened fingers. The bedroom smelt like a brew-ery and all Mashas' frillies were still scattered over the floor where she had thrown them in her haste to pack up and leave Vasilis. Onos the donkey had been wandering about in the kitchen with a miserable hangover, obviously pining for his best friend.

The undertaker was duly contacted and the Pappas was notified and began to make the funeral arrangements. The Pappas was most conflicted as he had really hoped for a good funeral to boost his dwindling congregation, but cursed it was that old fool Vasilis who had gone and kicked the bucket before paying up the blackmail money. The Pappas was too self absorbed to consider his own blackmail scheme may have hastened the early death of Vasilis from the stress.

Chatter was rife as the village folk drank coffee in Stavroulas. "That gold digger Masha she kill him by leaving him," was one popular point of view, but Tassia was quick to defend Masha declaring she had really loved him.

Mrs Kolokotronis was openly weeping and felt responsible for Masha's departure. "We insulted her by giving her all those hideous old lady dresses," she declared "and Vasilis forgetting her birthday must have been the last straw."

"He die of a broken heart," Petros the postman opined.

"It is all so dreadfully sad," Deirdre said. "Masha will be heartbroken I am sure when she hears."

"She 'ave no heart, she mail order gold digger," Stavroula offered. "Still he was far too young to die; he was only eighty four with lots of life still in 'im."

The only certainty was Masha must be notified of her husband's demise. No one knew where she had gone and the last person to see her was Adonis when he left her at the bus stop with her heavy suitcases. "I think she go 'ome to Russia," Adonis said "but wherever she is she must be told."

Luckily Evangelia from the beauty shop had the mobile telephone number of her most frequent customer and the village folks were able to leave a frantic voicemail message breaking the tragic news and urging Masha to return home in time for the funeral.

CHAPTER 55

A New Look For Toothless Tasos

Toothless Tasos was blissfully oblivious to the passing of that old fool Vasilis. Brimming with excitement over the prospect of his dinner date with Thea that evening he had driven into town to buy some new clothes to impress her. He decided to splurge on a new suit and tie as he wanted to look his very best and found a very shiny blue suit on sale for a massively discounted price.

The only suit he possessed was the one he had worn to his wedding with Stavroula and these days it only got an outing for funerals. Luckily the new very shiny blue suit was in the same style as his old one as Toothless Tasos did not want to experiment with anything too trendy.

He planned to take Thea to the nearby village of Marouli, named for lettuce, as the evening would be a disaster if the folk in Astakos were watching and gossiping about his every move. There was a nice little taverna in Marouli that served excellent souvlaki and best of all it was very cheap. Toothless Tasos was a bit of a skinflint if truth be told and moths were known to emerge from his wallet when he finally prised it open.

He hoped Thea would not mind travelling there in the ancient side- car that was welded onto his now vintage motorbike. He had an idea some women could be a bit funny about wearing a crash helmet on top of their hairdos. Toothless Tasos was very law abiding, as he didn't want to do anything to draw attention to himself after successfully getting away with faking his own death.

On his return to the village he had an appointment at the beauty parlour for a new hair cut and it was there Evangelia broke the news to him of Vasilis' death. His first reaction was most selfish as he hoped the bad news would not mean Thea felt the need to postpone their impending dinner date. He decided if she was distressed he would comfort her. He made a mental note to take a newly washed pocket handkerchief along on his date in case he had to mop up her tears of grief.

Evangelia scolded Toothless Tasos on the terrible condition of his hair, persuading him to have a drastic new cut revealing his ears. She sent him on his way with an expensive bagful of hair products he was clueless how to use. She sprayed his hair with enough products it failed to move in the breeze and was very stiff to the touch. She insisted on shaving the straggly beard from his face, leaving the bottom half of his face a sickly pale pallor compared to the rest of his weather browned features.

By the time he was dressed in his new shiny blue suit he felt quite different, even though he had kept his holey pullover on beneath the suit jacket for comfort. He was unable to assess his new look as his house lacked any kind of mirror and had no idea he looked quite ridiculous, not to mention too shiny.

He called for Thea with a bunch of wilting flowers in his

hand. Not recognizing her lovelorn suitor in his very shiny blue suit, sweeping brush stiff hair and newly shaved face, she attempted to slam the door in his face, saying she wasn't interested in buying any flowers.

"It is I Tasos come to take yous to dinner," he announced with one foot in her door, causing Thea to do a double take when she realised it was indeed Toothless Tasos and not a shiny, slimy door to door salesman.

She supposed it was a bit of an improvement over his usual bedraggled look but was nevertheless mortified to be stepping out with anyone tasteless enough to wear such an execrable excuse of a shiny blue suit over a holey pullover. As she climbed into his ancient side-car she supposed he had at least made an effort, though she noticed he had made no attempt to compliment on her appearance. Toothless Tasos thought Thea looked like a goddess but he was far too tongue tied to tell her.

The cheap taverna Toothless Tasos had chosen to impress Thea was overrun with cats. Luckily the motorbike side-car was equipped with Tasos' trusty old water pistol which he used to scare the cats away, thinking he was being most gentlemanly. As Thea was a great lover of cats Toothless Tasos went down even further in her estimation. Tasos stood out like a sore thumb in his shiny new suit as the other customers were dressed in typical farmer gear, having spent most of the day harvesting lettuces.

Conversation naturally turned to the death of Vasilis as it had been such an unexpected shock to all the villagers. "I wonder if mail order Masha will inherit his 'ouse and all his money," Thea mused, contemplating how much money she owed for all the tat she had been buying from the addictive home shopping channel.

"Well he's no one else to leave it to and she was his wife," Tasos said, "he never had any children, or at least none we 'eard of."

"She'll only get it if she 'ears he's dead and turns up," Thea suggested. "If she doesn't turn up it should go to the donkey home as you know how that old fool Vasilis was about donkeys."

Attempting to keep the conversation going Toothless Tasos asked Thea if any of her underwear had gone missing.

"I think the first date is a bit too soon to be taking an interest in my smalls," Thea replied.

The conversation dried up as their souvlaki arrived. Thea considered Toothless Tasos was showing no class at all by bringing her to this cheap taverna with only souvlaki, lettuce and keftedes on the menu. Gorgeous Yiorgos had gone to a bit more effort when he took her out and boasted a car with a sunroof, rather than an ancient bike with a side-car.

On the plus side Toothless Tasos was such an old miser he must have plenty of money saved up in the bank. Even if she could stop her shopping channel addiction cold turkey there were still a lot of bills to settle for the piles of tat she had been buying which necessitated her catching a fourth husband very quickly.

Thea suggested they leave early as they had to be up at the crack of dawn for Vasils' funeral and it didn't seem seemly to be out having fun so soon after his death. As Toothless Tasos bid her goodnight on her doorstep he gallantly presented her with a bottle of olive oil as a traditional gesture of courtship.

"Oh look," said Deirdre, hanging over the balcony to get a good view "Toothless Tasos has just taken Thea home, I hope they had a romantic date."

"Shush, it will be all round the village tomorrow if you say it too loudly," Quentin said "I've never known a place where people gossip so much."

CHAPTER 56

The Funeral

E veryone in the village turned out for that old fool Vasilis' funeral. The Pappas was in a most inappropriately cheery smug mood as the church was for once bursting at the seams and all the pews were full. Most of the congregation fell asleep as the Pappas droned on, and had to be nudged awake when it was time to line up and give the corpse in his open coffin a traditional kiss.

"No sign of mail order Masha," Stavroula noticed.

"We left plenty of messages on her mobile phone but she didn't respond," Slick Socrates told her.

Quentin and Deirdre couldn't understand what was going on but they joined the line of 'kissing the corpse' mourners as it seemed the right thing to do. Handkerchiefs were whipped out of pockets and used to cover noses as the mourners approached the corpse of old Vasilis who reeked of donkey and ouzo. "Do you really think I need to kiss him?" Deirdre whispered to Quentin "after all I hardly knew him."

"It seems to be the done thing," Quentin whispered back "just hold your nose and get on with it."

After the corpse of Vasilis had received its last kiss the lid of the coffin was lowered, sealing Vasilis tightly inside still clutching the glossy photograph of Masha in a bikini. The processional walk to the graveyard, where a newly dug hole awaited Vasilis, was led by the Pappas followed by Onos the donkey adorned with a wreath.

The six pallbearers followed next and then the rest of the mourners. The task of hoisting the coffin on their shoulders fell to Toothless Tasos, Fat Christos, Gorgeous Yiorgos, Prosperous Pedros, Tall Thomas and Takis. They stumbled along under the weight, trying to avoid slipping in the mess Onos the donkey left in her wake.

The funeral livened up a bit at the graveside when a hysterically sobbing woman appeared with her face encased in bandages. Even though the bandages concealed all the woman's features there was no doubt it was mail order Masha as the enormous silicone chest, long blonde hair extensions and tottering stilettos gave her identity away.

"It's too late her coming back now when it was her leaving him what killed him," Stavroula said loudly. "Heartbroken he was over that heartless loose hussy."

"I never leave him," mail order Masha cried out. "I only go to the clinic in Athens to 'ave my lips done. I would have been back sooner if the lips not go 'orribly wrong."

Mail order Masha was telling the truth. On the day of her birthday she had intended to surprise Vasilis by telling him he had bought her a pair of luscious new lips as a present and she just had to pop along to the clinic in Athens to have the filler injected. When he had disappeared on the day of the party she had flounced off to the clinic in a temper, leaving Vasilis to presume she had left him. She had always intended to return to her old fool of a husband and would have been back sooner if her lip operation hadn't gone horribly wrong.

Masha had suffered some kind of allergic reaction to the injection of filler and her lips had puffed up to four times their normal size, leaving her with the most grotesque 'trout pout'. She could not bear to look in the mirror and had insisted the incompetent clinician wrap her face in bandages until her 'trout pout' deflated.

Masha had only received word of Vasilis' tragic demise the day before as she had been ignoring all her telephone calls, presuming it was Vasilis who she was still very cross at and did not want to talk to.

As the grave digger began to shovel earth atop Vasilis' coffin, Masha's mobile phone began to ring. The mourners gave her dirty looks, telling her to turn the phone off as the graveside was no place for such disturbances, and as a supposedly grieving widow, she ought to know better. When Masha went to turn off the phone she thought it must be some sort of sick joke as the number flashing up on her mobile was that of Vasilis.

Frantically shushing the mourners Masha answered the phone and began screaming manically, telling the gravedigger to stop his shovelling. "Dig him up, dig him up," she screeched like a demented banshee. "Vasilis he on the phone and say he is alive in dark place."

"Don't be so absurd," the Pappas said, but Masha handed the phone to Slick Socrates who soon confirmed it was indeed Vasilis on the phone.

The coffin was hoisted out of the hole and everyone watched in collective awe as the lid was prised open. A furious Vasilis climbed unsteadily out of the coffin demanding to know what on earth was going on. It turned out he hadn't been dead at all but simply pickled from alcohol. The ouzo had knocked him into a comatose state. It was only as the coffin lid closed and he began to be deprived of air he had started to come round in a dreadful panic as he realised he was trapped in a dark box.

The mourners thought a miracle had taken place and began frantically making the sign of the cross and then leaping with joy as though they were in some evangelical gospel meeting. As Vasilis began to understand the predicament he had just escaped from the expletives started at a fast and furious pace as he cursed those gathered to give him a send off.

"Bury me alive would you, you malakas, can't a man have a drink in peace without being thrown in the grave? And why you no put no photo of Onus the donkey in my coffin you malakas?" Vasilis demanded to know

"We thought you were dead of a broken heart when mail order Masha leave you," Gorgeous Yiorgos said.

"I no leave yous my love, I am right here," Masha declared throwing herself into the arms of her husband. Seeing his wife encased in facial bandages Vasilis started to scream, accusing the mourners of beating her up and telling them they were dead men if they laid one more fist on her.

"No one 'urt me except with insults" Masha assured Vasilis "the bandages are to cover my 'orrible botched lip job."

"Remove them at once and let me kiss you," Vasilis said, but Masha refused, saying "they 'ave to heal before you get frisky."

Everyone was horrified when they realised Vasilis had actually been buried alive and was only saved from the grave as he happened to have his mobile phone in his pocket. Slick Socrates commented he must change his mobile phone provider as Vasilis' phone had remarkable service if it worked from an underground grave.

The finger of blame was pointed at Gorgeous Yiorgos as it was he who had proclaimed he had found Vasilis dead in his bed.

"Can't you tell the difference between a passed out drunk and a corpse?" Vangelis the chemist asked him.

"He was dead I swear," Gorgeous Yiorgos insisted "yous all thought so too when yous kissed him in church."

"Thank goodness they don't allow cremation in the village," Quentin observed "or Vasilis would be nothing more than a pile of ashes by now."

Catching sight of Stavroula by the graveside Vasilis recollected the awful blackmail letter from the Pappas claiming Stavroula was apparently his love child. Throwing his arms around Stavroula he said, "I am so touched yous came to my funeral, yous kind, thoughtful and lovely woman."

"Don't get carried away," Stavroula told him "you know we always give everyone a good send off, even if we hate them."

Sotiris, Vasilis' old neighbour who had spent the last thirty years feuding with him over the boundary of the disputed olive tree, sidled up to Vasilis and confessed he had been so grief stricken when he heard of his death he chopped the disputed olive tree down. "Yous malaka fool," Vasilis shouted "what we feud over now?"

The Pappas had quite enough of this graveside cock up that had deprived him of his rightful place as the centre of attention. "What I want to know is who is going to pay for this hole and the funeral service?"

"Yous can use the same 'ole to bury Tassia's old uncle in," volunteered Fat Christos "I 'ave just 'ad phone call to say he has snuffed it."

The Pappas cheered up a bit at the thought the hole

would not be wasted and he would have yet another funeral service to conduct. Tassia burst into tears as it was the first she had heard of the death of her old uncle.

CHAPTER 57

The Heiress

Tassia's ancient old uncle was the richest man in the village, having amassed a small fortune over charging unsuspecting tourists in the small store he preferred people grandly to refer to as a supermarket. Just like his brother, Tassia's deceased father, her uncle hated spending any of his money, so Tassia, as his only surviving relative, stood to inherit a sizeable amount, not to mention the supermarket, his house and a lot of olive trees.

Fat Christos gave himself a pat on the back for having the foresight to propose to Tassia before she became an heiress. He would hate for her to think he was after her money even though he was. As he comforted Tassia she confessed "I never even liked him, it was just a shock hearing the news on top of Vasilis rising from the dead. I suppose now I will have to take over the running of the shop or sell it."

"We could always run it together my love," Fat Christos suggested, thinking it would provide them with a most handsome living plus give him some gravitas in the village.

"I could scrap the fishing boat as the stupid government

are handing over cash bribes to stop fishermen from fishing. We must speak to the Pappas at once about bringing the wedding forward and make everything official."

Tassia agreed, reminding Christos of his promise to give her a baby as soon as they were married. Fat Christos said "All in good time, let us get the boat and finances sorted first. I will tell my mother to hurry up with your wedding dress."

"Well if she wouldn't be offended I could buy one from a shop now I am about to be a wealthy woman," Tassia shyly suggested.

"Nonsense we don't want to be wasting money on something you will only wear once, my mother is doing marvellous things with that bit of old polyester she dug out of the attic and dyed white," said Fat Christos, determined to put his foot down and let Tassia know he intended to control the marital purse strings.

Having made their plans for the future the engaged couple decided to join the other villagers at the wake for Vasilis at Stavroula's taverna. Mail order Masha had been in no mood to party as her lips were still painfully inflated and she could not drink anything without dribbling. She decided the bandaged mummy look didn't suit her at all.

Vasilis persuaded her to join the party by promising to give up the demon drink, and winning her round with the solid gold brooch in the shape of a donkey, with diamonds for eyes, he discovered had been buried with him in his breast pocket. He could not turn down the chance to be around Stavroula his love child, though he had not yet made up his mind to tell her he was her father.

He would discuss it with Masha first he decided. He also had to determine what approach to take with the Pappas who he had no intention of paying any blackmail money to. He had to play it carefully as he did not want Stavroula to hear of her parentage from such a malicious source.

Gorgeous Yiorgos was fed up with being the butt of everyone's jokes as they teased him endlessly about confusing a passed out drunk with a corpse. He slunk away quietly, deciding to call on Petula and give her some more help with the tricky hill start manoeuvre she kept stalling on.

Moronic Mitsos decided to launch his unofficial investigation into the disappearing underwear. He received plenty of slaps across the head as his offensive line of questioning upset the village women, putting his big foot into delicate underwear matters without any tact. After one slap too many he too slunk away, taking refuge in the hardware store where he discovered Bald Yannis' underwear catalogue stash.

Not quite managing to put two and two together, he presumed Bald Yannis was planning to expand into ladies underwear to go with his hideous old lady dresses and missed the glaringly obvious clue Bald Yannis was in fact the elusive underwear thief.

Prosperous Pedros was most put out Stavroula's cold buffet had no vegetarian options and got into a heated argument with her when she insisted snails were vegetables. "Po po these non vegetarian snails are only good for fish bait," he said, sticking them in his pocket to take home to put on his fishing lines.

Masha was becoming most suspicious of the amount of attention her husband was lavishing on Stavroula, paying her endless compliments. She wasn't in the slightest bit jealous as she believed no one could compete with her in the beauty stakes, even with the disadvantage of a bandaged face and dribbling lips. Nevertheless she suspected Vasilis was up to something and planned to have it out with him when she got him home.

"I think being buried alive has left that old fool Vasilis not right in the 'ed," Stavroula confided to Mrs Kolokotronis. "He's been fussing around me saying nice things, which is 'orrible, all afternoon. It's not normal I tell you."

"Well it must 'ave been a traumatic experience waking up in a coffin," said Mrs Kolokotronis. "I don't think I could have survived a hole in the ground if I wasn't really dead."

Spotting Tassia she called her over and suggested they retire to make some alterations to the wedding dress, pointedly noting "just as my Christos is getting thinner you are putting on weight Tassia and your bosom is growing most bigly."

CHAPTER 58

Bald Yannis' New Hair

Bald Yannis was having a ghastly time of it at the hair transplant clinic. Not having bothered to read any of the glossy brochures before making his appointment he hadn't realised his recent back wax and his early morning facial shave had left him with limited options in the donor hair department. The hair transplant surgeon informed Bald Yannis his only options were to have either the hair from his legs or the hair from his chest grafted onto his bald head.

"If only I hadn't paid good money for that torturous back wax in the beauty parlour yous would have had my hairy back to take grafts from," Yannis said. As he had a surfeit of chest hair growing wildly he reluctantly told the surgeon to take the donor hair from there.

The result was nothing like the photos in the glossy brochure. The surgeon made lots of small holes in Bald Yannis' by now bright red scalp and plugged them with chest hair in a curved line reaching from ear to ear. The front and back of his head remained bald on either side of the newly planted weed like strip of wispy hair.

Bald Yannis was apoplectic with rage when he looked in the mirror and saw how ridiculously clown-like he looked. "Malaka what 'ave yous done to me?" he screamed. "I paid yous good money for this, yous incompetent hair butcher."

Worried he was about to be attacked the surgeon reassured Bald Yannis he would soon get used to his new look and if he still hated it tomorrow he would sell him a toupee.

"Now one thing I should have mentioned before I started," the surgeon explained "is the area of your chest I took the donor hair from will remain bald as that patch of hair will completely refuse to grow back."

Bald Yannis looked at his still very hairy chest which now featured a prominent large bald circular spot in the centre between his nipples. "How can I go without a shirt in summer with that ridiculous bald spot showing and how will I explain it away if I manage to lure any unsuspecting woman to my bed?" Yannis questioned.

"Well you could always have your chest waxed at the beauty parlour to make the rest of it match the bald spot," the surgeon suggested. Yannis blanched at the very thought of waxing any more of his body and lamented he was hairy in places he didn't want hair and bald in places he wanted it.

"I thought this hair transplant would give me a full 'ead of hair," he complained. "Instead I have ended up with a wiry wispy landing strip between my ears. I'd better take that toupee now in case anyone is rude enough to comment on this awful hair transplant and I suppose it will cover the enormous scar you have left me with. Don't bother with the toupee glue, I have plenty of superglue in the hardware shop at cost price without wasting any more money."

CHAPTER 59

A Quiet Evening in the Wake of the Wake

After all the excitement of the funeral and the wake it was unusually quiet in 'Mono Ellinka Trofima' that evening. There were only a few straggles of fishermen sitting around eating tripe soup and they were happy to have the company of Quentin and Deirdre to relieve the monotony.

"I 'ear Fat Christos is going to scrap his fishing boat and take government bribes to stop fishing. It madness, 'is boat is in better condition than mine," Prosperous Pedros said.

"Only 'cos you never spend any of your money, yous skinflint," Takis reminded him. "We must 'elp Fat Christos strip all things of value from the boat before the government send tax inspectors to make it a bigly bonfire."

"A curse on Fat Christos the malaka, inviting the tax inspectors to the village," Vangelis the chemist complained, knowing he would need to rush to his pharmacy shop to make sure he had a receipt roll on show in the cash register.

"A curse on that malaka indeed," agreed Takis, making a mental note to start handing out paper receipts instead of writing up bills on the paper tablecloths.

"Ave yous bought that falling down 'ouse yet K-Went-In?" Tall Thomas asked. "Not yet," replied Quentin "we were at the funeral today."

The thought of that old fool Vasilis buried alive in that coffin was too awful for everyone to contemplate and they hurriedly turned to a more cheerful topic.

"Did you 'ear Toothless Tasos is walking out with Tassia?" Quentin decided to stir things up with the bit of juicy gossip he had been sitting on since the night before, as he was very nearly one of the locals now.

"What yous say?" screeched Gorgeous Yiorgos "that two-timing hussy has a date with me tomorrow."

At that exact moment Thea was sat at home surrounded by piles of tat she had amassed from the home shopping channel. Contemplating a debt laden future she picked up a hammer and violently destroyed the television set to remove the temptation of any more ill-advised impulse purchases from the addictive home shopping channel. With the television destroyed she then began to compile a list of pros and cons of each of her suitors.

CHAPTER 60

A Confession

S it down my love, we must 'ave the serious talk," Vasilis said to the bandage wrapped and drooling mail order Masha when they returned home after the funeral.

"You want divorce me as I look 'orrible with botched lip job," Masha shouted.

"No, of course not," Vasilis told her "but yous know how yous keep saying you would like children...."

"Ah the Viagra is working at last and yous want go bed to make baby," Masha interrupted before Vasilis could finish his sentence.

"No, well maybe, but not yet. I 'ave a confession, yous possibly 'ave a fifty year-old step-daughter and it is Stavroula," Vasilis revealed.

"What, 'ow can that be, I am too young to be a mother to that old shrew Stavroula? Vasili yous make me laughing stock, making me mother to unpleasant nasty woman," mail order Masha exploded, continuing "it impossible I be related to a woman with no clothes taste and bad 'air, Vasili what you thinking, must be mistake yes?"

Vasilis explained to Masha the first he had learned Stavroula may be his daughter was in a blackmail letter from the Pappas who had heard this from Stavroula's mothers' death bed confession.

"Po po, you better not be thinking of leaving 'alf of everything to her," Masha said, before the enormity of Vasilis' news began to sink in.

"Whoever 'eard of a blackmailing Pappas before?" Masha said. "It not right, it not decent, it not churchly. People should be able to take their deathbed confessions to the grave without interfering Pappas's causing havoc. Are no murky secrets safe? No way you give that malaka Pappas one cent of my, I mean our, money."

"And if it is true Stavroula he is my daughter?" Vasilis asked.

"We say nothing till you 'ave, 'ow you say, the DNA proof," Masha advised. "If is true he is your daughter then I play step Mama and Stavroula will be big sister to baby we go make."

As the pair pondered how they could secretly obtain a sample of Stavroula's DNA without her knowing Masha came up with an excellent idea. She told Vasilis as soon as her bandages were removed she would invite Stavroula to join her for an afternoon of pampering at the village beauty parlour and then remove the hairs from the hairbrush Evaneglia used on her client.

With the matter settled to their mutual satisfaction Masha slipped Vasilis another tab of Viagra, realising the best way to secure her own inheritance was to start reproducing as quickly as possible.

CHAPTER 61

Presumed Dead

Whilst Vasilis and Masha were contemplating how to get their hands on a sample of Stavroula's DNA the policemen from Pouthena, the up north village of 'nowhere', had returned to Astakos and were at that moment asking Stavroula to provide a DNA sample "to rule you out of our enquiries," they explained.

Kostas' car, which Stavroula had driven to the top of an overgrown ravine and then pushed over the edge on the night she poisoned her second husband with weed killer laced homemade chicken soup, had at last been found. A search party was combing the area surrounding the car in the hopes of retrieving his body, but the ravine was an area well known to be frequented by brown bears, wild boars and the odd wolf, any of which could have long gnawed away any evidence.

Slick Socrates was on hand to advise Stavroula against handing over any of her DNA, telling the policemen it was bound to be all over the car as Kostas had driven her in it many times.

"You think Kostas he dead?" Stavroula asked the policemen who told her they thought it was possible as his car had been found in the middle of nowhere, not even close to the 'nowhere' village of Pouthena, and no one had seen sight of Kostas for ages.

"Maybe he crash off the road and there is no foul play," the policemen told her. "Katerina, the sister of Kostas, is making lots of noise since she returned from the island to discover her brother missing, and we have to put on a show of investigating as she is too loud."

As the policemen were being quite pleasant and there had been no mention of handcuffs or interrogations, Stavroula decided to once again butter them up with platefuls of free food. As long as their search was concentrated on the ravine there was no reason to suppose they would ever think to dig up the new concrete floor she had lain in the chicken coop. The policemen did not seem terribly bright and were way too easily distracted by tempting plates of home cooked food.

She served the two policemen heaped plates of pastitsio which they ate with relish. She was eager to get rid of them as she thought if Kostas was presumed dead she would not need a divorce from him and would be free to marry Slick Socrates. The lawyer put a spanner in her thoughts by reminding her even if Kostas was presumed dead, thus leaving her a free woman, there was still the matter of her marriage to Toothless Tasos which had never been legally dissolved since Tasos faked his own death at sea.

Stavroula had been the innocent party in Toothless Tasos' deception, but Slick Socrates advised her if she pursued legal channels to rectify the situation then her marriage to Kostas, even if he was now presumed dead, would be revealed as bigamous. Stavroula really could not afford to have anyone looking too closely into her marriage with Kostas.

Stavroula was stuck with one useless husband who was supposed to be dead but wasn't, and one dead husband who was only presumed to be dead but was actually buried under the chicken coop. It was all enough to make Stavroula's head explode and she began to seriously consider getting rid of Toothless Tasos. After all she thought, murder was quite easy once you got the hang of it and getting rid of Toothless Tasos would free her once and for all to marry Socrates.

As she banged her pots and pans in the kitchen whilst contemplating the next day's menu her thoughts turned to where she might get her hands on some cyanide and where might be a good place to hide a body. Throwing some oregano in a pan of lamb Stavroula began singing happily to herself.

CHAPTER 62

Don't Trust the Collection Plate Condoms

A s Tassia stripped down to her underwear for her wedding dress fitting with her soon to be mother-in-law Mrs Kolokotronis, the older woman could not help commenting, "Your chest is nearly as bigly as mail order Masha's and you are getting a thick middle Tassia."

The older woman stuck a foot into Tassia's back in an effort to fasten the buttons. Tassia made a frantic dash to the bathroom where she threw up. Mrs Kolokotronis was quick to surmise the problem and proclaimed her delight at becoming a grandmother.

"We were supposed to wait until the wedding night but Christos was overcome with passion on the night he proposed," Tassia admitted.

"You must bring the wedding forward so no one knows yous in the pudding club," Mrs Kolokotronis advised, asking what Fat Christos had to say on the matter. Tassia admitted she was too shy to tell him, but was over the moon she had got pregnant on her very first sexual encounter.

"All the book say it's difficult to get pregnant the first

time," she said, but Mrs Kolokotronis assured her the old rumour only applied if the couple were standing up or in a car. "That explains it then as we made the passion lying down in the garden shed," Tassia elaborated.

Mrs Kolokotronis telephoned her son, telling him to come home from the taverna as there was good news to celebrate. On hearing about Tassia's remarkable pregnancy Fat Christos announced "I knew it was a mistake to use the condom from the church collection plate."

Too late he realised he should have feigned delight at the prospect of becoming a father and hurriedly assured his mother and fiancée he was indeed overcome with joy at the news. He wondered if Tassia's pregnancy would interfere with her running her dead uncle's supermarket alone when he went into the clinic to have his stomach stapled. He must mention his weight loss operation and get Tassia to hand over the cash for the doctor's brown envelope the moment the ink dried on their wedding certificate.

"I 'ave the busy day tomorrow," he said, "after my harbour jog the tax inspectors send someone to make the fishing boat a bonfire. It leaves no time to see the Pappas so I go now to church and tell him we marry this weekend."

"Kala, if we wait any longer Tassia will be too fat for dress," Mrs Kolokotronis said as Tassia dashed to the bathroom to be sick again.

CHAPTER 63

A Bigly House Decision

Adonis drove Quentin and Deirdre back to the neighbouring village of Rapanaki to have yet another look at the 'Lemoni Spiti'. As they pulled into the 'Lemoni Spiti' they could hear the old crone next door, Fotini, screaming loudly. Dashing to peer over the wall they encountered the sight of Fotini hanging on for dear life to the branch of an olive tree. The three-legged wooden olive ladder had toppled over, leaving her precariously caught mid-air with a good half-meter drop beneath her dangling feet.

"Get over 'ere quick Adoni," she screamed "I cannot 'ang on much longer, my arms is weak. I been stuck here for hours with no malaka to 'ear me shout."

Adonis leapt over the wall and putting his arms around Fotini's hips he lowered her onto firm ground. "Watch where yous putting your 'ands yous pervert," Fotini warned "yous is far too fresh yous young whipper snapper."

"What yous doing up the tree?" Adonis asked. Fotini explained she had been peering over the wall to spy on a new set of potential house buyers when the ladder toppled over and she grabbed onto the branch.

"I no bring any other 'ouse buyers here," Adonis said, wondering if he had a rival about to cash in on the commission.

"K-Went-In this not goodly news, if someone else buy 'ouse yous no can buy. Let me telephone 'ouse owner and see if he reduce price for yous." As he dialled the number of the house owner Adonis confided "Achilles the borrowed builder 'as lots of ideas to decorate windows with shower curtains, it the bigly new fashion in Athens he say."

"This house is already such a bargain. If Adonis can get the price reduced even more it would practically be a steal," Quentin whispered to Deirdre.

"We would still need to pay for the costs of the renovations," Deirdre pointed out, to which Achilles insisted "I comes very cheaply," surprising them as he had popped up out of nowhere.

"You really want to buy his house?" Deirdre questioned Quentin, and he admitted he really did, in fact his heart was set on it even though his head considered the downfalls of owning property in this foreign country.

"Quentin you have spent our whole married life putting my happiness first and if this is what you really want then yes, I am all for it. We will buy this falling down old ruined house and engage Achilles the borrowed builder to make it habitable. We will spend our vacations in our new 'Lemoni Spiti' in the village of a radish in Greece. "

Quentin picked Deirdre up in his arms and spun her round, no mean feat as his impulsive action nearly gave him a hernia. Adonis joined them and told them the new reduced price of the house, and the amount of the deposit needed to secure it.

When Quentin told Adonis they had agreed to buy the 'Lemoni Spiti' Adonis picked Quentin up in his arms and spun him round, forgetting all about his bad back momentarily. Achilles the borrowed builder brashly kissed Deirdre on the cheek, assuring her he would do a bigly good job, while Adonis mentally calculated his commission.

CHAPTER 64

A Sticky Afternoon

Back in Astakos Stavroula was most surprised to receive an invitation from mail order Masha to join her for an afternoon of pampering at the beauty parlour. Stavroula remembered her cunning plan to lure mail order Masha as a regular customer to her taverna to attract all the men back as customers, and grumblingly accepted the beauty parlour invitation.

Mail order Masha removed her facial bandages to reveal a pair of lips blown up totally out of proportion. The Botox she'd had injected into her face had deadened all feeling so poor Masha could not even feel the drool dribbling down her chin.

Mail order Masha persuaded Stavroula to have a wash and blow dry, hoping to acquire her DNA from the hairs in the hairbrush. Their attention was riveted on Bald Yannis as he entered the beauty parlour with a ridiculous new strip of hair reaching from ear to ear across his bald head. He confided in a deep whisper to Evangelina he was in dire need of help to conceal his disastrous hair transplant, but the toupee he had bought was much too big for his head and not the right fit.

Plonking the toupee on his head Evangelia told him she would cut it down to size to make it less obviously fake. When she had finished cutting and coifing the toupee Bald Yannis dropped the tube of super glue he was passing her to make the rug secure.

Stavroula's attention was fixated on Bald Yannis as mail order Masha made a furtive move to remove Stavroula's hair from the hairbrush. Stavroula was most perturbed to catch mail order Masha in the act and threatened her with a pair of salon scissors as she accused her of stealing her hair to put a curse on her.

As Stavroula stood waving the scissors she slipped on Bald Yannis' tube of superglue and landed on mail order Masha, puncturing one of her silicone boobs with the point of the scissors. There was a horrified silence as the silicone boob deflated; leaving mail order Masha decidedly lopsided. Masha grabbed the nearest thing she could find to stuff down her bra to disguise one flat side, which happened to be Bald Yannis' toupee.

"Come back with my wig," demanded Bald Yannis as mail order Masha ran from the salon shoving his toupee into her bra and clutching the hairbrush full of Stavroula's hair. Stavroula was prevented from chasing after mail order Masha because her shoe was super glued to the salon floor.

CHAPTER 65

Good for Business

I never knew a woman could run so fast in such ridiculous stilettos," Quentin said, watching mail order Masha totter up the street at great speed.

Mail order Masha arrived home in a furious temper, demanding that old fool Vasilis telephone the police and have Stavroula arrested for grievous bodily harm for deflating her silicone boob. Vasilis was desperate to calm his wife down and promised to have Stavroula arrested if the DNA sample proved she was not his daughter. In the meantime he appeased Masha by ordering a taxi, at horrendous expense, to take her to the clinic in Athens to have her deflated silicone boob re-inflated.

To keep her sweet he promised to pay for her to have yet more plastic surgery as Masha was keen to have filler injected into her bottom to make it even bigger. Apparently it was all the rage in more cosmopolitan places than backwater Astakos. Mail order Masha was so happy at the prospect of more body transforming surgery she agreed to take the DNA sample along with her so they would know once and for all if the blackmailing Pappas' words about Stavroula's parentage were true.

Bald Yannis temporarily resigned himself to the loss of his toupee, acknowledging to himself it had looked quite ludicrous and not at all realistic. As he opened the hardware shop he was surprised by the request of those two peculiar American tourists to look at his full collection of shower curtains.

He noticed the woman Deirdre always appeared nervous around him and decided to amuse himself at her expense by offering to demonstrate his finesse with a chainsaw by giving the hardware shop cat a haircut. "That rude man is quite mad," said Deirdre running from the shop. "And what on earth was that ridiculous strip of hair on his head."

"That must be the new hair transplant he squandered a small fortune on," Quentin replied "we may be the first people to have seen it so we can spread some juicy gossip around in true Greek style."

Bald Yannis soon realised his new hair transplant was good for business by the queue of village men clamouring to buy nails and screws as an excuse to take a closer look at the revolting hair he had sprouting on his head. He even managed to shift a few more hideous old lady dresses to his captive audience.

CHAPTER 66

Goat Loving Malakas

F at Christos had a busy afternoon stripping anything of value he could potentially sell from his fishing boat before the tax inspectors sent someone official to burn it. With the help of Prosperous Pedros and Tall Thomas he soon had the new-fangled computer guidance system removed, along with the rudder, the sun canopy, his plastic relaxation chair and all the fishing paraphernalia of buckets, bait boxes and nets.

"It is the end of an era," he declared, bidding goodbye to the fishing life and contemplating his new career as a supermarket owner and husband of an heiress.

By the time the government officials arrived with Fat Christos' cash bribe for agreeing to the boat burning there was nothing left but the bare wooden bones of the stripped down hull that was worth nowhere near the agreed on price. The Pappas arrived to officiate over the boat burning ceremony, wafting some burning basil as was customary and confirmed the wedding was set for the day after tomorrow.

Fat Christos was disappointed Gorgeous Yiorgos had

failed to turn up to help with the boat stripping as promised. He didn't know Gorgeous Yiorgos and Petula had suffered an overheated engine just outside the neighbouring village of Rapanaki while on their driving lesson with the goat. They had been forced to abandon the car and hike off in the unseasonable scorching heat wave in search of water to cool the engine, dragging the goat Krasi behind them on a bit of old washing line.

They spotted the house of Fotini, the old crone mother of Prosperous Pedros, and were most relieved they would soon have a bottle of water and would be able to drive merrily on their way. However they had no way of foreseeing Fotini suffered a morbid fear of goats. The sight of two people approaching her house with a goat in tow threw her into a terrible panic. Fotini barricaded herself into the kitchen, refusing to open the door.

"Kyria Fotini, please bring us some water we implore you," Gorgeous Yiorgos pleaded, but his pleas were met with resistance as Fotini started lobbing lemons at them through the kitchen window and cursing them as goat loving malakas.

Gorgeous Yiorgos telephoned Prosperous Pedros to tell him his mother was having some kind of hysterical fit and needed locking up. Prosperous Pedros pointed out his mother had already locked herself in the kitchen and would surely calm down if they would only remove the goat from her sight. He had no intention of leaving the boat burning ceremony as he was busy haggling with Toothless Tasos over the price of the 'up for grabs' sun canopy.

Gorgeous Yiorgos suggested they try the neighbouring house in their quest for water, exclaiming "This is the 'Lemoni Spiti' the Americans buy." The pair clambered over the wall dragging the reluctant goat behind them and helped themselves to a bucket of water sitting on the abandoned kitchen floor.

Gorgeous Yiorgos, being ever the gentlemen, suggested Petula carry the water back to the car and hydrate the engine, then drive back to collect him and the goat. Petula was touched he had not suggested leaving her alone in the abandoned old ruined house next door to the deranged old mad woman and set off walking back to the car in the unseasonable sweltering heat wave.

Returning in the car the inexperienced driver Petula crunched the gears into reverse. The car slipped backwards towards the ruined house and she drove right over the Pappas' pride and joy, his pet goat Krasi, leaving it in a flattened and bloody heap on the ground. As she and Gorgeous Yiorgos looked in horror at the run-over goat they could hear cackles of delight whooping from Fotini's kitchen.

Petula implored Gorgeous Yiorgos to telephone her cousin Adonis as he would know what to do. She was in a total panic over the Pappas' reaction if he ever discovered she had inadvertently murdered his beloved pet.

Adonis speedily came to the rescue. He was feeling rather guilty he'd not yet managed a word with the Pappas over the disgraceful way he treated his cousin Petula, but his time had been taken up charming the Americans.

"Petula you must tell the Pappas the goat wandered off," Adonis insisted. "I'll give the goat to cousin Yiota to serve at the taverna. The Pappas wont's discover the truth if all the evidence is eaten."

Adonis grabbed the blood stained blanket from the back seat of his pick-up truck and wrapped it around the dead goat. He passed Petula his hip flask of ouzo to cope with the shock and both he and Gorgeous Yiorgos swore to her no word of the truth would escape their lips.

CHAPTER 67

The Fake Dating Scam

Whilst Adonis was sneaking the Pappas' dead goat through the back door of Yiota's taverna, Thea was once again ensconced in the deckchair in Toothless Tasos' living room watching another gripping instalment of her favourite soap opera 'Seven Deadly Mothers-in-Law.' Now she had destroyed her own television set with a hammer she was relying on the generous nature of Toothless Tasos to facilitate her passion for the programme.

Toothless Tasos had finally confessed he too was addicted to the soap opera and he immediately went up in Thea's estimation. She encouraged him to pull up the plastic relaxation chair he had just purchased from Fat Christos' boat and join her in her viewing. It was pleasant to share mutual observations about the addictive soap opera characters.

Fat Christos interrupted their viewing by calling round to see if Toothless Tasos would lend him his new very shiny blue suit for his wedding. "I 'ave lost so many the kilos my cloths hang off me," he explained.

"You two look very cosy," he observed, prompting Thea

to stand up to leave, explaining she had a date with Gorgeous Yiorgos that evening. Toothless Tasos was overcome with jealousy at the thought of his goddess out with another man and plucked up the courage to ask Thea to accompany him to the wedding.

"But what will you wear," Thea asked "if Fat Christo 'ave your new shiny suit on? I don't want you showing me up by turning up in your smelly old fishing clothes."

Yiota was busy in the taverna kitchen scrubbing the tyre marks off the Pappas' goat and the Pappas was in the church counting the cash he had received from officiating over the boat burning ceremony and wondering if he should reinvest it in some fake silver cutlery.

Bald Yannis enjoyed a lucrative day in the hardware shop selling his overpriced goods to his captive audience. He was in such a good mood he decided to indulge Moronic Mitsos by pretending he'd received some written responses to the fake internet advert he had placed in his fake dating scam. Moronic Mitsos was nothing if not highly gullible and he had fallen for Bald Yannis' fake dating scam hook, line and sinker.

Although the completely deluded Moronic Mitsos was unhappily married it did not stop him from forever badgering Bald Yannis to set up an internet dating profile for him, grossly exaggerating his own attractions in a bid to lure some wealthy foreigner. He hoped to attract a beautiful and rich younger woman who would fall for his charms and keep him in a manner he is as yet unaccustomed to, in spite of his generous police pension.

Bald Yannis played along by pretending to knock up a fake dating profile, claiming Moronic Mitsos to be younger, slimmer, handsomer and hairier on his head than in reality, and the owner of a yacht no less, that sails elegantly in the clear blue Greek bays. In reality the yacht is a leaky rowing boat stinking of dead fish and even his own mother would not describe Moronic Mitsos as handsome.

The fake ad was penned in English, a language Moronic Mitsos had never had a desire to learn, and the trap to make a village laughing stock of him was underway. Moronic Mitsos waited in eager anticipation for Bald Yannis to receive the replies and translate them. Little did he suspect the hardware man was creating the replies himself and trawling the internet for photographs of attractive women to attach to the fake replies.

Even though Bald Yannis was universally unpopular in the village he attracted quite a large audience of local men in the kafenion who were eager to eavesdrop as he read the fake replies to Moronic Mitsos. Bald Yannis told Mitsos he'd had two replies to his advertisement of a handsome Greek god with a luxury yacht, and he must decide if he liked the look of the anorexic English granny posing in a bikini with wads of cash, or if he preferred the Moldavian gold-digger with voluptuous assets but no cash. He assured Moronic Mitsos there was no rush to decide as there were sure to be more replies the next day, when he had finished penning them.

The other men headed off to the tavena chuckling over Moronic Mitsos' gullibility. Moronic Mitsos had a fit of pique and had to be warned yet again if he insisted on putting on his former policeman's hat and fining people for driving through the village too fast when it was no longer any of his business, Pancratius the village policeman would be called out from his sick bed and forced to arrest him.

Meanwhile Bald Yannis took a shortcut home through Stavroula's back garden where he helped himself to a pair of voluminous lace knickers from her washing line.

CHAPTER 68

A Wedding Ban

After Adonis dropped the Pappas's now dead pet goat Krasi off at the taverna for Yiota to cook he called in at the church where he found the Pappas polishing his briefcase cutlery collection and muttering about the exorbitant price of Holy wine. Adonis scowled at his cousin's husband and told him Petula was most upset as the goat had wandered off and was apparently lost, and he Adonis, expected no repercussions to land on his cousin. The Pappas feigned innocence, pretending Adonis' subtle allusions to his wife beating tendencies went over his head.

Surmising Petula would be busy looking for the lost goat, the Pappas voiced his thoughts she may not have bothered to have a hot meal waiting for him on the table and perhaps he should dine at the taverna 'Mono Ellinka Trofima.'

Desperate to keep the Pappas away from any sight or smell of the goat his cousin Yiota would soon be serving, Adonis persuaded the Pappas to allow him to drive him home, promising to stop en route and buy him a large bottle of Holy wine and a bag of savoury sausage pies and some sweet bougatsas from the bakery. Adonis would also be on hand to ensure Petula did not accidentally walk into the Pappas' fist.

The Pappas found Adonis' presence in his home menacing enough to keep his fists off Petula. Once Adonis took his leave the Pappas satisfied himself by banning Petula from attending the wedding of Fat Christos and Tassia as a fitting punishment for her carelessness in allowing his darling pet goat to wander off. Petula was relieved not to feel his fists, but was most upset she had been summarily banned from the wedding celebrations.

After that old fool Vasilis had waved a tearful goodbye to his mail order bride by sending her on her way to the plastic surgery clinic in Athens in a taxi, he was about to climb onto the donkey and make his way to Stavroula's taverna when he had an unexpected visitor. He was desperate to be in the presence of his possible daughter and forge a special relationship with her to make up for all the years he had not known she was the fruit of his loins.

Vasilis' unexpected visitor was Bald Yannis who'd decided he wanted his toupee back after all, never knowing when it would come in handy. He had paid good money for his terrible toupee and hated to lose anything of value. Vasilis agreed to hand over the toupee if Bald Yannis agreed to say no more of the matter of mail order Masha stealing it. Finally rid of Bald Yannis, Vasilis climbed on the donkey and headed to Stavroulas.

"Stavroula my dear, how lovely you look this evening," he greeted her, adding "and as fragrant as these," presenting her with a bunch of wild flowers he had picked en route.

Stavroula's hackles naturally began to rise at the sight of that old fool Vasilis acting so nice. She had already discussed with slick Socrates any possible legal ramifications of inadvertently puncturing and deflating mail order Masha's silicone boob with the salon scissors, but was also suspicious of why mail order Masha stole her hair. Slick Socrates had warned Stavroula she may end up stuck with a large bill to repair mail order Masha's now botched silicone boob job, so Stavroula decided to keep her temper in check and keep on the right side of the mail order bride's foolish husband.

Vasilis brushed off Stavroula's fake concerns about the boob deflation and assured her Masha had been placated with his offer to pay for her to have her bottom extended. Stavroula could not resist asking why Masha had run off with her hair and Vasilis made the excuse Masha was so taken with the colour she had wanted a few strands to colour match the new dye for her hair extensions.

Stavroula beckoned Mrs Kolokotronis to join her in the kitchen where the pair muttered and mumbled Vasilis' behaviour was not normal. Sticking their heads out of the kitchen door they witnessed Vasilis gazing their way with a ridiculous smile on his face. They decided he may not yet have fully recovered from his hideous ordeal of waking up alive in the underground coffin.

CHAPTER 69

Eating the Evidence

S lick Socrates, the slimy lawyer and Stavroula's live in lover, was enjoying a rare evening away from his beloved in the rival taverna of 'Mono Ellinka Trofima.' Word had reached him the Pappas' pet goat Krasi was on the night's menu and he was now tucking into a plateful of goat with relish. Socrates did not share Stavroula's reverence for the Pappas as he considered him a drunken buffoon who was mean to his wife. He thought it quite ridiculous the Pappas kept a goat as a pet and thus had no qualms about eating it.

Fat Christos refused the goat as he was still sticking rigidly to his strict weight loss diet. The results were remarkable as he had already shed the twenty kilos needed to proceed with the stomach stapling surgery. He just needed to get his hands on Tassia's brown envelope after the wedding ceremony to bribe the surgeon. No word of his pending operation had seeped out as true to his plans everyone thought he was losing the weight in anticipation of looking dapper at his wedding.

Quentin and Deirdre had some exciting news to share,

telling the villagers Adonis had finally persuaded them to go ahead with the purchase of the ruined 'Lemoni Spiti' and they had paid him a deposit.

"I is glad you will be neighbours to my old mother, K-Went-In and Did-Rees," Prosperous Pedros told them, sending them wine.

"Such a charming old lady," Quentin said, having heard nothing of Fotini's behaviour when she locked herself in the kitchen.

"Has she been a widow long?" Deirdre asked.

"Yes, for more than ten years, but dont's tell her," Prosperous Pedros replied. "My mother believe my father is on a trip to Athens an' she would go mad with grief if she knew he was actually dead."

"What, she thinks he has been on a trip to Athens for ten years when he is really dead?" Quentin asked in amazement.

"Is true K-Went-In," Prosperous Pedros assured him "the truth would kill her with grief."

"But does she not ask why he never returns?" Deirdre queried, to which Pedros explained "She get confused about dates. Some days she think he only go this morning, other days she more lucid and curses him for staying away."

Deirdre was amazed the populations of two villages must be in on the lie that the husband of Fotini was away rather than dead, not realising the despised Fotini rarely left her house so was kept out of the gossip loop. She hoped their new elderly neighbour would not be problematic, erroneously presuming the old lady was merely a harmless eccentric.

Quentin and Deirdre shared the renovation plans they had for the 'Lemoni Spiti' and were reassured by the taverna regulars the borrowed builder Achilles was a master craftsman in great demand.

"He did marvellous things to the new chicken coop Stavroula just had built in the garden," Socrates said. "In my opinion it is far too good for the chickens."

Adonis made his entrance; reassuring all the goat eaters the Pappas was blissfully unaware they were all dining on his pet as he took a plateful of the tasty meat. Gossip focused on Bald Yannis' ridiculous new hair transplant but steered away from Stavroula's attack on mail order Masha as Socrates was present.

Everyone was enjoying the goat and taverna talk had just turned to the wedding when Mrs Kolokotronis burst through the door in hysterics.

"Socrates, come at once and call Pancratius the village policeman," Mrs Kolokotronis screamed "the underwear thief has attacked Stavroula and she's nearly dead."

Plates of goat were abandoned and chairs thrown to the wayside as all the taverna goers rushed to Stavroulas in hot pursuit of Socrates to find out what on earth was going on.

CHAPTER 70

A Near Fatal Attack

S tavroula and Mrs Kolokotronis had been hovering in the kitchen doorway observing that old fool Vasilis' abnormally nice behaviour when Stavroula heard something untoward outside in her garden.

Venturing outdoors Stavroula was quick to observe a shadowy figure removing a vast pair of her bloomers from the washing line, under the cover of darkness.

"Stop underwear thief," she screamed, making a grab at the shadowy figure. The thief, determined not to have his identity revealed, threw the huge knickers over Stavroula's head to obscure her vision and tried to make a quick getaway. Stavroula though held fast to his person and the pair grappled ferociously.

The underwear thief was desperate to get away before the alarm was raised and resorted to violence, clasping his hands around Stavroula's neck and squeezing tightly. As the life was slowly squeezed from Stavroula her hand caught hold of the soup ladle she used to scoop up chicken food and she used it in self-defence to hit the underwear thief soundly over the head. As his hands momentarily lost their firm grip around Stavroula's neck she emitted a shrill screech which alerted Toothless Tasos, who was just at that moment walking past her garden.

As the underwear thief heard the wary approach of Toothless Tasos he threw Stavroula to the floor and deftly tripped up Tasos who landed in an ungainly heap on top of Stavroula. The thief fled into the night at great speed leaving Stavroula gasping for breath and painfully bruised.

"Taso you save my life," Stavroula sobbed, pulling the knickers off her head. "That pervert thief malaka was so strong I thought for sure he would kill me."

All thoughts of murdering her former husband left her as she now owed him an eternal debt of gratitude for saving her from death by strangulation.

Vasilis was mortified his possible daughter had been in such danger and immediately jumped on his donkey to seek assistance from Vangelis the chemist and the local doctor. Mrs Kolokotronis dashed off to get Socrates, and Toothless Tasos carried Stavroula into the taverna and poured her a large glass of brandy for the shock.

In other circumstances Stavroula would have been delighted to see so many people gathered all at once in her taverna. Everyone had descended in outrage, horrified such violence had occurred in the village. Socrates arrived and took his beloved into his arms, appalled at the sight of the unsightly bruises that signified her almost demise. Pancratius the village policeman had hot footed it from his sick bed and was busy taking her statement.

Stavroula was furious she could not provide a description of her attacker beyond saying he was a shadowy figure with very strong hands. "He 'ad my knickers over my 'ead," she lamented. Toothless Tasos had been more concerned with rescuing Stavroula than in getting a close look at the attacker and was of no use at all in the description department. Vangelis the chemist prescribed cold compresses for Stavroula's bruised neck and Vasilis hovered close by, attempting to squeeze her hand in compassion.

Everyone agreed the underwear thief had been tolerated for far too long in their midst, leading to this near fatality. It would be terrible for the tourist trade if word got out there was a deranged strangler in the village. Something must be done to reveal his identity and ensure he was locked up.

Scurrilous accusations were made as the villagers suggested names of the possible culprit, each randomly accusing anyone they held a grudge against. The Pappas' name came up several times but Adonis reluctantly conceded the Pappas was at home with Petula eating spinach pies when the attack occurred.

Pancratius the village policeman drew up a long list of names of possible suspects, striking a line through the names of those who had been in either taverna at the time of the attack as they had concrete alibis. Quentin and Deirdre were very happy to realise they were not prime suspects, nor were their new friends Takis, Yiota, Prosperous Pedros, Tall Thomas, Fat Christos, Adonis and Socrates. It still left an awful lot of suspects to be investigated and the policeman had no way of knowing if the underwear thief was even a local pervert or from further afield.

Moronic Mitsos berated Pancratius the village policeman for failing to launch a serious investigation into the theft of the underwear. He concluded this failure had emboldened the thief to the point of almost deadly violence and announced from now on he would be on the case whether

Pancratius wanted his help or not. He organised a village meeting for the following day as he planned to initiate a village patrol whereby each of the men would take turns to guard the washing lines.

Toothless Tasos was proud to be hailed as the hero of the hour; having no idea by coming to Stavroula's rescue he had eliminated himself from her murderous thoughts. Stavroula squeezed his hand in gratitude as she had honestly believed she was about to be a goner in the garden, so close to the new chicken coop she had planned to dispose of the body of Toothless Tasos in.

CHAPTER 71

A Reward is Offered

T he next morning Bald Yannis surveyed the enormous red lump on his still almost bald head with dismay. Stavroula's aim with the chicken scoop ladle had landed him with an egg-like protrusion that may well give away his identity as last night's attacker. He realised the fun he'd had stealing underwear had left him in a very dire predicament if his identity as Stavroula's attacker ever came to light. He had never intended to hurt her but she had clung onto him like a limpet and he could not afford for her to discover his identity. His reputation would be ruined and he could well end up in prison.

Luckily he had retrieved the terrible toupee from Vasilis and was soon at work with a new tube of superglue, securing the ill-fitting wig to his head to conceal the egg-like protrusion. He decided with regret his underwear stealing days were over. He considered this a great pity as his secret hobby had afforded him hours of amusement. He supposed he had better dispose of the remaining evidence as his bedroom drawers were overflowing with frilly items which would be his downfall should they ever be discovered.

Satisfied the lump was covered by the ill-fitting toupee Bald Yannis headed to the hardware shop where he spouted his utter disgust at the unprovoked near fatal attack on Stavroula to anyone who would listen. His hardware shop was bustling with a transfixed audience as everyone had turned out to take a look at his terrible toupee. Bald Yannis soon realised the terrible toupee was good for business and he put his vanity aside as it served its true purpose in covering up his egg-like protrusion.

He was at the side of Moronic Mitsos when the former chief of police rallied the village men into signing up for the newly established washing line patrol. "This pervert must be caught," Bald Yannis thundered as he finally pretended to show some civic duty. A rota was drawn up by Moronic Mitsos and the village men were duly assigned their nightly spots on the washing line patrol duty.

Quentin was proud to be included on the rota and Deirdre promised him she would be by his side on his allotted night. Bald Yannis deflected suspicion from himself by offering a reward to the person who caught the underwear thief. "Is that a cash reward?" Toothless Tasos asked, only to be disappointed when Bald Yannis confirmed the reward would be paid in hideous old lady dresses.

Pancratius the village policeman had managed to remain up from his sick bed long enough to solicit statements about last night's shocking incident, though no one had anything concrete to report. The only sure facts established were the underwear thief turned strangling attacker was a shadowy male with strong hands who may be suffering a headache after Stavroula managed to clock him hard with the chicken scoop ladle.

News of Toothless Tasos' heroic moment had reached the ears of Thea who was most impressed with his bravery. Of course by the time she heard the story it had been exaggerated beyond all reality and Toothless Tasos had allegedly fought off a ten foot man with the strength of two hundred. His heroic act cast Stavroula in the unlikely role of the helpless damsel in distress and boosted his low confidence no end.

Whilst Thea rummaged through her pile of shopping channel tat looking for something to wear for the wedding the next day, she began to give serious consideration to taking Toothless Tasos as a husband. He was now higher on her list of potential suitors than Gorgeous Yiorgos who had stood her up the previous evening, claiming exhaustion after his driving excursion with Petula.

Thea decided she would impress Toothless Tasos with her culinary skills and set about baking some homemade baklava to take along to their soap opera watching rendezvous.

Slick Socrates was reluctant to leave the side of his beloved Stavroula. Instead of being laid up in bed taking care of her bruises she had returned to the taverna where she was enjoying being the centre of attention. That old fool Vasilis assured Socrates his woman would be safe with him and he would not leave her side. Slick Socrates had a queue of clients outside his lawyer practice so he left Stavroula to the pampering ministrations of Vasilis.

Toothless Tasos was first in the queue for lawyerly advice as he had a delicate subject to broach with Socrates. He wanted to know if there was any way he could legally disentangle himself from his marriage to Stavroula as he was thinking of getting married again.

"Well you're supposed to be dead and dead men can't wed," Socrates advised. "If you come clean you faked your death it could lead to terrible trouble for Stavroula as she married Kostas bigamously. I want you divorced so I can marry Stavroula, but we have to find a cunning way to proceed without drawing attention. Let me think on it."

Next up for his legal services were Quentin and Deirdre, with Adonis along to translate. "They are buying the old 'Lemoni Spiti' in Rapanaki and need papers drawing up," Adonis beamed.

"Tell them I hope they be happy in the falling down house," Socrates instructed, putting a legal stamp on the papers.

By the time Petula took a seat in Socrates' office she was nearly a nervous wreck, worried the Pappas may have spied her entrance from his window in the church. Socrates was very sad to see Petula sobbing openly as she admitted she did not know how much longer she could stay under the same roof as the Pappas. Socrates was shocked to hear the Pappas had banned Petula from the wedding of Fat Christos, but reassured her the Pappas had no inkling at all about the death of his goat.

"Patience Petula, my dear," he said "it is no easy matter obtaining a divorce from the Pappas without leaving yourself homeless with no money. Let me think on it some more."

Next up was Tassia who was calling in to discuss her substantial inheritance. She voiced her quiet concerns to Socrates that after fourteen years of courtship Fat Christos and she were finally to be wed, but now she had money she worried if she should protect her inheritance with a pre-nuptial wedding agreement.

As a traditional male chauvinist Socrates was shocked at the very thought of a woman protecting her worldly assets from her husband. He told Tassia "it is a good job no word of this conversation will reach Christos or he would have every right to call off the wedding. What is yours is his once you wed and you should put this pre-nuptial nonsense out of your head or resign yourself to remaining a spinster."

Tassia was horrified at the prospect of becoming an unmarried mother and apologised to the lawyer for ever suggesting the pre-nuptial thing. Socrates patted her knee fondly and said it was a shame she had no male relatives to look out for her, but she could always trust him to look out for her best interests.

CHAPTER 72

Pre-Wedding Nerves

Tassia was busy comforting her future mother-in-law Mrs Kolokotronis who was suffering a serious attack of the vapours following the horrid excitement of the previous evening.

"To think my dearest friend Stavroula was nearly murdered in her back garden, now I won't feel safe when Christos moves out to marry yous, leaving me all alone."

Tassia naturally felt duty bound to offer old Mrs Kolokotronis a home with them if she felt the need of it. Mrs Kolokotronis considered the invitation showed Tassia to be a respectable daughter-in-law in spite of her reputation for being a dirty housekeeper and told her she would think on it.

Meanwhile Achilles the borrowed builder was due at any moment to put the finishing touches to her son's bedroom which she was converting into a sewing room. Apparently he had some wonderful shower curtains he planned to nail up as a decorative feature and she found the idea most elegant.

All the wedding plans for the following day were in order. Tassia's too tight dyed white polyester wedding dress was finally finished and her veil concealed the gaps in the back where the buttons strained to meet. All the guests had received their invitations and Stavroula was putting the finishing touches to the wedding cake.

Tassia had no idea where Fat Christos planned to whisk her off to for their honeymoon. She had overheard him on the telephone making travel plans for the evening of their wedding and was beside herself with excitement at the prospect of her first ever real holiday. She hoped he would prove to be a good husband and felt ashamed she had bothered the lawyer Slick Socrates with all that pre-wedding nerves pre-nuptial nonsense.

Life was looking very good to Tassia. After so many years of tending her ailing grouching father her life was about to take a turn for the better. She had a baby on the way and a supermarket to run with her new husband. While it was true Fat Christos had never exactly swept her off her feet he was often considerate and his weight loss had left him less sweaty. He hadn't questioned how her pregnancy was already showing, even though it was less than a week since their first and only sexual encounter.

Tassia hoped her new friend mail order Masha would return from the plastic surgery clinic in time to attend her wedding, though she hoped she would not turn up in an outfit to outshine her on her special day.

CHAPTER 73

The Wedding

The day of the wedding dawned bright and clear. Fat Christos was relieved to be able to lie in his bed beyond the crack of dawn as he no longer needed to take his boat out and haul the fishing nets in. He breathed in the fresh salty air and took his final jog as a single man in the company of Quentin, watching Prosperous Pedros' fishing boat head back to shore.

He presumed after his stomach stapling surgery he would have the energy and vigour of a much younger man and looked forward to being trim and slim, imagining he would even be able to turn heads in a good, rather than disgusting, way. He hadn't realised until he began his weight loss journey just how much effort it took to drag his lard-like frame around.

The two men parted ways after their jog as Quentin and Deirdre were meeting Adonis and driving over to the 'Lemoni Spiti' before the wedding. Fat Christos went off to allow his mother to make some last minute alterations to the very shiny blue suit he had borrowed from Toothless Tasos, as it was already beginning feeling too loose.

Quentin and Deirdre were all dressed up in their wedding finery when Adonis pulled up in his pick-up truck to take them to another meeting with Achilles the borrowed builder. Deirdre wanted to discuss tiles with the borrowed builder. She had found a stunning picture of a recently discovered ancient Greek mosaic floor and wondered if Achilles could recreate it in the bathroom.

"Po po," said Achilles. "Did-Rees that floor is two thousand years old, yous is better off with somethin' more modern I am thinking."

"But I love this particular style of a circle of sage old Greek heads embedded in tiles," Deirdre insisted, to which Achilles replied,

"Did-Rees, believe me yous no want the head of Plato watching yous on the toilet. Now let us study these lovely shower curtains and I look yous some good new tiles at the hardware shop, not this second hand rubbish."

Suddenly realising time was getting on Quentin and Deirdre told Adonis they needed to be back in Astakos for the wedding. As they reached the pick-up truck they were shocked to discover the neighbouring old crone Fotini had installed herself in the passenger seat, dressed to the nines in the very finest the hardware shop had to offer in hideous old lady dresses, matching black pop socks and an oversized hat brimming with garish plastic flowers.

"What are you doing in 'ere Kyria Fotini?" Adonis questioned.

"I am waiting for my husband to take me to the wedding," Fotini replied.

"Yous husband is in Athens," Adonis told her, to which she demanded he accompany her to the wedding instead. A long argument ensued as Adonis tried to persuade the old crone to return to her house, but she was having none of it. She was quite determined to go to the wedding and ended up sitting on Quentin's knee as the four of them squeezed onto the front seat of the pick-up.

"No frisky business," Fotini warned Quentin as her hat stabbed him painfully in the eye with a plastic tulip.

The foursome made it to the church with only minutes to spare before the bride arrived. Fotini left the others in her wake as she strode decisively to the very front pew, taking a seat beside Mrs Kolokotronis who unsuccessfully tried to shoo her away.

"No one invited you," Mrs Kolokotronis hissed at Fotini who replied "you think at my age I care. I come to spit on the bride," referring to the traditional custom of spitting on the bride for good luck.

Thea was seated beside Toothless Tasos looking suitably goddess- like in a tasteful pastel suit she had secured at a very good price from the home shopping channel. Thea wondered if she would be next up the aisle and began to fantasise about her fourth wedding dress. Stavroula was sporting a floral scarf to hide her extensive bruising and was accompanied by Slick Socrates in an expensive slick suit which put the groom's borrowed attire to shame.

Mail order Masha had made it back to the village just in time to attend the service with Vasilis. Masha's surgical interventions had been most successful. Her punctured and deflated boob was once again full of silicone and standing up to attention, her disastrous trout pout had deflated to a perky moue and her bottom was voluptuously full although admittedly difficult to sit on. She wore a green velvet evening gown covered in donkey hairs and looked most out of place at a noon time wedding.

The fishermen had all made an effort to spray their fishy clothes with air freshener to disguise the smell and Gorgeous Yiorgos had even run a handful of extra virgin olive oil through his boot polished hair.

Quentin and Deirdre could not understand everything that was going on, yet Deirdre still managed to shed a tear as the Pappas pronounced Fat Christos and Tassia man and wife. Deirdre thought Tassia looked delightfully old fashioned in her home made dress, but she seemed to have put on a lot of weight very quickly.

As the Pappas stepped forward to bestow a blessing on the newlyweds he caught sight of the engagement ring on Tassia's finger and exploded in sudden anger, accusing the bride of theft and demanding the police come and lock her up.

"You steal my wife's engagement ring you 'orrible woman," he screamed, shoving her violently into a pew. Tassia burst into tears as Fat Christos assured her he could explain and Gorgeous Yiorgos tried to calm the situation down.

"Po po, you think that woman bad," Fotini piped up, grabbing hold of the Pappas's skirt. "Your 'orrible wife ran over your goat with 'is car," she said, pointing an accusatory finger at Gorgeous Yiorgos "and they all eat it at taverna," she cackled manically. Fotini had not had so much fun in years and as Tassia fled down the aisle in tears Fotini spat repeatedly all over her new dress.

Fat Christos hurried after his new bride to console her while the Pappas was frozen to the spot with horror at the thought his congregation had gorged themselves on his darling pet goat Krasi, murdered by his deceitful wife. He imagined how they must have all laughed behind his back and felt the sharp pang of humiliation.

Storming from the church he left a shell shocked congregation behind him. Each spectator was mortified at the events that had just unfolded but were collectively relieved the marriage was at least made official before the Pappas officially lost it.

CHAPTER 74

The DNA Sample

F at Christos caught up with the tear and spit sodden Tassia outside the church. He was filled with shame at the turn the wedding had taken and was keen to reassure his new bride the matter of the stolen ring was all a misunderstanding. Gorgeous Yiorgos was quick to back Fat Christos up and confessed he had been remiss in not making more effort to recover Petula's ring as she had requested once the Pappas had realised it was missing.

Tassia was most relieved to hear Petula had sold her own ring and it had not ended up on her own finger through an act of theft. She took the engagement ring off her finger and implored Gorgeous Yiorgos to please return it to Petula. Fat Christos promised to buy Tassia another ring but made it clear to Gorgeous Yiorgos he expected his money back for the other one.

As the rest of the wedding guests exited the church and began to make their way to Stavroulas for the celebration they spotted Fotini being physically carried from the church in a fireman's lift by her totally embarrassed son Prosperous

Pedros. Pedros was furious his mother had turned up uninvited at the wedding and made such a horrendous scene. He was determined to get her back to Rapanaki and lock her up in the kitchen.

"Did you see the way our new neighbour spat all over poor Tassia's lovely new dress?" Deirdre said in disgust to Quentin.

"Ah it is old tradition to spit," Adonis assured them "it meant to bring good luck. Only the old people do it now and after this old generation gone will be no spit left."

"Well I think it is just awful," said Deirdre, pulling out a handkerchief and rushing over to dab the spit up from Tassia's wedding dress. Tassia was overcome with the older woman's kind gesture and managed a half-hearted smile, hoping the events in the church had not totally ruined her special day.

Tassia smiled a real smile as she saw her new friend mail order Masha posing provocatively for the wedding photographer.

"I like your new bottom," Tassia told her "but what a pity you couldn't have just injected some of my new husband's fat into it instead of that potentially toxic chemical mix."

Mail order Masha pulled her husband aside and whispered to him the clinic had just phoned with the results of Stavroula's DNA sample. The meddling Pappas had been correct and Stavroula was indeed the result of that old fool Vasilis' long ago passionate fling in an overgrown olive grove with the lovely Melina.

"Better she 'ear it from you than the foul blackmailing drunken Pappas," Masha wisely advised.

Vasilis was overcome with emotion at the news that at the age of eighty four it had just been definitively confirmed he was a father for the very first time. As he begged his wife's forgiveness Masha assured him there was nothing to forgive as his indiscretion had occurred long before she was even born.

"We make best of it," she told him in the level headed Russian way that made him adore her.

After the wedding party had dined on Stavroula's finest offerings of delightful mixed meze the tables were pushed back for a vigorous bout of Greek dancing. Vasilis took Stavroula aside and told her he needed a quiet word of great importance.

"Stavroula I have some news that may shock you my dear," he began "but your parentage is not all as it seems. I have just learnt that without a doubt I am your father, the DNA it prove it."

Stavroula did not appear to be as shocked as Vasilis had expected at this sudden news.

"How long have you known?" was her first question, to which Vasilis truthfully told her he had only recently heard but it had that very day been confirmed by indisputable scientific DNA evidence.

"Ha, that is why Masha wanted my hair," Stavroula surmised. She wanted to know how Vasilis had heard and the story of her mother's death bed confession and the blackmailing Pappas came out.

"He know all this time and never a word the malaka," Stavroula said, disgusted by the Pappas' deceitful behaviour.

Stavroula told her new father many years ago her mother had admitted she had never loved her husband Gregoris, the master butcher. It had been an arranged and loveless marriage, but Melina told her daughter she had experienced love and romance just once and the memories of it had kept her going for her lifetime. She had never revealed the name of the man she had loved nor revealed the fact she had strayed in an overgrown olive grove, but Stavroula had harboured a secret suspicion Gregoris was not in fact her real father.

Never in Stavroula's wildest imagination could she imagine that old fool Vasilis was the love of her mother's life and he was indeed her father. He was hardly the noble figure her imagination had conjured and she told Vasilis she needed time to come to term with the news.

"Oh my, this means mail order Masha is now my stepmother," she sighed in horror, as she went inside to break the shocking news to Socrates.

CHAPTER 75

Shirley Valentine

For some strange reason Bald Yannis could not fathom he had not been invited to the wedding. It irked him he appeared so unpopular when even those strange American tourists had been included in the celebration. Mindful of his new civic duties Bald Yannis had volunteered to take the first nightly patrol on washing line duty, even though he knew it was a waste of time as he had no intention of catching himself.

He still had his large stolen collection of women's underwear to dispose of and he wondered if he could use it to lay a false trail. Even though no finger of suspicion had pointed his way he would feel more secure if someone else took the blame. The gossip at the kafenion centred on who exactly had an alibi for the night of the attack and Bald Yannis realised he may well need an alibi in addition to a fake suspect.

He soon eavesdropped Gorgeous Yiorgos had stood up Thea on the night of the attack, pleading exhaustion after his secret driving lesson with Petula. This gossip gem had been revealed as part of a conversation about the increasing closeness between Toothless Tasos and Thea, rather than about Gorgeous Yiorgos' lack of an alibi, yet Bald Yannis decided to turn the information to his advantage.

He would wait until he was on his nightly washing line patrol duty and under cover of darkness he would plant some of the stolen underwear in Gorgeous Yiorgos' chicken coop. He would also plant some in Moronic Mitsos' rowing boat he decided, and perhaps some more in the garden of the Pappas. That would keep the village snoops busy and deflect all suspicion from him.

Bald Yannis greeted Moronic Mitsos most heartily as a fellow reject from the wedding celebrations. Moronic Mitsos openly scoffed at the terrible toupee Bald Yannis was wearing, which irked his sense of vanity no end.

"Another woman answer your online advert looking for a Greek god with a rowing boat, I mean yacht," Bald Yannis told Mitsos. "Would you like me to read you her reply as it is English?"

Moronic Mitsos ordered them both a coffee and settled down to hear the letter Bald Yannis had penned which he pretended was from a middle aged English woman called Shirley Valentine who professed she was a bored housewife looking for a romantic interlude with a handsome Greek with a yacht. Bald Yannis had even printed off a photograph of the actress Pauline Collins who had taken the eponymous role in the film 'Shirley Valentine', which he knew full well Moronic Mitsos had never heard of.

Moronic Mitsos seemed very keen on this Shirley woman. He instructed Bald Yannis to write her a reply saying he would love to meet her and whisper sweet nothings in her ear as they sailed the coast in his yacht. Adonis was sitting quietly in the corner and overheard this exchange. He reflected it didn't take much to keep small minded villagers amused.

Promising to compose a reply to Shirley at his earliest convenience Bald Yannis announced he was off on his washing line patrol duty and woe betide any perverts he should come across. Instead he scuttled home to collect the stolen underwear and under cover of darkness left a fake trail of 'frillies' in the chicken coops, gardens and rowing boats of his fellow villagers.

CHAPTER 76

A Honeymoon Let Down

G orgeous Yiorgos was showing off his Greek dancing skills with great panache at the wedding reception when he received a dark and disturbing phone call from Petula. Without even bidding farewell to the newlyweds he hastened out to his car and drove straight to the home of Petula.

There he discovered the broken and beaten body of his childhood friend who had experienced the worst bout of anger the Pappas had ever displayed. After discovering his wife's deception over her engagement ring and the awful truth of the sad demise of his beloved pet goat Krasi, the Pappas had lost all control and beaten his wife into a bloody pulp.

Gorgeous Yiorgos gently scooped Petula up and drove her to hospital. Seeing her tucked neatly and safely into a hospital bed and in receipt of the very best medical attention he returned to the wedding to gather the village men together. He demanded they collectively do something for once and for all to put the Pappas in his place and discourage his nasty ways.

Socrates had just heard of the Pappas' blackmailing scam from Stavroula and he was eager to vent his own form of retribution on the drunken priest. The village men all agreed the Pappas had gone too far and needed to be taught a lesson. They did not think of summoning Pancratius the village policeman from his sick bed as this was something they felt the need to take care of themselves.

The Pappas was discovered skulking in the back of the church, drinking from a bottle of Holy wine. He knew his fists had gone too far with Petula but had hoped she would keep her mouth shut and pretend she had walked into the proverbial door as usual. On seeing the posse of approaching village men he knew for sure he was about to receive their rough and ready version of retribution.

The Pappas made the sign of the Holy cross as they roughly threw him into Gorgeous Yiorgos' fishing boat and cast off from the harbour. The men were seething with quiet anger. They waited until the boat was well away from the harbour before unceremoniously tossing the drunken snivelling Pappas into the sobering water with a warning if he survived he should stay well away from Petula. Leaving the Pappas floundering in the sea the men headed back to shore to re-join the wedding celebration.

Back at the wedding celebration Fat Christos had one eye on the clock as he needed to be ready when the taxi arrived to take him to the clinic for his stomach stapling surgery. He had yet to break the news to his bride he expected her to hand over a large brown envelope of cash to bribe the surgeon and he had no idea she was expecting him to whisk her away on a romantic honeymoon.

Tassia was distraught when she learnt the truth there was not going to be a honeymoon, nor was there not even going to be a proper wedding night.

"But you are already pregnant," Fat Christos reasoned "and it will be better for the baby if I have the stomach stapled and lose the rest of this excess weight very quickly."

"This should be the most romantic night of my life," Tassia wailed "and instead I will be all alone while you have your fat stomach stapled."

"You can always revert to tradition and share the wedding bed with my mother," Fat Christos argued lamely, realising he had not made the best start to married life and perhaps should have handled things a little differently.

"Now don't stay up too late partying," he advised his new bride, reminding her she would need to be up bright and early to open the supermarket. He even forgot to kiss Tassia as he stepped into the waiting taxi clutching the large brown envelope he had managed to wheedle out of his new bride.

CHAPTER 77

The Curse of the Pappas' Fishing Curse

Prosperous Pedros did not return to the wedding celebrations after taking his mother Fotini home in disgrace. He had found her behaviour most mortifying, yet she cackled triumphantly at causing so much trouble. He escorted her into the house and threatened to stop doing her shopping and buying sweet treats unless she showed some contrition.

Fotini assured her son her outrageous behaviour was one of the few perks left to someone of her advanced years and she had no intention of mending her obnoxious ways. She was secretly looking forward to having the new American neighbours to terrorise and pondered how long it would take them to put the house back up for sale to escape her meddling ways. The very thought emitted another series of cantankerous cackles, driving her long suffering son away.

Prosperous Pedros retired to his small fishing cottage for some peace and quiet as he painstakingly threaded the bait onto his numerous fishing lines. He reflected he'd had a narrow escape by staying single as women brought nothing but trouble, as evidenced by his odious mother.

As he cast his fishing boat from the harbour that moon-free evening he was at peace in his solitude and did not regret his decision to go fishing rather than return to the wedding. As he headed back to shore with a magnificent catch he caught sight of what appeared to be the Pappas floundering helplessly in the deep water with his dress ballooning around him.

His first instinct was to ignore the Pappas and let the nasty drunk drown. He had no idea how the Pappas came to be out at sea but realised now he had seen him his run of good fishing luck was already doomed by the Pappas' fishing curse.

Prosperous Pedros considered he may as well rescue the Pappas as it may give him heavenly favour at some future point. Cursing under his breath he steered the fishing boat towards the drowning priest and hauled him unceremoniously into the boat. Raising his palm in a gesture of rude dismissal Prosperous Pedros simply told the Pappas "I don't want to hear it malaka."

CHAPTER 78

The Pappas' Fake Religious Renaissance

The Pappas had spent an uncomfortable night in his wet black dress, tangled up in the fishing detritus that lay at the bottom of Prosperous Pedros' fishing boat. He felt extremely sorry for himself at the rough way he had been treated and reflected he would most certainly have drowned if Prosperous Pedros had not hauled him out of the water. Mindful of the village men's warning to stay away from Petula he did not dare to return home, nor dare he risk any of his congregation catching him looking so undignified and revolting in the church.

He spared not a thought for his poor beaten wife who he considered had got everything she deserved. However his lack of contrition would not go down well in the village and he realised if he was to survive in his priestly job he had better simulate repentance.

The Pappas came up with a cunning plan to increase his standing in the village. He decided now would be a good time to have a religious Renaissance and he would concentrate all his efforts on going round being insufferably Godly. Of course he would need to swear off the demon drink, but he considered he was clever enough to dupe the dullards in the village and convince them he was a reformed character.

With a plan decided on the Pappas pulled a bit of old prawn bait out of his liturgical garments and wrung the sea water out of his socks. He would make a discreet entrance to the church and spend the morning cramming up on biblical quotations about the evils of wine and then inflict the pious quotes on his unsuspecting heathen congregation.

CHAPTER 79

An Impending Visitor

Fotini was beside herself with excitement having just received a telephone call from her second cousin Nitsa. Nitsa had moved away from Astakos many years ago, at the time of her marriage, and settled in the up 'north village' of Pirouni, named for a fork. At the sprightly young age of eighty two Nitsa was four years younger than Fotini, but she had been widowed first. Now she lived with her son Apostolakis and his family as it was the proper thing for a son to take in his old widowed mother.

Fotini was pleased she wasn't widowed or she might be forced to live with her son Pedros who could be most impatient. Luckily her old husband was only off in Athens, though he did seem to have been gone rather a long time she pondered. She decided she would ask Pedros if he knew when his father was coming home.

In the meantime Nitsa was coming to visit and Apostolakis had insisted on paying for her trip. The best thing about the impending visit was Nitsa was driving her own car down and this would mean Fotini would have wheels at her disposal. Her miserable son Pedros never took her anywhere she wanted to go. Just look at how the killjoy had put his foot down over her attending that wedding, she muttered. It was quite disgraceful she had been forced to gate-crash rather than attend as her son's plus one.

Fotini telephoned Pedros to tell him the wonderful news about Nitsa's impending visit and told him to get himself over immediately as the spare room needed a good cleaning out. Pedros had already been warned of the situation by Apostolakis who had been so desperate to have a break from his batty old mother he had even bought her an old Mercedes taxi for the journey, then booked himself and his wife on a cruise to celebrate their new found freedom.

Prosperous Pedros presumed the visit could be a disaster as his mother would be gadding about all over the place in Nitsa's car and Nitsa could not be trusted to not blurt out the news Fotini's husband had really been dead for the last ten years.

CHAPTER 80

Bleeding Borscht

Vasilis and Masha were expecting the arrival of Stavroula and Slick Socrates for a dinner party at their home. They had extended a familial invitation in order to better relations between father and newly discovered daughter. Mail order Masha had a big pan of borscht simmering in the kitchen which Vasilis liberally laced with vodka when she wasn't looking. He had promised her he would not touch alcohol after the funeral debacle, but felt the need of some Dutch courage for this pending occasion.

"What else yous cooking?" Vaslis demanded. "We can't just give them red soup, my daughter he is experienced cook you know."

"Po po, yous know I no cook nothing but borscht," Masha reminded him "if you wanted a wife who cook you should have married a village peasant." With that she flounced out of the kitchen, saying she was going to glam up before the guests arrived.

Vasilis was most disappointed when Stavroula telephoned to cancel the dinner party, claiming she had far too many customers in the taverna to leave them to their own devices. Masha was most put out as she had glammed up in a gold sequin mini dress with matching platform shoes. She suggested they put the borscht in a Tupperware box and take it to Stavroulas. The mismatched couple climbed onto Onos the donkey and balancing the Tupperware box of vodka laced red soup they headed into the village.

As soon as the pair climbed down from the donkey Stavroula immediately went on the defensive. It seemed Masha's newly inflated silicone boob was now bleeding heavily and she would no doubt attempt to pin the blame on Stavroula and her recent slip up with the salon scissors.

"Malaka the borscht is bleeding all over my new sequin dress," Masha exclaimed, to the relief of Stavroula who realised the spreading red wound was actually some nasty smelling Russian soup and not blood.

Hoping to improve relations between Vasilis and his newly discovered daughter Masha air kissed Stavroula and insisted she call her Mama.

"I ave been telling my husband 'ow much I want the children and you come along as a readymade one, is good, you not ruin my stunning figure," she laughed.

Stavroula was only too mindful Slick Socrates could seemingly not get enough of Masha's voluptuous figure and slapped him sharply round the head as a warning to keep his eyes off his new step-mother- in-law to be. Stavroula was not partial to sampling foreign foods and she eyed the borscht with sinister suspicion as she demanded to know what was in it.

"Beets and Smetana," Masha told her.

No matter how many times Stavroula tried she could not get her tongue to pronounce the strange sounding Smetana which translated into sour cream.

"If I want sour cream I leave the milk out in the sun as a cure for sunburn," Stavroula said "and I would not put gone off milk in the soup and expect people to eat it."

Socrates politely downed a generous bowlful of the suspect red soup, but Stavroula stuck to her guns and refused to sample the foreign muck.

"The Greek food is the best and more healthiest in world," she declared, making a rash promise to teach her new step-mother to cook proper Greek food.

"Father Vasilis, yous 'ave many lost years to make up for financially," Stavroula declared. "Yous should 'ave paid for the cost of my wedding to Toothless Tasos and the cost of my wedding to Kostas. I give yous the bills to pay."

"It will be my pleasure," that old fool Vasilis surprised her by saying, immediately receiving a sharp kick under the table from his mail order bride who was horrified he had no apparent qualms about sharing her fortune.

Stavroula excused herself from the family dinner as Mrs Kolokotronis was banging on the kitchen door. The pair huddled in the kitchen together as Stavroula voiced her opinion on her new step-mother's suitability.

"Mail order Masha likely kill my new father with her 'orrid cooking," she lamented to her neighbour. "'Ow can anybody be expected to eat that foreign muck and survive. No wonder that old fool Vasilis, I mean my respected new father, is nothing but skin and bone."

Mrs Kolokotronis had more pressing concerns on her mind as it had suddenly struck her that her new daughter-in-law appeared to be far more pregnant than her recent encounter with Fat Christos in the garden shed would explain.

"Maybe he didn't wait till the night he proposed to make

romance," Stavroula suggested, but Mrs Kolokotronis was adamant Fat Christos had not made free with Tassia until the night he put a ring on her finger.

"This baby business is odd as Christos used condom from the church collection plate. I worry Tassia may be a loose hussy and marry my Christos to give a good name to some other man's baby."

Stavroula was suddenly sensitive to the subject of questionable paternity, not surprising considering Vasilis' recent announcement.

"Well either way he marry an heiress and get his hands on Tassia's money," Stavroula consoled her friend "and it would be no bad thing if the baby not look like Fat Christos."

Mrs Kolokotronis, taking offence at Stavroula's remark as she considered her son to be very handsome, slammed the door loudly on her way out. She decided to visit Tassia to see if she could get to the bottom of her sudden suspicions. She would take her a present of a new shower curtain as an excuse to visit.

CHAPTER 81

Bald Yannis Flogs Some Patriotic Shower Curtains

Whose bra is this?" Thea demanded to know, extricating an ample lace push-up bra from Toothless Tasos' front door knocker. Toothless Tasos blushed unbecomingly, stammering he had no idea who the underwear belonged to, but it definitely wasn't his.

Thea soon forgot about the suspect bra as her mind was filled with considering the pros and cons of Toothless Tasos as her fourth husband. As she settled into the deckchair to catch up with the latest gripping instalment of her favourite soap opera 'Seven Deadly Mothers-in-Law' she suggested a few home improvements Toothless Tasos should undertake to make his home more comfortable.

"You need a curtain over that window," she declared "as every Thomas, Adonis and Harris can peer in as they pass and may get the wrong idea about me visiting yous 'ouse."

As soon as the soap opera finished Toothless Tasos hotfooted it over to the hardware store as Thea's comments on his need for home improvements had hit home. Living the bachelor life he had no idea about decorative home touches, though he thought he had done his best without the help of a womanly touch and considered the stuffed swordfish noses a decorative success. For no other reason than he ran a successful hardware store he presumed Bald Yannis would be the man to give suitable advice.

Bald Yannis was feeling almost cheery as he'd had a very productive evening laying a false trail of stolen underwear throughout the village, while pretending he was on washing line patrol duty. He was busy trying to work out why there was a sudden rush on shower curtains and mistakenly surmised it could be the foreign influence of that strange American couple. He decided to promote the shower curtains with a large profit margin as a must-have item. It was a great opportunity to sell off a large pile of useless old surplus stock gathering dust in the back room.

"I 'ave come to purchase a curtain for my living room window," Toothless Tasos announced to the great delight of Bald Yannis, who whipped out a plastic shower curtain with a decorative lobster border.

"This is finest curtain I 'ave," Bald Yannis declared, adding "not only is it decorative and functional, but is unique one of a kind. No one else 'ave one. It is also patriotic to the village as it is adorned with lobsters."

Toothless Tasos was completely clueless about interior design and was delighted the hardware shop stocked such a fine item. He handed over his euros and rushed home to nail the lobster embellished shower curtain over the living room window where he thought it added a homely touch that would undoubtedly impress Thea.

Bald Yannis was feeling very smug over his shower curtain sale and settled down behind his cash register to pen a letter to Moronic Mitsos from a lonely hearted woman in

China who he claimed was descended from the Ming dynasty. He laughed to himself at the thought of Moronic Mitsos becoming insufferably boring about luring a woman with a classic lineage. He wondered if the made up woman would declare Moronic Mitsos' yacht was a bit 'minging'. He reluctantly put his letter to one side as Quentin and Deirdre entered the shop in a quest for some ancient floor tiles.

"We are looking for floor tiles that are intrinsically Greek, very tasteful, with a magnificent history," Quentin said.

"What, you no want something modern?" Bald Yannis queried, adding "hold on, I 'ave just the thing, so old they are practically ancient."

Bald Yannis flounced off to his stockroom where he unearthed a pile of chipped floor tiles covered in goat and chicken poop he had recovered from that old fool Vasilis' outmoded outside toilet. The tiles had been salvaged when the ancient outside toilet was knocked down to make way for mail order Masha's new wooden sun deck.

"They aren't quite what we had in mind," Deirdre said, turning her nose away from the dreadful pile of smelly old rubbish Bald Yannis was offering. "We want something mosaic and historical."

"These old tiles are steeped in history, they was put down before the war," Bald Yannis insisted, though he realised this pair may be a tad too worldly to be taken in by his nonsense.

"The tiles won't do at all," Quentin insisted as his eyes fell on the pile of shower curtains. "However our borrowed builder Achilles will be most delighted if we purchase one of these lovely shower curtains, he just can't get enough of them."

"Ah I 'ave just the one for you, completely unique, no other shower curtain with the same design of a lobster border.

You know the lobster is the patriotic symbol of the village?" Yannis said, brandishing an identical shower curtain to the one he had just sold Toothless Tasos.

"Perfect, just the ticket wouldn't you say Did-Rees?" Quentin said, adding for Bald Yannis' benefit "the patriotic state fish of Idaho is the cutthroat trout, don't you know?"

The Americans purchased the one off unique lobster adorned shower curtain, identical to the one just purchased by Toothless Tasos. They ran into Adonis as they left the hardware shop with their purchase.

"Ah good news my good friends K-Went-In and Did-Rees," Adonis told them "my cousin Adonis the mechanic he finish drying the mobile refrigerated fish van of Tall Thomas and is this minute repairing the car what you broke down in."

The three of them were all smiles as they headed off to Stavroulas for coffee. Deirdre was particularly delighted to have survived an encounter with the dreadful Bald Yannis in which he had not wielded a chainsaw or a cat in her direction.

CHAPTER 82

Nitsa Arrives

P rosperous Pedros had endured a horrible afternoon being bossed around by his mother, the old crone Fotini, as they got the house ready to receive Fotini's guest, her second cousin Nitsa. Prosperous Pedros had scrubbed and mopped under the critical eye of his demanding mother. As a final touch Fotini insisted on laying a new waterproof bedspread over the bed Nitsa would sleep in, but to Pedros' untrained eye the new bedspread looked suspiciously like a shower curtain with a lobster border.

Prosperous Pedros was just about to take his leave when a large old Mercedes taxi, like the ones used in Athens, crawled at a snail's pace into the yard. Nitsa was sat behind the wheel propped up on a large pile of old magazines as she was too short to comfortably see out of the windscreen.

Despite the slow pace of the car Nitsa only managed to stop its progress by bumping into the rear bumper of Prosperous Pedros' pick-up truck. Nitsa and Fotini embraced, each declaring the other looked not a day older than the last time they had seen each other over sixty years before.

GOAT IN THE MEZE

Nitsa was amazingly sprightly for her advanced years and was full of plans for her visit. After demanding Pedros carry all her luggage inside she said to him "I 'ope you won't be staying 'ere as we don't want you cramping our style."

Prosperous Pedros felt a glimmer of hope the much dreaded visit of Nitsa may actually relieve him of some of his endless obligations to his mother. Feeling suddenly lighter he took his leave, forgiving Nitsa for the unsightly dent she had left in his bumper.

CHAPTER 83

Underwear Everywhere

G orgeous Yiorgos was looking forward to an evening in the company of friends in 'Mono Ellinka Trofima'. He had spent the afternoon visiting Petula in the hospital and tomorrow he would return to drive her home. Petula had recounted the phone call she had received from her husband the Pappas, in lieu of a visit. He had apologised profusely for losing his temper and left Petula half convinced he was a reformed character as he begged her to take him back. Gorgeous Yiorgos was not convinced the Pappas could change his spots, but he would support Petula in whatever she decided.

On returning home Gorgeous Yiorgos had found a silk thong draped over his chicken coop and wondered if someone had been up to something romantic in his garden. When he removed his work boots he was most put out to discover he did not possess a single pair of socks that were not full of holes. His toe nails had grown so shockingly long they protruded through all his socks, but when he sat down to cut them he could not reach them for his bulging stomach.

This reminded him he was missing his good friend Fat Christos who had unexpectedly left the village on the night of his wedding to book himself into a clinic for stomach stapling surgery. For one moment Gorgeous Yiorgos considered following Fat Christos' example and losing some weight so he could reach his toe nails.

Yiota emerged from the kitchen carrying heaped platefuls of grilled lamb chops. At the sight of the temptingly tasty food Gorgeous Yiorgos cast all thoughts of a diet aside and decided he would make an appointment to have his toe nails clipped in the beauty parlour instead.

Tall Thomas was happy to announce his mobile refrigerated fishing van had been nicely dried out by Adonis the mechanic and was now back in action on the road. He had been surprised to find a pair of black lace knickers wrapped round the steering wheel, but used them to wipe up the leaking brake fluid Adonis had forgotten to fix.

Prosperous Pedros was heartily hailed when he arrived in the taverna bearing freshly caught fish to share with everyone. For the first time he could remember his mother Fotini had not insisted he eat one of her awful home cooked meals before he headed to the taverna. He asked Yiota to prepare the fish and she promised to make a nice lemon dress for it, assuring Prosperous Pedros it would be a vegetarian dress.

Prosperous Pedros told everyone when he had gone to his outside bathroom to perform his shower he had found a frilly pair of panties hanging from the rusty nail on the wall. As the others absorbed this news they each began to reveal they too had discovered discarded women's underwear in the strangest of places and wondered what it was all about.

Moronic Mitsos volunteered he had found a bra in his rowing boat and told the others Bald Yannis had uncovered a pair of knickers draped over the hardware shop cash register. The ex-chief of police was not astute enough to surmise the underwear thief was leaving a false trail and was completely baffled. He noted Vangelis the chemist was performing his civic duty of washing line patrol person this evening and hoped they would soon catch the pervert in action.

Everyone was sipping wine and tucking into Prosperous Pedros' freshly caught fish with a lemon dress when the Pappas sheepishly entered the taverna. Taking a deep breath and smoothing his dress the Pappas announced to the room at large "drink no wine or strong drink, and eat nothing unclean."

Yiota stormed out of the kitchen brandishing a frying pan and screamed at the Pappas that she kept a squeaky clean kitchen.

"I 'ave found God again and am a new man," the Pappas declared, hoping the taverna goers would fall for his fake Holy act. "I say to you all do not get drunk on wine which leads to debauchery," he thundered, reading aloud the Biblical quotes he had written on the inside of his arm. "I promise to be good 'usband to Petula if you give me a second chance," he begged on his way out.

"He's as insufferable sober as he was drunk," Tall Thomas said. "Yous should have left him to drown in the sea, Pedro."

"I always thought he was an odious little man," Deirdre said, to which Yiota told her, "Yous good judge of character Did-Rees."

The villagers decided it was really Petula's decision whether to take the Pappas back or not, but they vowed if the Pappas ever indulged in wife beating again they would toss him far out to sea and definitely let him drown. As for his discovering God they rather questioned if that was something he ought to have done before signing up for a career in the church. Luckily for the Pappas the details of his blackmailing scam had not been disclosed to the villagers at large as this would surely have put the final nail in his coffin.

CHAPTER 84

Secrets Shared

V asilis and his mail order bride Masha did not make it to the taverna of 'Mono Ellinka Trofima' that evening. Vasilis was enjoying a quiet evening sharing surreptitious ouzos with Onos the donkey in the kitchen, while his wife was out of the house. Mail order Masha was visiting her new friend Tassia who was feeling rather despondent after being subjected to endlessly probing questions by her new mother-in-law Mrs Kolokotronis, who appeared doubtful as to the paternity of Tassia's unborn child.

Tassia confided to Masha she had hated to tell so many lies. The truth was in fourteen years of courtship Fat Christos had never laid so much as a finger on her and had never even tried to kiss her. Tassia had been so desperate to have a baby she had engaged in an unwise one night dalliance with a totally unsuitable man.

When two months later Fat Christos had finally proposed marriage she forced herself on him in the garden shed in order to pass off the baby, which had resulted from the one night unsuitable dalliance, as his. The fumbling coupling had been a sweaty disaster. It was only Fat Christos' total inexperience that led him to think he had used the condom from the church collection plate wrongly and got his new fiancée pregnant on their first and only sexual encounter.

Tassia knew she had deceived Fat Christos, but was painfully aware he in turn had only proposed marriage to get his hands on her fortune. A loveless passionless marriage to Fat Christos was, she considered, better than the shame of being an unmarried mother, and as long as he accepted the baby she would try to make him happy.

Tassia had not expected Mrs Kolokotronis to try and stick her nose in these private matters and the constant questions were wearing her down. Mrs Kolokotronis noticed Tassia was much further along than the fumble in the garden shed would explain. She told Masha she would take to the grave the name of her unsuitable lover and sought her advice in distracting Mrs Kolokotronis from finding out the truth.

"It seems to me Fat Christos is too fat to think of the sex and just not into the women," Masha suggested. "He no ladies' man but a mother's boy, maybe he like more the fish or the goat than the woman. He maybe not care he not father of baby as long as he get the money and the status of supermarket. He only want wife for money and to look after him. As for his mother it none of her business and you tell her if she keeps sticking nose in your business yous rescind the invitation to live with yous."

Tassia was very grateful to have such a wise and concerned friend. She realised she had been living a fantasy expecting Fat Christos to change after the wedding and suddenly take a romantic interest in her. As long as he was prepared to accept the baby and treat her with kindness she would go out of her way to be a good wife to him. If he didn't actually want to engage in marital relations with her then that was all to the good, if her revolting experience with him in the garden shed was anything to go by.

As the two friends relaxed in Tassia's garden surrounded by her beautiful roses Masha shared a secret too. "I am new mother to that old shrew Stavroula," she confided "keep it under your 'at but Vasilis is her father."

The two women almost rolled off their deckchairs with laughter as they suggested Vangelis the chemist could make a fortune selling do-it-yourself paternity kits.

CHAPTER 85

Lunch in the Car

Q uentin and Deirdre were enjoying morning coffee in
the sunshine at Stavroulas as they waited for Adonis
to bring them some more papers to sign relating to
the house purchase. "I have to say I will be sad to leave
Astakos once all these legal dealings are out of the way," Deirdre said.

"Oh it won't be long until we return and by then the borrowed builder Achilles will have made speedy work with the
renovations on our new falling down house. Could you have
ever imagined Did-Rees after breaking down on the mountain we would end up buying a holiday home here?"

"Never at all," Deirdre agreed "but I have to say this place
is really something special. Look how kind it was of Prosperous Pedros to share his freshly caught fish with us last night
and even the most awful villagers like the Pappas and Bald
Yannis provide endless amusement."

"Good grief, what is that?" asked Quentin as an old Mercedes taxi drove into view, stopping and starting jerkily as the
tiny old woman driving it could not reach the pedals to

control the clutch. The old Mercedes taxi drove past the taverna and lurched right into the back of Tall Thomas' newly dried out mobile refrigerated fish van which was parked on the incline above the harbour. The violent collision of the two vehicles forced Tall Thomas' van down the incline and straight into the sea. The collision brought the old Mercedes taxi to a halt and Quentin noticed their neighbour Fotini cackling uproariously in the passenger seat.

Tall Thomas ran into view, swearing and cursing at the top of his lungs at the sight of his mobile refrigerated fish van once again landing in the sea. As everyone watched transfixed the van at first bobbed buoyantly on the water and then began to sink. The fishermen drinking coffee outside the kafenion once again joked to Tall Thomas he had better not expect them to re-catch the fish they had already sold him that morning.

Once again all hands were on the ropes used to tug the van out of the water. Adonis' timely arrival in his pick-up van was fortuitous as his van was used to tow the mobile refrigerated fish van from the sea and back to the garage of his cousin Adonis the mechanic. Prosperous Pedros lost his grip on the rope as he heard his mother's second cousin Nitsa screeching at him from the driver's seat window of the Mercedes taxi.

"Oy, young Pedro, we 'ave 'ad the 'orrible accident and is in shock, fetch us two brandies to settle our nerves," she called, while calmly unwrapping a packet of homemade sandwiches she proceeded to share with Fotini. Neither of the two old ladies moved from their seats in the car as they tucked into their sandwiches and knocked back the brandies, while enjoying the entertainment of the mobile refrigerated fishing van being hoisted from the sea.

Tall Thomas demanded Pancratius the village policeman be summoned from his sick bed to arrest the old woman who had caused such havoc. He was stopped in his tracks as the old woman suddenly laughed "What Thoma, yous would have your old aunty arrested would you, go ahead and I cut yous out of my will."

Tall Thomas had no clue the driving menace was his aunty Nitsa and dutifully approached the old Mercedes taxi to allow her to kiss him.

"Now keep an eye on my taxi," she instructed "as Fotini and I are going off to do a spot of shopping." With that she left the Mercedes in the No Parking place outside Stavroulas and climbed down from the stack of magazines she was balanced on.

"I suppose this means Adonis the mechanic will now be spending his time drying out the mobile refrigerated fish van of Tall Thomas again, rather than fixing our car," Quentin lamented. "What is it these Greeks say, meth-avrio will do I suppose?"

CHAPTER 86

Havoc in the Hardware Shop

Nitsa took a sharp intake of breath as she spotted that old fool Vasilis drinking coffee outside the kafenion. Marching over to him she slapped him soundly round the head, saying "I been waiting more than sixty years to do that you letch, that's for trying to lure me into that overgrown olive grove with yous when yous 'ad dishonourable intentions."

Vasilis had no clue as to the identity of the old woman who had struck him and he tried to recollect the parade of pretty faces he had attempted to lure into the overgrown olive grove back in the day. Sighing wearily he realised his memory wasn't as good as back in the day and he went along to see how much longer mail order Masha would be in the beauty parlour.

Entering the beauty shop he could hear mail order Masha screeching at Evangelia. She sounded like an old fish wife as she berated Evangelia for cutting Gorgeous Yiorgos' disgusting yellowing toe nails in full sight of her regular paying customers. Gorgeous Yiorgos was so embarrassed by this scene he left the beauty parlour with only one toe nail cropped foot, muttering he needed to get to the hospital to collect Petula.

With Gorgeous Yiorgos gone, mail order Masha instructed Vasilis to make his way home on Onos the donkey as she intended to stay and have her hair extensions coloured. She said she fancied going red and would then need her finger nails doing to match, so she wouldn't be home until much later.

"There is a pan of borscht simmering in the kitchen so you won't go hungry my love," she said, blowing Vasilis a kiss "but don't give any to the donkey, yous know how it upsets 'is stomach."

Leaving the beauty parlour Vasilis hid in the jewellery shop doorway to avoid passing the mad old woman who had just slapped him. Nitsa and Fotini were enjoying their day out as they headed into the hardware shop to buy some hideous old lady dresses.

"What is that 'orrible thing on your 'ead?" Nitsa rudely asked as she surveyed Bald Yannis' terrible toupee with mirth.

Bald Yannis scowled at these new customers as they demanded he show them his full collection of hideous old lady dresses which they expected to try on before buying. "No one try on dresses before buying," he insisted, but he had finally met his match in these two indomitable and cantankerous women. They started to brazenly strip off their clothes in the middle of his shop floor, giving him a horrifying flash of their hairy chests, before he hastily showed them into his filthy stock room to try on the dresses they had chosen.

"Oh look, the malaka sells waterproof bedspreads," Nitsa said, pointing at the shower curtains and giving Bald Yannis another idea for marketing his shower curtain stock.

Nitsa picked up a shower curtain and asked Bald Yannis if he could cut two holes in it for armholes as she thought it would make a most elegant and patriotic raincoat. "Anything to oblige," Bald Yannis agreed, using his chainsaw to cut two circular holes in the shower curtain. These two elderly ladies were giving him a wealth of ideas for flogging off his surplus shower curtains in imaginative and profitable ways. He was actually smiling as he totted up the total for the sale of several hideous old lady dresses, another waterproof bedspread and a raincoat. He remembered to charge extra for his chain sawing services and then uncharacteristically offered to carry their purchases to their car.

As they walked back to the car Fotini suggested they could have some fun at the expense of those two strange Americans as she had heard they were due back to have another viewing of the 'Lemoni Spiti' they had just bought.

CHAPTER 87

Policemen Return from Nowhere

Heading back to his hardware shop after escorting the two old ladies to their car, Bald Yannis ran into Moronic Mitsos who demanded to know if Shirley Valentine had replied to his billet-doux. Bald Yannis told him Shirley was keen to visit the handsome rich Greek with a yacht, but she expected him to pay for her airline ticket.

"Po po, I thinks the Shirley is after my money," Moronic Mitsos complained, to which Bald Yannis told him "well you did try to pass yourself of as an almost millionaire. I 'ave just 'ad a reply to your fake advertisement from someone who is rich," he lied.

Moronic Mitsos got suitably excited until Bald Yannis delivered his punch line, telling him the rich suitor was a man rather a woman. "Po po I no want no men after me," Moronic Mitsos declared "better ask the Shirley how much she need for the ticket."

Having amused himself completely at the expense of Moronic Mitsos, Bald Yannis had a brainwave and stopped to chat with Stavroula. Ten minutes later she left his hardware

253

shop clutching a large pile of lobster adorned patriotic shower curtains Bald Yannis had convinced her to buy as easily wiped down tablecloths for her taverna.

As Stavroula was putting the new shower curtain table-cloths on her taverna tables she was perturbed to notice the return of the two policemen from the up 'north village' of Pouthena, named for nowhere. "I wonder what those malakas want now?" Stavroula muttered to herself while attempting to disarm them with a fake smile.

"'Ave you found Kostas?" she asked, knowing full well unless they had dug up the chicken coop his body would not have been discovered.

"Your 'usband Kostas appears to have disappeared with no trace," the policemen told her. "His body was not found in the ravine and while it is true the body could 'ave been eaten by wild animals there is no evidence to suggest it was there. Katerina is really worried about her brother and nags us end-lessly to find out what 'appened to him."

Stavroula forcefully made her position clear, saying to the policemen "I told you everything, that no good malaka Kostas playing round with another loose woman hussy and leave me abandoned and alone in 'up north' village of Pouthena where I 'ave no friends. The 'ouse in my name so I sells it and returns to Astakos where I 'ave the many friends to comfort me over the philandering ways of the run off 'usband."

The policemen were satisfied Stavroula sounded most convincing and hoped she would rustle them up some tasty food in her kitchen. However Stavroula's patience over the matter was wearing thin as she considered three visits from the constabulary to be excessive and she had no intention of providing them with a third free meal. She launched into a tirade against police ineptitude, telling them they should have put as much effort into catching the perverted underwear thief who had savagely attacked her in her own back garden and was still on the loose. "Left me for dead he did. What yous doing about that, yous malakas?"

The policemen explained the case of the attacking underwear thief was unfortunately out of their jurisdiction, but they were quite aghast this lovely woman who could cook up a dream had been a helpless victim of some kind of pervert. They assured Stavroula they would speak to Katerina and tell her unless some vital new evidence came up they would have to consider the case of the missing Kostas closed.

Stavroula relented as the policemen had evidenced such good sense and served them some freshly cooked yemistas. They admired her new patriotic tablecloths adorned with lobsters and regretted now the case was closed they would miss the opportunity to sample any more of Stavroula's delicious cooking.

CHAPTER 88

Goats in the Inheritance

When Gorgeous Yiorgos drove Petula home from the hospital he was on hand to help her receive several concerned visitors. Slick Socrates stopped by, shocked by the lurid bruises still decorating Petula's face. He was not happy Petula seemed prepared to take the seemingly contrite Pappas back and he knew Petula was unaware of the Pappas' blackmailing scam, which would have disgusted her.

Mail order Masha arrived, tossing her newly bright red hair extensions. She brought generous gifts of some concealing make-up to cover the lurid bruises and a Tupperware bowl full of her by now infamous borscht. Yiota dropped by with a competing bowlful of tasty stifado and suspiciously sniffed the borscht with an amused expression.

Petula confided to her visitors she was prepared to give the Pappas one final chance, explaining if she left him she would be homeless and destitute. Socrates confirmed the Pappas had tied up his assets in such a way Petula would find it difficult to access them.

Poor Petula still partially blamed herself for the beating she had received from her husband, as she had deceived him by selling her engagement ring and she had been responsible for inadvertently murdering his beloved pet goat Krasi. She decided it would go some way towards mending her sorry marriage if she made a gift to her husband of a new pet goat, and enlisted the help of her visitors to secure a suitably cute animal. Gorgeous Yiogos took it upon himself to find a cute pet goat as it had been his car involved in the murderous accident.

Mail order Masha appeared suddenly distracted as she noticed to her horror one of her new bright red nail extensions was missing. She hoped it hadn't fallen into the Tupperware bowl of borscht she had brought along to Petula as it would be awful if Petula choked on the nail extension and ended right back in the hospital.

Petula was not the only Astakostan to return to the village that day. Fat Christos returned from the clinic where the surgeon had received a handsome brown envelope to perform the stomach stapling surgery. He was already looking decidedly trimmer and his new diet of only liquidised foods would help him to quickly shed his remaining excess kilos.

Toothless Tasos ran into Fat Christos as the latter headed towards the supermarket to be reunited with his new bride. Toothless Tasos promised to give him plenty of tips on liquidised foods as they had been his staple diet for years, before he had invested in his new false teeth.

Tassia was a little apprehensive about the return of her new groom as she worried his mother would be putting suspicious ideas in his head about the paternity of the baby. She hoped her warning that she was prepared to rescind the invitation of having Mrs Kolokotronis come live with the newlyweds was enough of a threat for the older woman to keep her mouth shut.

Tassia complimented her husband on his drastic weight loss and promised him she would learn to become a whizz with the blender. Fat Christos confided as he lost more weight his excess skin could present a problem as his stomach was already sagging down to his knees. Not only was it proving very heavy and sweaty to cart around but it also gave him a nasty itchy rash.

Tassia had a happy announcement to make as she had just received the legal copy of her old uncle's will. In addition to the supermarket, she had inherited his rambling old house in the neighbouring village of Rapanaki, eight hundred olive trees, a herd of goats and a fishing boat.

"What no cash?" questioned Fat Christos.

He was relieved when Tassia told him her family had a history of hiding cash in obscure places as they didn't trust banks and there may well be bags full of the stuff hidden in his house, the chicken coop and even the goat pen. She suggested they instigate a search for any cash and this delighted Fat Christos who needed to wangle another brown envelope to bribe the surgeon for an operation to have his excess skin removed.

"I never knew your old dead uncle had a fishing boat," Fat Christos said.

"He kept it down at Gavros apparently," Tassia told him "but now we can bring it home and you will be able to fish again whenever you fancy."

Fat Christos was really happy he would once again own a fishing boat and considered this gave him one up on the meddling tax inspectors.

"I wonder if I can get my plastic relaxation chair back

from Toothless Tasos?" he pondered.

He was a tad worried when Tassia said there was no need as she would treat him to a new one, as he did not want her throwing their new found wealth around indiscriminately.

The newlyweds decided to close the supermarket early. They were not heading home for a romantic interlude to make up for missing a proper wedding night. Instead they planned to get the keys to Tassia's dead uncle's house and go searching for any hidden bags of cash.

CHAPTER 89

Picking Weeds

Prosperous Pedros felt duty bound to call on his old mother Fotini and check everything was going well with her and her house guest. Nitsa greeted him at the door and told him Fotini was down the garden perched up on the three-legged olive tree ladder to spy on her soon to be new neighbours. Prosperous Pedros decided with his mother out of earshot this would be a good opportunity to broach the subject of his dead father with Nitsa.

"I would be 'appy if yous don't mention to my mother my father is dead as the grief would kill her," he said.

"What you talking nonsense about, yous father not dead, he gone to Athens?" Nitsa replied. "If he was dead yous would be living 'ere with yous mother, like what a dutiful son would."

Prosperous Pedros was greatly relieved Nitsa was actually under deluded the impression his dead father was in Athens. It was in truth the only aspect of her visit that had unnerved him and now he knew she believed the Athens nonsense he couldn't really care less how much havoc the two elderly ladies could potentially cause. Embarrassment was after all a small price to pay to avoid dutifully moving in with his mother.

"Those must be those strange Americans," Nitsa said, pointing next door, "be off with you Pedro while I goes and climb the ladder with Fotini."

Deirdre and Quentin were quite disturbed to discover not one, but two, eccentric old ladies perched up the three-legged olive tree ladder peering down at them.

"Isn't that the old dear from the old Mercedes taxi who drove into the back of Tall Thomas' mobile refrigerated fish van?" Quentin asked, nodding to himself as he spotted the now dented old Mercedes taxi parked outside the neighbouring house. "I wonder what they find so fascinating."

Deirdre was engrossed in conversation with Achilles the borrowed builder who was busy suggesting he build her an outdoor bread oven.

"I think I would prefer an electric one in the kitchen," Deirdre told him, only to have Achilles reply "but I thought you wanted ancient traditions in 'ouse. Is old custom to bake bread outdoors. I not understand you Did-Rees, one day yous want the old and I says get modern, then I suggest the old and yous demand modern. Yous is a difficult confusing woman."

Eager to placate the borrowed builder Deirdre assured him she loved his suggestions and between them they would come up with a compromise she could live with.

"No one in Idaho has ever come up with anything as imaginative as the marvellous things you plan to do with shower curtains Achille. K-Went-In really likes the idea you had of building a secret room off the kitchen to hide from unwanted visitors in, that was a stroke of genius."

Quentin had indeed liked the idea as he envisaged it

would be very handy if any of Deirdre's relatives turned up uninvited for a free holiday.

Their conversation was interrupted by the uninvited arrival of Fotini and Nitsa who had managed to scale the neighbouring wall without breaking any bones. They made quite a sight in their hideous old lady dresses, with their pop socks revealing hairy legs that matched their moustaches. Armed with plastic carrier bags they made a grab for Deirdre's arm, gesticulating at the ground and muttering "horta, horta."

"I thinks the old crones wants show yous how to forage wild greens," Adonis translated as Fotini dragged Deirdre into the thigh high weeds and started shoving nettles and poppy leaves into her plastic carrier bag.

"Oh how kind," Deirdre commented. "I have seen Yiota serve horta, but am yet to try it."

"Is easy," Adonis told her "yous boil green weeds for three hours and put on the lemon and olive oil dress. This garden give yous free food, very tasty, horta very goodly with road-kill goat."

Fotini emitted a high pitched screech as she heard the word goat and gambolled back over the neighbouring wall at a terrific pace, taking the bag of wild greens she had picked with her.

"She probably see snake," Adonis explained, to the consternation of Deirdre who was not used to living in close proximity to snakes.

Nitsa told Adonis to tell the two Americans they should pop by tomorrow to sample the horta once it had been boiled. Quentin and Deirdre warily expressed their acceptance of this invitation though they were not convinced the two eccentric elderly ladies were completely compos mentis.

CHAPTER 90

The Missing Cat

T oothless Tasos had just received a shock to his system when he discovered the perfect goddess he had put on a pedestal of worship, actually had feet of clay. Thea had called on Toothless Tasos in a bit of a tizzy as she had lost her cat. She was convinced the cat was still inside the house as it hated going outdoors. She was having trouble locating it behind the vast mounds of tat she had impulsively purchased from the home shopping channel before destroying her television set with a hammer. She was worried the cat might suffocate amidst the clutter or suffer some other ghastly fate.

Toothless Tasos was of course delighted to come to the assistance of Thea and hoped it would increase his heroic status in her eyes. He had never before been invited to cross the threshold into Thea's home and was rather floored by the sight that greeted him. There was not a centimetre of space not covered in piles of tat and Thea's many excessive impulse purchases.

The realisation hit Toothless Tasos his beloved was a

hoarder, a habit he personally deplored, preferring a mini-malistic approach to his living space, as his possession of a solitary deckchair demonstrated. The hoarding habit revealed Thea to be a weak willed spendthrift in his eyes. However even with this glaring personal failure revealed he could not stop loving Thea as it was his personal weak willed habit to adore her unconditionally.

Climbing precariously over the top of a sofa piled high with boxes Toothless Tasos hissed "Gata Gata," in a desperate effort to locate the missing cat. He hoped it would not startle him by springing out suddenly as he had a personal loathing of cats which he considered to be thieving creatures. Far too many of the things had made off with parts of his fishy catch by hovering and pouncing, something he did not appreciate after a hard night's graft fishing.

"Thea this impossible, it's impossible to move, to find anything, to even breathe. Much as it pains me to tell yous an unpleasant 'ome truth, yous 'ave way too much clutter. Something must be done to reduce all this tat so yous have space to move and find the cat," he pronounced.

"Oh I know you are right Taso, but I must confess I had a terrible habit of buying things impulsively from the home shopping channel. All this tat has racked up huge debts and I just want rid of it all. I have controlled the bad habit and buy no more. I don't want to be a hoarder, will yous help me?" Thea sobbed uncontrollably, embarrassed that her compulsive shopping habit had been discovered.

Toothless Tasos made an uncharacteristically bold move and took the weeping Thea into his arms to comfort her. "Now dry you eyes, I have dealt with worse than this," Tasos assured her as he scrubbed her face dry with a fishy smelling hanky. He remembered the extraordinary lengths he had been driven to in order to get out of Stavroula's clutches all those years ago and compared to that Thea's current problems were miniscule.

"You owes debt money, so we clean out 'ouse and 'ave a sale of all this tat to raise money to pay debt money back," Tasos decreed. "For a start I buy that arm chair with cat hair to replace the decorative plastic chair I got from Fat Christos, as he wants it back to put in Tassia's dead uncle's fishing boat."

With that Tasos hoisted the cat hair covered armchair onto his back and carried it home, returning immediately to help Thea sort through the rest of the junk.

After several hours of hard work sorting through tat the pair returned to Toothless Tasos' house to catch up with the latest gripping instalment of their favourite soap opera 'Seven Deadly Mothers-in-Law.' As they entered his living room Toothless Tasos was surprised to discover Thea's missing cat was curled up fast asleep in his new cat haired covered armchair. He suspected he may have difficulties in encouraging it to leave.

CHAPTER 91

Vinegar in the Taverna

P rosperous Pedros tucked into his vegetarian meal of tasty horta in the taverna 'Mono Ellinka Trofima.' He was surprised to discover he was still hungry after finishing his meal and realised for only the second time ever he had not feasted on one his mother's home cooked meals before coming out to eat at the taverna. Fotini wouldn't brook any of his vegetarian nonsense and always made sure he had a big slab of meat on his plate, which made it much easier for him to insist he was a vegetarian in public. Prosperous Pedros decided to order a plate of vegetarian chicken to quell his rumbling stomach.

Fat Christos and his new bride Tassia had enjoyedd a productive afternoon searching through the filthy nooks and crannies of the dead uncle's house. They had discovered a thick wad of cash stuffed under the mattress and a bag of coins hidden in the toilet cistern. Their strangest find was a collection of gold teeth stashed in a teapot. They planned to return the next day to find out what else the old dead uncle had been hiding.

Insisting his pregnant bride needed her rest Fat Christos sent Tassia home and went on alone to the taverna where he discovered there was nothing he could eat with his new strict dietary restrictions in force. Yiota hadn't bothered cooking any soup and Fat Christos was reduced to drinking water. He telephoned Tassia who had just gone to bed for a well deserved rest and asked her to get up and liquidise him some dinner.

Toothless Tasos told Fat Christos he could have his decorative plastic chair back as he had acquired a new arm chair from Thea. Fat Christos was delighted to be able to offer Gorgeous Yiorgos the pick of his herd of newly inherited goats to give to Petula to gift to the Pappas as a peace offering. They arranged to pick out a goat the next day.

Everyone sat upright and sucked in their stomachs when mail order Masha entered the taverna with that old fool Vasilis. Her new red hair extensions were certainly eye catching, but her perfection was marred by a stubby bandage on the end of her finger which she had wrapped around it to disguise her missing red nail extension, which was quite possibly languishing in the pot of borscht she had given Petula. Poor Masha still found it uncomfortable to sit down after the noxious chemical injection she'd had injected in her posterior to make it even larger.

"Did-Rees stop scratching," Gorgeous Yiorgos advised her, noticing she could not stop messing with a very prominent mosquito bite. "Yiota bring Did-Rees some vinegar for bite," he instructed, telling Deirdre to rub the vinegar in well to deter anymore mosquitoes from biting, in addition to soothing the current itch.

"Vinegar sounds a bit odd as a cure," said Deirdre, thinking it would make her smell most unpleasant.

Yiota assured her Greeks had invented vinegar as a cure for anything you could think of. "Strange foreign people put it on fried potatoes instead of lemon and oregano, but Greeks use it for nits, bites and stomach problems. Never mind the smell Did-Rees, it is better than scratching."

"I still think you smell lovely darling," Quentin told her.

"I never thought of it till now but perhaps vinegar goodly for the nasty rash round my excess skin," Fat Christos said, experiencing a light bulb moment.

Toothless Tasos announced Thea was having a house clearance sale the next day and everyone was invited. "She 'ave some lovely things to get rid of," he said, leaving the others wondering if Thea was clearing her things out in preparation for moving in with Toothless Tasos. They knew from experience if they started to question him on his love life he would clam up and leave the taverna in embarrassment, so they kept their thoughts to themselves and agreed to turn up at the clearance sale, hoping to snag a few bargains.

Mail order Masha made a note to be sure to attend the clearance sale the minute she was finished in the beauty parlour having her false nail extension doctored. She imagined Thea had some lovely things as she wasn't quite as provincial as some of her neighbours.

"Petula found one of my lace bras in her garden," she told everyone "it seems underwear is no longer disappearing, but turning up in strange places."

Tall Thomas came in and tackled Prosperous Pedros, demanding to know if that awful old woman who claimed to be his aunty and had driven into the back of his mobile refrigerated fish van, was in any way connected to Fotini.

"She's a second cousin staying with my old mother," Prosperous Pedros explained "but definitely related to yous.

She's yous old aunty. Be nice to her, she's rich," he advised, knowing Tall Thomas placed a high value on material things. Eyebrows were raised in amusement when Quentin revealed he and Deirdre had been invited to partake of horta with Fotini and Nitsa the next day.

"Keep yous wits about yous when you go in 'er 'ouse," Takis advised, hoping Prosperous Pedros could not hear him. "She can be strange woman."

"Yes we gathered she is a tad eccentric, but consider her quite harmless," Quentin quipped. Eyebrows were once again raised in amusement at Quentin's obvious naivety in the ways of Fotini. She had not become the mortal enemy of everyone in two villages by being harmless.

The Pappas followed his new regular habit of wandering into the taverna to spout a Biblical quote on the dangers of the demon drink. "He who loves wine and oil will not be rich," he shouted, to which Tall Thomas replied, "it depends if he has a rich old aunty."

"Not to mention if he's just inherited eight hundred olive trees," Fat Christos added for good measure.

Gorgeous Yiorgos told the Pappas he would like a private word outside. He told the Pappas Petula had decided to take him back and he could return home the following afternoon. He advised the Pappas if he hit or insulted Petula he would be out on his ear and a bigly sea waited.

CHAPTER 92

The Beautiful New Pet Goat

The goat Gorgeous Yiogos chose from Fat Christos' newly inherited herd was a beauty. She was milky white with large floppy ears, a kissable nose and intelligent eyes.

"As the Pappas' new favourite tipple is water we call this goat 'Nero,'" Gorgeous Yiorgos announced, wrapping a large pink bow round the creature's neck and dragging it to the car. Nero was no trouble at all as Gorgeous Yiorgos drove to Petula's with the goat sticking its head out of the sunroof.

"Oh look at that attractive goatly specimen," Quentin commented to Deirdre. They both waved enthusiastically at Gorgeous Yiorgos and the goat as they drove past.

Petula was most happy with the choice of such a beautiful and amicable goat. She hoped by gifting it to the Pappas it would help to repair relations between her and her husband. He was due to return home at any moment and Petula implored Gorgeous Yiorgos to stick around to help calm her nerves.

"Yous 'usband has got insufferably Godly," Gorgeous

Yiorgos told Petula, which surprised her as he had never been the religious type before.

"Perhaps it is contrition for the way he treated me," she considered, but Gorgeous Yiorgos kept his own counsel on the matter as Petula had no idea the Pappas had suffered a near fatal drowning at the hands of the village men. She was so sweet natured she may not have approved.

The Pappas trudged wearily home. He was exhausted from spending hours looking up Biblical quotations on the demon drink and from sleeping uncomfortably on the floor of the church. He had reduced his intake of Holy wine instead of giving it up as he claimed, but told himself it was medicinal to cope with the trauma he had experienced of being tossed so roughly into the sea. He had stopped at the bakery to buy Petula a peace offering of some cream cakes, announcing "sweets for my sweet," as he handed them over.

"I 'ave a surprise gift for yous too 'usband, this is Nero, yous new pet goat," Petula said, pushing the pink ribbon bedecked creature into view. On sight of the Pappas Nero's hackles rose up and she bleated threateningly. Nero refused to go to the priest, instead nestling her head into Petula's skirts and stamping a hoof derisively.

"It is most considerate gift of a most handsome creature," the Pappas said, stepping backwards as Nero tried to take a bite out of his clerical dress. Gorgeous Yiorgos was delighted the goat had unwittingly stepped into the role of Petula's guard dog and felt quite assured of Petula's safety as he took his leave, promising to check in on her again the next day.

"I 'ave special dinner for you of Russian borscht," Petula told her husband. The Pappas had heard of mail order Masha's infamous soup and was quite relieved when Petula exclaimed, "Oh dear, the goat appears to 'ave eaten yous dinner."

"Is no worry, it is late and I'm tired," the Pappas oblig-ingly said, surprising Petula who was used to receiving a slap if his dinner wasn't waiting for him on the table. With a las-civious glint in his eye the Pappas suggested they retire early to bed and Petula apprehensively agreed, hoping her hus-band was not planning a night of fumbling passion.

His fumbling plans were thwarted though when they reached the bedroom as Nero had claimed his side of the bed and refused to let the Pappas climb in, snapping fiercely at him with surprisingly sharp teeth. The Pappas had no choice but to retire to the downstairs sofa while Petula cuddled up safely in bed with his new pet goat.

CHAPTER 93

Tourist Tat

F at Christos was settling happily into married life. Tassia was proving to be far easier to live with than his mother and she made an excellent job of liquidising his dinner, though the doctor recommended liquid slop was not exactly tasty. He was relieved she wasn't making demands on his body as he considered that sort of thing was really overrated.

Even if his mother's suspicions were true that Tassia's baby was fathered by another man, he could live with it. He was just relieved Tassia was actually pregnant and would not be expecting him to perform nightly marital duties to fulfil her wish of an instant family. Tassia was expecting the baby she wanted and he had grand plans to use the sizeable inheritance to make himself a man of stature in the village. He hoped his mother would be prepared to undertake grandmotherly babysitting duties as she was such a gossip she would be less than useless serving in the supermarket.

Fat Christos considered his new wife would be an excellent asset in the newly inherited supermarket and he was excited to transform the dusty old shop with its antiquated stock into something he could be proud of. Tassia was very supportive of his ideas to branch out into tourist tat as the tourists would soon be descending on the village in droves. He commissioned Achilles the borrowed builder to revamp the interior of the shop and as Achilles got busy banging up new shelves Fat Christos placed his first orders for tourist tat.

"Look Tassia, I is loving the electric lamp light up Parthenon and the glow in the dark plastic Acropolis. These plastic statues of armless Aphrodite will sell like hot cakes and we can get some Apollo and Aristotle 'eads," he enthused.

"Tourists love cats so order some of those Greek cat calendars too," Tassia suggested.

"An excellent idea, I wonder if they do a Greek goat one as well," Fat Christos agreed. "Perhaps we should venture into patriotic shower curtains as Bald Yannis seems to be making killing on 'em," he added, but Tassia advised it may not be wise to go into direct competition with the malicious hardware man.

"Let us leave Achilles to it and go back to dead old uncle's 'ouse in neighbouring village of Rapanaki and see if we can find more hidden money," Fat Christos suggested, "we can use it to pay for all this tourist tat what will turn us an 'andsome profit."

CHAPTER 94

Useless Million

I was sure old dead uncle would 'ave 'idden something of value under the chicken coop," Tassia told Fat Christos as they fruitlessly searched the stinky coop. They had already discovered a substantial stash of Euro notes in the sofa stuffing, an unexplained collection of very expensive looking jewellery hidden under a loose floorboard and another bag of coins stuffed up the chimney.

"I think we are not the first to look," Fat Christos declared, noticing some obvious scuff marks amidst the chicken dirt. The newlyweds started to follow the fresh trail marks which led from the dead uncle's chicken coop and ended up quite some distance away at the door of the old crone Fotini.

"I wonder what she 'ave to say for herself," Fat Christos pondered, hammering on the door.

Fat Christos was not deterred by the heavy lobbing of lemons which greeted their arrival. He was determined to have it out with Fotini, even if it did mean accusing Prosperous Pedros' old mother of being a thief. Fat Christos finally persuaded Fotini to open the door by threatening her he would summon her son if she insisted on being so stubborn.

"'Ave you been rummaging round in the dirt of Tassia's dead old uncle's chicken coop?" Fat Christos demanded to know.

"So what if I 'ave?" Fotini responded. "'Ow was I supposed to know his rightful heirs would suspicion something was buried there? You is too clever by 'alf Fat Christo, yous want to go halfs on my findings?"

"No, we want it all as we is rightful heirs and yous 'ave no claim on the buried fortune," Fat Christos decreed. "What yous dig up anyways Kyria Fotini?"

"See for yourself," Fotini told him, throwing him a hefty olive sack stuffed with old and worthless Greek drachma notes.

"Po po, there is more than a million of old useless money 'ere," Fat Christos said. "Yous old dead uncle stupid not to change it at the bank 'fore it became useless Tassia."

"A million drachma is worth less than three thousand Euros," Tassia quickly calculated, impressing her husband no end that she had a sharp brain that worked like a cash register.

"Not such a bigly loss considering all the other money we found. Kyria Fotini you keeps it," Tassia offered, pleasing the old crone greatly as she planned to get Prosperous Pedros to nail the old bank notes to her living room wall as decorative wallpaper.

"I 'ears yous is pregnant, let me spits on yous for good luck," Fotini said with a calculated smile, as Tassia fled away in disgust to the sound of Nitsa and Fotini cackling manically behind her.

CHAPTER 95

The House Clearance Sale

T
hea's house clearance sale was proving very popular amongst the villagers who were eager to snap up a bargain. Toothless Tasos had enlisted the help of Gorgeous Yiorgos and between the two of them they had carried all of Thea's bulkier items onto the pavement outside her house, allowing room for the bargain hunters to move relatively freely inside and rummage through the contents of the many overflowing boxes.

Fat Christos cast his savvy eye over the stuff for sale, wondering if he could sell any of it profitably in his new supermarket. "Why you 'ave eight dozen jars of lemon stuffed olives?" he queried, snapping them up for half-price.

"I was 'ungry one night when watching the 'ome shopping channel," Thea confessed guiltily, finally understanding a normal shopper would perhaps have only purchased one jar of lemon stuffed olives to keep hunger at bay.

Stavroula was pleased to purchase a new set of pans to replace the ones which were covered in dents from her constant banging. Some of her old set were worn thin with the indentations from Slick Socrates' head.

Bald Yannis was mightily tempted as he rummaged through Thea's extensive collection of silk underwear, but exercised remarkable self restraint as he did not believe in paying for underwear when there were so many washing lines to plunder.

Quentin and Deirdre were fascinated as they probed through Thea's boxes of tat in the still cluttered house. "Do you think all Greek people live like this?" Deirdre questioned. Fat Christos was quick to assure her Thea was one of a kind as she suffered from a compulsive shopping addiction.

"Very soon I 'ave some lovely things in the supermarket yous buy as souvenirs to take 'ome to Idaho, Did-Rees. I thinks the glows in the dark Acropolis will look magnificent in yous 'ouse back 'ome and yous gets another one for falling down 'ouse 'ere if you like. Very tasteful," he promised as Deirdre looked rather horrified at his tacky suggestion.

"We will definitely be buying some patriotic souvenir shower curtains from the hardware shop," Deirdre mentioned. This did not please Fat Christos and he immediately determined to override Tassia's advice and start stocking patriotic shower curtains in the supermarket, in direct competition with Bald Yannis.

Mrs Kolokotronis snapped up some comfortable cushions to gift to her new daughter-in-law in case she developed an aching pregnancy back. She was mindful the newly married couple did not welcome her unsolicited interference. She had not yet decided whether to move in with them or not so she considered it best if she did not antagonise them any further until she had reached a decision. She was filled with motherly pride at the way Fat Christos had taken advantage of the supermarket inheritance to finally make something of himself

and conceded his loss of blubber was giving him more purpose in life.

There were mutters of irritation all round as Fotini and
Nitsa arrived at the house clearance sale and immediately el-
bowed all the other bargain hunters out of way. "Age before
beauty," Fotini snapped at mail order Masha, yanking what
she thought was Thea's perfumed body spray out of the
younger woman's hands and spraying herself liberally with
it.

"Why yous spray yourself with oven cleaner?" mail order
Masha asked as the skin began to bubble and peel off Fotini's
arms.

Vasilis had come along to carry any bargains Masha spotted, but was not nimble enough on his feet to avoid the slap
Nitsa inflicted on his head.

"Take that yous letch," she screeched. "I 'ave been waiting more than sixty years to do that, that's for trying to lure
me into that overgrown olive grove with yous when yous 'ad
dishonourable intentions." It struck Vasilis this mad violent
woman had a remarkable long distance memory but had
seemingly completely forgotten she had already slapped him
just the day before.

"Keep your 'ands off my 'usband," mail order Masha
warned Nitsa "or yous 'ave Russian mafia to answer to."

Petula had quite skilfully applied the generous gift of
mail order Masha's bruise concealing make-up and it had
given her enough confidence to venture out of the house. Her
husband had even parted with a ten Euro note and told his
wife to enjoy her shopping spree at the house clearance sale.

Petula had recovered mail order Masha's missing bright
red fake finger nail extension from the vomit the new pet goat
Nero had thrown up inside the Pappas' shoes. The borscht

appeared to have disagreed with the goat's stomach and Petula was most happy to be able to return the missing nail extension, imagining it was quite valuable to Masha.

The Pappas had shown remarkable restraint controlling his temper when he discovered his vomit filled shoes. He had automatically raised his arm in a familiar gesture of violence, but one vicious head butt from the goat had given him pause for thought and he lowered his arm to pat the new pet, only to receive a sharp bite on his hand for his trouble.

"This was such a clever idea yous 'ad Taso," Thea told him "we 'ave got rid of lots of tat and got back some money for debts." She was particularly pleased to have sold the television set she had destroyed with a hammer to some old fool who thought it was a fish tank.

"What they doing 'ere?" Toothless Tasos queried, spotting his ornamental stuffed swordfish noses being snapped up by Petros the postman.

"They smell bad," Thea told him. "I give yous lovely ornamental mirror instead. I cannot abide stuffed smelly swordfish looking at me when watching my favourite soap opera."

Toothless Tasos considered Thea had gone too far by purloining and selling his decorative home features, but he did not have the heart to reprimand her in case it brought on another bout of uncontrollable sobbing. Still her act rankled him so he quickly popped home, returning with Thea's cat displaying a 'For Sale' sign round its neck.

CHAPTER 96

The Cookery Lesson

Stavroula was manically scratching her ample bosom when mail order Masha walked into the taverna kitchen for the promised Greek cooking lesson from her new step-daughter.

"Po po, these minging myrmingi ant things are itching me something 'orrible," Stavroula complained, explaining "Toothless Tasos gives me apricots from 'is tree and theys is crawling with ants, the nasty things got under my shirt and inside my vest."

Mail order Masha had no interest in the goings on of Stavroula's amply sagging bosom. She was far more interested in checking out her fake finger nail extensions than in examining Stavroula's rash.

"What we cooking?" mail order Masha asked her new step-daughter with a disinterested air, as she really was not inclined to expand her culinary skills. She considered herself an accomplished borscht cook and if she fancied anything different they could eat at the taverna.

"What yous know to cook already?" Stavroula asked her

281

new step-mother. She was quite amazed when mail order Masha nodded her head in the local style and clucked to indicate she had no clue how to boil an egg, cook traditional moussaka, nor fry a simple aubergine.

"I knows 'ow to cook borscht," Masha said emphatically. "I cooks best Borscht in Russia," not confessing it had made the Onos the donkey and the Pappas' new pet goat violently sick.

Stavroula told Masha "here take this knife; I shows you goodly way to peel potatoes."

Masha reluctantly picked up the knife to copy her example, but was overly concerned she may knife off another fake nail extension. The two women attempted to make small talk with mail order Masha asking her new step-daughter how she felt when she discovered Vasilis was her father.

"It shocked me," Stavroula confided "but always I 'ave the feeling Gregoris not my real father. He was a difficult man but teach me 'ow to kill and pluck chickens and butcher goats. I thinks Vasilis an old fool to marry a gold digger, but I needs to get used to calls you Mama. It not comes easy."

Mail order Masha confided to Stavroula she and Vasilis were trying for a baby. Stavroula was shocked at the very thought of her ancient father indulging in the necessary act, exclaiming it would likely kill him off. Stavroula regretted having no children of her own but blamed her two useless husbands for both being infertile.

"I goes now," mail order Masha announced mid potato, "I promised to pick up treats for the donkey on the way 'ome." She considered it a kind gesture when Stavroula gifted her a bagful of potato peelings to take home to the donkey. Clutching the bag of potato peelings mail order Masha flounced out with a flick of her hair extensions, refusing to commit to anymore tedious cookery lessons.

CHAPTER 97

Quentin and Deirdre Have Lunch at Fotini's House

Quentin and Deirdre were feeling rather nervous about the impending late luncheon of boiled wild weeds at Fotini's house, not least because of the communication problem. The usually always obliging Adonis had flatly refused to come along and translate, telling them to take a phrasebook instead. Adonis pleaded a prior engagement rather than admit to his loathing of Fotini.

As the American couple left Stavroulas to head over to Fotini's house they were surprised when Nitsa pulled up in her old Mercedes taxi, gesticulating for them to get in the back. Nitsa came to a halt thirty seconds later outside the hardware shop, driving into a wheelbarrow Bald Yannis had for sale. Holding up one finger to indicate Quentin and Deirdre should wait, she kept them captive in the car by utilising its central locking.

Bald Yannis was relieved to see Nitsa was alone rather than in the company of Fotini. The two women together were more than a match for him.

"I needs wall paper paste and a brush," Nitsa requested, as it was taking far too long to decorate Fotini's living room by using a hammer and nails to attach all the old drachma notes to the wall. "Put them on tab of Prosperous Pedros," Nitsa demanded, striding quickly to the door with her unpaid for purchases.

Bald Yannis was quick on his feet to cut her off in the doorway, wielding his chainsaw menacingly and pointing to the prominent sign reminding his customers not to ask for credit as the war is over.

"Look, that mad Bald Yannis is threatening the harmless old lady with a chainsaw," Deirdre cried in horror, wondering just how low the hardware shop man could stoop. Quentin would have leapt to Nitsa's defence as he was a gentleman, but the car's central locking kept him captive in the back seat.

"I ave no cash on me," Nitsa told Bald Yannis who was trying to grab back the unpaid purchases Nitsa was holding onto for dear life. An unseemly struggle ensued as Tall Thomas rushed to his new aunt's rescue by proffering a fish from the borrowed car he was using while his mobile refrigerated fishing van was drying out, in lieu of a cash payment.

Bald Yannis quickly calculated the fish was worth more than the cost of the wallpaper paste and brush, and Tall Thomas gladly accepted his change in the form of a patriotic shower curtain. He thought it would make an excellent sunscreen for the windscreen of his mobile refrigerated fish van to prevent it from becoming too hot.

Nitsa climbed back in the old Mercedes taxi and settled herself on the pile of old magazines so she could better peer through the windscreen. As the old Mercedes taxi ploughed along at a crawl in jerky fits and starts Deirdre wished she had taken a travel sickness pill.

"Look out," Quentin screeched as Nitsa swerved to try and hit Onos the donkey who was ambling along with that old fool Vasilis on his back.

"Malaka I missed 'im," Nitsa swore as she failed to connect with the donkey, though she managed to give old Vasilis a nasty fright.

The rest of the drive to the neighbouring village of Rapanaki was hair-raising but uneventful, though Nitsa had a decided tendency to aim directly for every pot hole they passed. Deirdre whispered to Quentin they would have got there much faster if they had walked. Nitsa managed to bring the old Mercedes taxi to a halt by driving into an olive tree in Fotini's garden. Leaning over from the front seat towards her reluctant passengers she gave an evil smile and holding out her hand demanded "yous pay, is taxi."

Quentin and Deirdre did not realise they were honoured to be among only a handful of visitors ever to cross Fotini's threshold. Fotini was so unpopular it was rare for anyone to visit and unexpected callers were usually greeted with a handful of forcefully lobbed lemons.

Fotini was delighted to receive a gift from her visitors of a new waterproof bedspread which exactly matched the one she had put on Nitsa's bed. The gift pleased her so much her guests went up in her estimation and she decided to be on her best behaviour for the duration of their visit. This was a huge concession by Fotini's usual standards as she considered it one of the few perks of old age to be as deliberately obnoxious as she liked.

The American pair were taken aback to enter a living room partially papered with nailed up old drachma notes.

They considered it a most unusual style in home decor.

"Fotini must be very rich and eccentric if she can afford to paper her house in bank notes," Quentin whispered to Deirdre, having no idea the old drachma notes were valueless.

The American couple almost passed out from the stifling heat as they entered Fotini's kitchen where she had been boiling a pan of wild weeds over an open fire for the last several hours. Quentin considered it quite quaint Fotini favoured a traditional method of cooking rather than using her electric cooker, having no way of knowing the electric company had cut off her supply when she greeted the meter reading man with a forceful lobby of lemons.

Four places were set at the kitchen table, in close proximity to the open fire. Fotini heaped huge amounts of boiled horta onto her guest's plates and liberally doused it with her very finest extra virgin olive oil. Nitsa was sent out into the garden to collect some of the lemons that been lobbed from the windows and these were squeezed over the plates of horta to add the final delicious finishing touch.

The conversation consisted primarily of exaggerated gestures due to the language barrier, but Quentin and Deirdre managed to convey their enjoyment of the appetising food. In truth they at first found the horta a tad bitter as it is an acquired taste, but they began to acquire a taste for it as they tucked into the second plateful Fotini heaped on them.

"Yous yitonas," Fotini repeated over and over, stabbing a finger at her guests. Quentin thumbed through the phrase book and was happy to discover she was telling them they were neighbours rather than insulting them.

"I thinks they a bit gormless," Fotini said to Nitsa, not caring if the word for gormless could be found in Quentin's phrasebook.

After lunch Quentin and Deirdre gesticulated to their hosts they planned to call in at the neighbouring 'Lemoni Spiti' to have another look at their recently acquired falling down house. Fotini very kindly offered them the use of her three-legged olive tree ladder to facilitate their climb over the garden wall.

"Well that went quite well," Deirdre said to Quentin, who agreed the experience had hardly been unpleasant at all. Deirdre was most relieved Fotini hadn't spat on her as she still had nightmares about the old lady spitting all over Tassia at the wedding.

CHAPTER 98

Washing Line Patrol Duty

T all Thomas was driving Adonis the mechanic quite mad by pestering him endlessly to hurry up drying out his mobile refrigerated fish van. The borrowed car was not a great substitute as it lacked refrigeration and Tall Thomas worried his lucrative fish selling business would suffer. Some of the fishermen had taken to selling their own catch and there were rumours his business model was about to be copied by a rival from the village of Gavros.

The sudden appearance of his old aunty Nitsa from the 'up north' village of Pirouni had so far proved a disaster. It was her inept driving that had caused the second sinking of his fish van. However he was mindful he had been brought up to be polite to old family members. Prosperous Pedros' words about her supposed wealth left him thinking he should pursue an amicable relationship with her, just in case she included him in her will.

Tall Thomas was exhausted, having spent the whole of the previous night sleeping upright in an olive field with one eye open for any sign of the elusive underwear thief. He decided to tackle Moronic Mitsos in the kafenion about the need to continue with the washing line patrol duty rota. The elusive thief turned strangling attacker appeared to have stopped stealing. No new underwear had been reported missing and none of the patrolling villagers had spotted anything even slightly suspicious.

Bald Yannis was the first to second Tall Thomas's motion the washing line patrol rota should be abandoned as a waste of time. Moronic Mitsos was not convinced; pointing out the thief may only have stopped stealing as he was aware the washing lines were being watched so scrupulously.

"My wife is 'appy her knickers are no longer under attack," the moron declared, while conceding "it possible the thief is bored of bras and knickers, an' is stealing somethin' else."

The Pappas, who was trying his best to inveigle his way back into the good graces of the villagers, piped up with one of his newly cribbed Biblical quotes, saying "A thief might not get caught by the law, but God knows."

Slick Socrates fired a filthy look in the direction of the Pappas, muttering to himself about God knowing all about blackmailing malakas. He would love to expose the Pappas as a scheming blackmailer but had promised Stavroula not to gossip about her newly discovered paternity. The villagers decided to keep up the washing line patrol for one more week and then hold a vote on its future.

"I 'ave a new woman interested in your online advertisement, very attractive," Bald Yannis told Moronic Mitsos, showing him a glossy photograph of the current Miss World.

"'Ang on I knows her," mail order Masha butted in, as she religiously watched all the televised beauty pageants for inspiration "why Miss World want to meet this moron?"

Bald Yannis was annoyed mail order Masha, who was not in on the dating scam, was about to potentially put a spoke in his fake scam fun. Thinking quickly Bald Yannis told Moronic Mitsos "most likely some woman use the photo of the real Miss World to make yous like 'er. She probably 'ideously ugly and use fake photo, best you not bother reply to 'er letter."

As he spoke he felt the piercing glare of mail order Masha who was looking at him with deep suspicion. She thought Bald Yannis was shifty and up to no good, fleetingly wondering if it was possible Bald Yannis was the elusive underwear thief.

Before mail order Masha had time to think further on the matter she spotted her new step-daughter Stavroula making her way along the harbour. Desperate to avoid the threatened cookery lesson on 'ten things to do with an aubergine' she fled at great speed, wobbling precariously on her stiletto heels.

"Was that the mail order hussy?" Stavroula questioned the village men outside the kafenion, to which they all denied ever seeing her that morning.

CHAPTER 99

Toothless Tasos and Thea Enjoy a Day Out

Toothless Tasos was taken aback with shock when Thea, his goddess with the now feet of clay, boldly suggested they go out together for the afternoon. Thea told him she thought it would be most pleasant if they drove down the coast to the village of Gavros on his ancient motorcycle and side-car, and take a walk by the sea. Toothless Tasos had never in his life been invited out by a woman. He worried if this made Thea too forward and pushy, but hastily cast his negative thoughts aside at the prospect of spending more time in her company.

Thea was emboldened by her desperate need to catch herself a fourth husband. Having carefully weighed up all the potential suitors the village offered, she came to the pitiful conclusion Toothless Tasos was the best of a bad bunch.

Gorgeous Yiorgos appeared to have lost interest in her and was taking far too much interest in the Pappas' wife Petula, in Thea's personal opinion. Thea had even dressed up in her finest clothes from the home shopping channel and sprayed herself with too much perfume, making up an excuse to go in the hardware shop to see how the land lay there.

Bald Yannis looked too ridiculous for words in his terrible toupee, yet he had the nerve to snub her, taking no interest in her whatsoever beyond his pathetic attempts to sell her a ghastly cheap looking plastic shower curtain emblazoned with lobsters he tried to pretend was patriotic. Thea was happy to put a line through the name of Bald Yannis as a prospective suitor, realising these were desperate times indeed that she had even briefly considered him.

Tall Thomas appeared completely indifferent to Thea's many charms and Slick Socrates had already been ensnared by Stavroula. Pancratius the village policeman was too sickly for her taste and Vangelis the chemist was far too free with his gossip about the villagers' various ailments, a trait she found off-putting as she wasn't a gossip. That left Toothless Tasos as the man she had set her sights on, but she found it hard going contending with his painful shyness.

Toothless Tasos found it impossible to put into words his adoration and devotion to Thea, leaving her oblivious to his true feelings for her. She suggested an afternoon out together in the hope it would make him realise she was an attractive woman worthy of an honourable marriage proposal. He had proved himself to be a considerate confidant over the home shopping compulsion that resulted in her hoarding, but he'd failed to grasp just how pressing her monetary worries and debts were.

Toothless Tasos was rather annoyed when, upon their arrival in Gavros, Thea suggested they go into a taverna for ouzo and meze. He had not envisaged spending any money as he thought her idea of a walk would be free. Thea seemed far too much of a spendthrift and was now making free with his money it seemed. Thea made a mental note that he ordered the cheapest meze on the menu for them to share, but reflected he was such an old miser he must have plenty of money saved up in the bank. Thea poured Toothless Tasos plenty of ouzo before boldly broaching the subject on her mind.

"Taso, I need to know your intentions," she said "it is not good for my name to be gadding about with yous and being seen in your 'ouse if yous don't plan to make an honest woman of me."

"Surely you knows 'ow much I loves you, I loves yous for years but never catch yous between 'usbands before to tells yous," Toothless Tassos declared, suddenly emboldened by ouzo to declare his true feelings and overcome his usual tongue-tied state.

Thea was amazed by his declaration as she'd truly had no idea of the depths of his feelings. She was flattered and immensely pleased she appeared to have ensnared him. However her bubble was soon burst when Toothless Tasos went on to say "but surely you knows my situation with Stavroula stops me making an honest woman of yous."

"What, yous means yous 'ave not extricated yourself yet from the situation with Stavroula? I thought yous got out of that marriage long ago," Thea proclaimed, seeing her expectations of an imminent fourth wedding slipping away.

"It is bigly complicated," Toothless Tasos explained "we could continue courting while Slick Socrates looks into a lawyerly solution. He wants to marry Stavroula and I wants marry you Thea."

Thea was devastated to realise the situation was far more complicated than had ever occurred to her. She now had Toothless Tasos eating out of her hand and declaring his undying love, but it wasn't enough to bag her a much needed wedding.

"Maybe yous buy me a bigly engagement ring as sign of your intentions," Thea suggested, considering an engagement was the next best thing to marriage and an engaged man would feel some financial responsibility towards his intended.

"We engage then, my beloved most beautiful Thea," Toothless Tasos exclaimed, amazed at the turn the afternoons events had taken.

"Not till I get a bigly diamond ring on my finger," Thea reminded him, waving her hand in the air. She planned on dragging him into the jewellery store on their immediate return to the village.

CHAPTER 100

Diet Sabotage

F at Christos convinced his new wife Tassia the sensible thing to do with their newly found money was to deposit it in the bank. He had no truck with the peasant habit of hiding bags of money all over the place, considering it could be an invitation to thieves. In his efforts to improve himself Fat Christos had taken remarkable steps in a very short time. He had exchanged a life of fishing for one as a supermarket owner and the single life living with his mother to being a married man with a pregnant wife.

The most remarkable change was of course to his obese physique. The combination of dieting and the stomach stapling operation had left him almost half the size he was before. He was tempted to splash out on a wardrobe of business suits and flashy ties, but decided it would be prudent to wait until he had his excess skin removed in another expensive operation.

He had started to study a business course, determined to turn his newly inherited shop into a successful supermarket, envisaging it as just the first step in his imagined retail empire. Tassia was most supportive of all his plans and had volunteered to hand over the necessary brown envelope when the doctor decreed the time was right to cut off the excess skin.

Mrs Kolokotronis was finding it hard to come to terms with all the changes she was witnessing in her son. She was proud of his efforts to improve himself, but worried she would lose her influence over him now he was on his way to becoming a thin man. She could not really account why she felt it necessary to sabotage Fat Christos' diet plans, as her intentions were really not malicious. It was rather the only way she imagined of exerting some remaining control over him. She turned up at the shop where Fat Christos was busy supervising Achilles the borrowed builder as he knocked up some nifty new shelving and built a new cheese counter.

Mrs Kolokotronis arrived bearing a bottle containing a liquidised meal. Fat Christos had described his new strict dietary requirements to her, explaining the need for small portions of liquidised lean proteins. Mrs Kolokotronis had ignored these needs as she threw pork souvlaki, fried kalamari and a bar of shop bought chocolate into her blender.

She was pleased to see Fat Christos drink it up with more enthusiasm than he had shown for Tassia's lean and healthy, doctor recommended, liquidised meals. He complimented his mother on the very tasty liquidised meal and agreed it would reduce Tassia's burden if his mother liquidised his evening meals as well.

Relations between Tassia and Mrs Kolokotronis were nicely back on track since the latter had decided to keep her own counsel on the subject of the baby's paternity. Mrs Kolokotronis offered to supervise Achilles the borrowed builder if Christos would like to do some business course studying and if Tassia would like to pop home for a rest and put her feet up.

The newlyweds happily accepted her offer and Mrs Kolokotronis settled down behind the cash register and whipped out her knitting. She was determined to complete a wardrobe full of knitted baby clothes before the baby was born as she was looking forward to becoming a grandmother and having a baby to fuss over.

Achilles the borrowed builder was mightily impressed with Mrs Kolokotronis' exceptional skill with the knitting needles and asked her if she had time to knit him a warm hat for when he worked outdoors.

Toothless Tasos stopped by for some air freshener as Tassia was complaining about the lingering smell of the stuffed swordfish noses she had sold to Petros the postman. Seeing his holey pullover caused Mrs Kolokotronis to "po po" at his disgraceful appearance and she asked if he would be interested in buying a new pullover if she knitted one. As he did not imagine knitting was quite Thea's thing Toothless Tasos readily agreed to commit to purchasing a newly knitted pullover.

Prosperous Pedros came in to buy some choice morsels of chicken to use as fish bait and was most impressed at Mrs Kolokotronis' exceptional skill with her knitting needles. He asked her if she would be interested in teaching him to knit as he could not face the prospect of going into a strange shop when he needed to replace his pullovers. Instead of agreeing to teach him to knit Mrs Kolokotronis offered to knit him a pullover if he would be willing to buy it. As he agreed Mrs Kolokotronis realised she had the seeds of her own business plan and decided to start her own clothing line of knitted pullovers, hats and scarves. She would persuade her son to sell them in the supermarket and if it proved successful she could expand into socks, gloves and dresses.

She was full of her new plans when Fat Christos returned to relieve her of her duties supervising the borrowed builder. She had quite a spring in her step as she headed home and gathered up all the ingredients for Fat Christos' liquidised dinner. She threw in a fatty sausage, some doughnuts from the bakery and a large portion of chocolate ice cream, whipping them all together into a revolting liquid pulp.

CHAPTER 101

The Pappas Walks the Goat

P etula was naturally still rather suspicious of her husband's new and improved mood, having lived under the shadow of his bad temper for far too long. She had heard all about his thundering delivery of Biblical verses in the village, but he had never been one to bring his work home with him. Fortunately she was spared his hypocritical moralistic preaching within the four walls of their house.

The Pappas had ceased raising his voice in anger towards her as it caused his new pet goat Nero to react very antagonistically towards him. He had already suffered some agonisingly sharp nips. The Pappas found his new goat to be rather formidable and was wary of provoking her, though he greatly admired her beauty, considering her a most handsome creature. Nero was excessively taken with Petula, serving as her guard dog and following her round everywhere like a devoted sheep.

In order to try and inveigle his way into Nero's good graces the Pappas had taken to bringing home little treats for her. He could not resist the attractive picture she presented when he tied a new shiny bow round her neck and the goat's collection of decorative ribbon bows was rapidly increasing in varied colours. Still the goat could see right through him and showed no signs of warming towards him.

Petula was constantly harried by the destruction Nero wreaked on the Pappas' possessions. The goat had eaten the seat out of the Pappas' best clerical dress and chewed up his slippers. Next the goat ate and then regurgitated his pyjamas inside his waterproof rubber boots. Nero appeared to have an innate sixth sense which kept her from chewing things belonging to Petula as she only targeted items used exclusively by the Pappas.

The Pappas arrived home from the church in a surprisingly good mood as he had counted more bottoms on pews than he had seen for a long time. The villagers' innate respect for the church was winning back those members of his congregation who were prepared to overlook his scurrilous behaviour and give him a second chance, following Petula's kind hearted example. It had slowly dawned on the priest people would look at him with more respect if he followed his own Biblical advice and lay off the demon drink. He had started to reduce his intake of Holy wine which he now referred to as the 'grapes of wrath'.

Petula felt a sinking feeling when the Pappas arrived home, announcing he planned to take Nero for a walk. He told her to make sure the goat was suitably dressed in the fuchsia bow he had bought her. Petula had completely forgotten the goat had copiously thrown up the Pappas' pyjamas in the waterproof rubber boots he was now putting his feet into prior to taking Nero for her walk. Petula was too late to warn him and his feet slid into the vile and slimy mess the goat had deposited.

The Pappas displayed his peasant origins by showing no compunction about sticking his vomit laden feet, still encased in his sweaty socks, into Petula's newly scrubbed kitchen sink, for a quick wash. Petula rushed to hosepipe out the rubber boots and then luckily managed to find him an old pair of vomit free boots. The Pappas said not one word about his insulted dignity as he put on the old boots and dragged a reluctant Nero, who looked so stunning in her fuchsia bow, off for a walk.

The Pappas needed the peace the walk offered to contemplate some interesting news he had heard on the village gossip vine. Apparently those two odd American tourists who always looked so hapless had been spreading the word the walls of Fotini's house were extravagantly papered with bank notes. Having lost the projected income the blackmailing scam should have earned him the Pappas was eager to come up with another quick source of money.

He ruminated to himself obviously Fotini did not need the bank notes if she could afford to wastefully nail them to her walls. His own need was far more deserving he considered. Having a bit of wealth at his disposal may allow him to command more respect in the village as he was sick to death of being treated like a poor church relation. It would take considerable cunning to come up with a foolproof plan to break into Fotini's house and strip her walls, but the Pappas was determined to conjure up an efficacious plot.

It started to drizzle as the Pappas dragged the reluctant Nero back home. He was disappointed to see the light rain had left Nero's new fuchsia bow looking rather bedraggled. Throwing his arm round the goat's neck in an unwelcome affectionate gesture the Pappas promised "when I is rich I will buy you the best goat's clothes there is."

CHAPTER 102

Cat for Ransom

"Taso, I can barely see the diamond," Thea complained, peering through a magnifying glass at the miniscule gem set into the engagement ring, the smallest and cheapest one Mr Mandelis, the jewellery shop owner, could offer.

"We must be sensible an' prudent," Toothless Tasos cautiously advised, contemplating how many fish he would have to catch and sell to pay for the diamond ring gracing his beloved's finger. "Remember it was your spendthrift habits that got you into this 'orrible debt ridden mess in the first place."

Thea ungraciously accepted the new miniscule diamond engagement ring and flounced off; announcing the cat Gata had gone missing again and she must find it. Toothless Tasos' irritation at Thea's ingratitude and her lack of money sense gave way to guilt as he knew full well where the cat was. He worried Thea may not forgive him if she discovered he had accidentally sold the cat to Bald Yannis during the house clearance sale.

"Yanni I want the cat back," Toothless Tasos forcefully

said, striding determinedly into the hardware shop, quite prepared to stand his ground against the larger man.

"I bought the cat in good faith," said Bald Yannis, who
had been wondering how long it would take for Toothless
Tasos to come crawling back to reclaim the cat. "Is very good
cat for demonstrating close haircuts with the chainsaw," he
added, while picking up a chainsaw for a quick lick and
polish.

"I need the cat back," Toothless Tasos declared emphatically. "I will give yous what yous paid, is fair."

"Po po the cat is more valuable than that now; if yous
want it back yous pay 'andsome ransom," Bald Yannis insisted, staring the smaller man down.

"'Ows much yous want?" Toothless Tasos asked, blanch-
ing a terrible color when Bald Yannis named his ridiculous
price.

Toothless Tasos realised he had got himself into a terrible
pickle as he left the hardware shop catless. If Thea found out
what he had done his life would not be worth living, but there
was no way he would even contemplate handing over the
ransom sum Bald Yannis had demanded.

"Why yous looking so down in the dumps?" Stavroula
asked him, telling him to sit down and take a coffee on the
house. Relations between Stavroula and her former yet legally
still married husband had improved immensely since the
night he had saved her from strangulation by the elusive underwear thief.

"I've done a stupid thing. I sold Thea's cat to Bald Yannis
and now he's demanding ransom money to give it back,"
Toothless Tasos confessed, swearing Stavroula to secrecy.

Sly Stavroula came up with a devious solution to the
problem. "My cat Boukali is so attractive to other cats we will

use it to lure Thea's cat from the 'ardware shop, then bag it."

"Bravo, that's a brilliant plan," Toothless Tasos enthused, promising to look after the taverna whilst Stavroula went off to put her plan into action.

Stavroula carried Boukali across the road, leaving it on the doorstep of the hardware shop while she went inside to distract Bald Yannis. She requested some obscure pan scourers that could only be found in his filthy back stockroom. As he moved out of sight she encouraged Thea's cat Gata to pick up the scent of the attractive potential mate she had left on the doorstep. The plan worked like a dream as Gata picked up the cat enticing scent of Boukali and went tearing out of the door, chasing the other cat all the way back to Stavroulas, where Toothless Tasos niftily bagged it.

"Forgets it Yanni," Stavroula yelled. "I bet the pan scourers are cheaper at Fat Christos' new supermarket."

Bald Yannis was furious to think he had lost a potential sale to a rival shop. He lifted his leg to kick the cat, then cursed as he realised it was suddenly no longer there. By the time he gave up the fruitless search for the cat Toothless Tasos had already returned it to a grateful Thea, claiming he had found it wandering the street.

CHAPTER 103

Taxi to the Hospital

Bald Yannis marched over to Fat Christos' new super-market craftily disguised in some concealing dark glasses and a baseball cap over his terrible toupee, planning to do a bit of surreptitious snooping. He had a note-book at the ready to discreetly write down the prices of any-thing Fat Christos was selling which were a duplicate item of his own hardware shop stock.

He was just about to enter the newly renovated shop when Fat Christos collided with him on the doorstep. "I'm sick, I need the 'ospital," Fat Christos screamed, doubling over in violent pain and vomiting all over Bald Yannis' shoes. Bald Yannis was totally unsympathetic to the other man's plight. He was furious at the state of his shoes and called the other man a malaka before storming back to his hardware shop to hose down his feet.

Tassia finished serving a customer and dashed outside to offer assistance to her husband who was suffering excruciat-ing pain. "Quick get in that conveniently handy passing taxi," she suggested, sticking her arm out to hail the old Mercedes taxi which happened to be driving by.

"Yous 'ad better stay to watch the shop," Fat Christos told his wife, collapsing on the back seat of the taxi.

"I will get yous mother to watch the shop and follow yous to 'ospital soonest," Tassia promised her husband.

Nitsa and Fotini were delighted to have picked up such a lucrative fare as it was quite a distance to the hospital. As the taxi jerked fitfully along in fits and starts Fat Christos was far too ill to take much notice of the incompetent driver balanced on a stack of old magazines behind the wheel. He fell off the seat when Nitsa took aim at Onos the donkey, carrying Vasilis into the village. "Got you that time yous old fool," she screeched in delight as Vasilis fell off the donkey.

Nitsa managed to bring the old Mercedes taxi to a halt outside the hospital by driving into the back of an ambulance. "That's extortion," Fat Christos complained when Nitsa demanded an exorbitant amount for the taxi fare. She adamantly refused to let him out of the taxi to go into the hospital until he had handed over the contents of his wallet.

"Quick grab that doctor, they always 'ave lots of money," Fotini advised Nitsa, spying their next unwitting fare.

Mrs Kolokotronis felt terrible when she heard her son had dashed off to hospital in considerable pain. She refused to watch the shop for Tassia, claiming it was her right as his mother to be beside him in his hospital bed. "Gets me to 'ospital as quick as yous can," she demanded, climbing into Achilles the borrowed builder's van.

She had an awful suspicion the contents of her liquidised dinners may be in some way responsible for her son's sickness. She had patently ignored the doctor's recommendations on the strict limits of Fat Christos' post stomach stapling surgery diet and had been shoving all manner of forbidden fatty and sweet treats into the blender.

Fat Christos was tucked up in a hospital bed with a drip in his arm when his mother arrived. "I must speak to the doctor," she exclaimed, giving the white coated young physician a detailed list of the all the forbidden food items she had furtively been feeding her son.

"You know that disgusting fatty and sweet diet could kill your son?" the doctor scolded her. "And if he gets fat again the fat will kill him. This is a serious matter Kyria Kolokotronis and you should be ashamed of yourself."

Mrs Kolokotonis sat by her son's hospital bed sobbing and begging his forgiveness. When the doctor assured him he would survive he forgave his mother, but told her from now on Tassia would be solely responsible for liquidising his meals.

"She's as batty as a hatter, nutty as a fruitcake, mad as a box of frogs, first she tries to kill me then yous use her taxi to bring me to the 'ospital, what's yous thinking Masha?" that old fool Vasilis shouted, shuffling into the hospital room and helped into the bed next to Fat Christos.

"What happened to you Vasili?" Mrs Kolokotronis enquired, surprised to see a fellow Astakostan in the adjoining bed.

"That old crone Nitsa what is staying with that old hag Fotini knocked me off the donkey deliberately with 'er taxi an' broke my arm. Then Masha stops a taxi to bring me 'ospital and that 'orrid old crone is driving it and wouldn't let us out till she emptied my wallet. Masha ring the police and report her for deliberately driving into the donkey."

"Calm down Vasili, it may have been an accident," mail order Masha advised her husband, adding "she's too old to be driving that bigly car though."

"I tell you she done it deliberate Masha, ring the police and get her arrested," Vasilis demanded, asserting his husbandly authority. "Ring Stavroula too," he whispered, "she will want to be by the sick bed of her newly discovered father."

Masha stepped outside to telephone Pancratius the village policeman and her new step-daughter Stavroula. She embraced her good friend Tassia warmly as her friend arrived at the hospital to rush to the bedside of Fat Christos.

Returning to her husband Masha announced she hated hospitals and would be off as she had a pressing appointment at the beauty parlour and he only had a broken arm. She had seen much worse injuries back in Russia when the wolves were on the prowl. Tassia and Mrs Kolokotronis were perfectly capable of fetching and carrying for Vasilis at the same time as they fussed over Fat Christos.

Promising she would look after the donkey Masha fled the hospital as quickly as her wobbling stilettos would carry her. Her old fool of a husband was becoming obsessive in his ludicrous claims about that batty old woman she thought.

CHAPTER 104

Liberated Women

I'm not responsible for old cousin Nitsa," Prosperous Pedros insisted when Pancratius the village policeman confronted him in the taverna 'Mono Ellinka Trofima' that evening.

"It's not right she's driving round in an unlicensed old taxi picking up paying customers," the policeman asserted. "She's causing havoc on the road, and extorting exorbitant fares."

"It's not my business what my old cousin does," Prosperous Pedros insisted again, beginning to lose his temper at the assumption he could control the batty old crone.

"Your mother was with her," pressed Pancratius the village policeman.

"So, since when is it illegal to sit in the passenger seat?" Prosperous Pedros shouted, getting decidedly hot under the collar of his pullover. "Yous is disturbing my dinner, leave me alone." he said, calling "Taki, come throw 'im out."

The other customers leapt to the defence of Prosperous Pedros, agreeing it was not his responsibility what his old cousin got up to. "Don't look at me neither," Tall Thomas told the policeman "I 'ave no control over my nutty old aunty. This is that 'ere women's liberation imported from foreign countries, it's not politically correct if we tell our women what to do these days."

"She is probably just trying to earn some extra money to supplement her meagre pension," Quentin suggested, receiving a kick under the table from Deirdre who had not enjoyed the experience of being held captive in Nitsa's taxi.

Yiota emerged from the kitchen carrying a Tupperware box full of salad and souvlaki. She told the policemen if he was heading to the hospital to question Vasili about his accident he could deliver the food at the same time.

"No need, I cook 'im 'is favourite borscht," Masha piped up, piling a Tupperware box of her infamous red soup she had retrieved from under the table, onto the policeman. "Tell him to share with Fat Christos," she instructed. "Tassia say the doctor approve goodly borscht for 'is strict diet."

Pancratius the village policeman felt outnumbered and left the taverna clutching both boxes of food. Something had to be done to prevent Nitsa picking up unwilling paying passengers in her old Mercedes taxi. However he dreaded to think of the stink she would create if she was arrested and locked up in a prison cell. His reputation would suffer if he acquired a name for locking up helpless old ladies.

"Why yous not at 'ospital with yous 'usband, Masha?" Vangelis the chemist queried, thinking it was bad form she was dining out while her husband needed her.

"I look after 'is donkey and cook 'is borscht," Masha said, adding "I is supposed liberated woman like what Thomas said, yet yous expect me to chain myself to 'usband's 'ospital bed, yous chauvinist."

With that Masha stood up to leave, feeling duty bound to report on Vasilis' progress to her new step-mother Stavroula and to take legal advice from Slick Socrates to determine if Vasilis would be due any monetary compensation for being knocked off the donkey.

CHAPTER 105

Fire!

The Pappas waited until Petula was tucked up asleep in bed with his new pet goat before venturing outdoors into the moonless night. He hoped his black clerical robe would blend well into the darkness and he used a black balaclava to conceal his face. He admitted to himself his cunning plan to break into the house of Fotini and steal her moneyed wallpaper was making him a tad nervous as it involved stepping out of his usual comfort zone. His previous money making scams had not involved anything quite so physically challenging or outright criminal.

All the lights were off inside Fotini's house, the Pappas noticed, as he approached. He took this as a good sign, having no way of knowing the electric company had cut off her supply. Noticing the downstairs shutters had been left unlatched the Pappas muttered to himself "Po po, Fotini deserve to lose her wallpaper money if she is so stupid to leave the window open with riches inside."

Hoisting himself in through the window left the Pappas sweating with the effort. He could hear the distant drone of

313

old ladies snoring upstairs and congratulated himself on his perfect timing for his first foray into house breaking and burglary. He landed silently on his feet in the living room. Whipping out his torch and an olive sack for his money stash he prepared to start prising the bank notes from the wall.

When the torchlight revealed the mass of useless and worthless drachma notes the Pappas emitted a furiously loud "malaka." In utter frustration he hurled the torch from his hand, only to have it land in the still glowing embers of Fotini's living room fire where the batteries exploded with an almighty bang.

"What's that?" Fotini and Nitsa screamed in unison. Jumping out of their beds they wrapped themselves in their waterproof bedspreads and made remarkably nimble progress down the stairs, where they were just in time to spot an unidentifiable shadowy figure climbing out of the living room window.

"Follow 'im quick," Fotini screeched as Nitsa simultaneously screamed "Fire, fire." The torch exploding in the fire embers had caused the fire to roar and spread.

It was obviously a more pressing matter to put out the flames lapping at the moneyed wallpaper than pursue the shadowy figure through the window. Fotini ran into the kitchen to grab a bucket of water to throw over the fire, which had been made much worse by Nitsa attempting to douse the flames with her waterproof plastic bedspread. Their lives were in terrible danger as the house could burn down around them.

Nitsa dashed out through the kitchen door, returning instantly with the hose pipe. Demonstrating incredible bravery she tackled the out of control flames, while instructing Fotini to telephone Prosperous Pedros and the police.

Prosperous Pedros turned up quickly and was genuinely alarmed at his first assumption his mother and her cousin had very nearly managed to burn the house down. He was closely followed by Pancratius the village policeman who imagined he was being dragged from his sick bed over nothing more than the hysterics of two old women who had caused him nothing but trouble all day.

"We didn't start the fire, the arsonist was the thief what come through the window to rape and murder us in our beds," Fotini insisted, stridently backed up by Nitsa.

Pancratius the village policeman soon confirmed there were indeed muddy footprints all over the windowsill and living room floor, and a burnt and mangled torch on the edge of the fireplace. Fotini quickly confirmed she had never once in her life owned a new-fangled torch as she always used candles, and she would never think of wearing muddy boots in the house.

"We tell yous it was an intruder what wanted 'is wicked way with us," Nitsa cried, instructing Pedros to go and get them two brandies for the shock.

"This is a very serious matter," the policeman said earnestly, pondering the possibility the elusive underwear thief could have struck again. The underwear thief's modus operandi had only been to steal from washing lines up to now, but perhaps his perverted tendencies had got the better of him and now he was breaking and entering with rape in mind. Mind you it would need to be one brave pervert to consider attacking these two cantankerous and formidable old ladies, he thought to himself.

He did not blame Fotini for leaving the shutters unlatched as apart from the washing line thefts there was no other criminal activity in the village and Fotini had nothing of value worth stealing to attract thieves. It did not occur to any of the four of them the worthless bank notes had provided the thief's motivation for his illegal entry, which left them each convinced a deranged and very unfussy sex pervert was on the loose.

CHAPTER 106

Ruled Out of the Enquiry

Word of the pervert intruder who was obviously intent on the rape and murder of two innocent old ladies was the talk of the village by the next morning. The villagers vented their outrage vociferously, most alarmed at such skulduggery in their midst. Even though they despised Fotini they would not wish such a frightful fate on her.

Deirdre voiced her fears that they had recently purchased the falling down house next door to the one where this grisly crime had occurred, but the villagers were quick to emphatically reassure her criminality was not the norm and the area was safe. Petula recommended Quentin and Deirdre acquire a guard dog goat if they were worried as she had never slept so soundly since Nero moved in.

The Pappas was dumbfounded when he heard from his congregation his bungled bout of house breaking and burglary had been misinterpreted as a perverted attempt to rape and murder those two cantankerous old women in their beds. His relief that the accidental fire he had started had distracted the ladies from pursuing him through the window was immense. It had given him the opportunity to escape undetected under the cover of darkness.

The only evidence of his misconduct was the singed hemline on his clerical dress, but fortunately the goat had chewed it up as soon as he returned home. Petula had not the least suspicion he had left the house the previous night and he had taken the precaution of hosing down his muddy boots rather than demanding she do it.

Moronic Mitsos felt nostalgic for the days when he would have been at the centre of the police enquiry and called a meeting of the village men to discuss the matter. He suggested putting additional men on washing line patrol duty as the general consensus was the elusive underwear thief must be last night's prime pervert suspect.

Bald Yannis was for once lost for words. He knew full well that although he had enjoyed his bit of fun pilfering 'frillies' in his unsuspected role as the elusive underwear thief, he knew for certain he had nothing to do with the events of the previous night. While murder may be a harmless fantasy he occasionally indulged in, the very thought of raping those ghastly old women was enough to turn his stomach.

Tall Thomas wondered if the good nephew thing to do would be to offer to sleep over on Fotini's living room floor to protect his aunty Nitsa, but decided against it. Prosperous Pedros knew the right thing to do would be to offer to move in to protect his mother but he was having none of it, worried once Fotini got him into her clutches he would be stuck there for the duration until she was dead, which could be years off yet. He preferred the idea of ensuring his mother's house was secure and solicited the services of Bald Yannis to accompany him and Tall Thomas to the house to discuss installing security measures.

Fotini and Nitsa had been up half the night, unable to sleep after their terrifying experience. When Prosperous Pedros drove up with Tall Thomas and Bald Yannis they were immediately ordered upstairs to double check there were no pervert rapists lurking under the beds. Fotini stridently demanded Prosperous Pedros tell his father to come home at once to protect her. Pedros lied through his teeth, promising his mother he would try to contact his dead father in Athens.

The living room was still stuffy with smoke from the accidental fire as Bald Yannis took his measure of the window and considered how best to secure it. Fotini favoured the extreme method of electrifying the window so any intruder would be instantly electrocuted. This idea was dashed when Prosperous Pedros reminded his mother the electric supply had been cut off, rendering any such plan useless.

Bald Yannis offered to solder iron bars on the outside of the window, but demanded cash up front after his last encounter with Nitsa. "'Ow much you want?" Nitsa asked as she started to pull the useless bank notes off the wall to pay him with, hoping he would be too thick to notice they were worthless.

"Don't touch that money," Bald Yannis suddenly shouted, having had a rare stroke of genius. "It could be a clue the police should investigate. 'Ow many malakas know yous have bank notes all over walls but don't know they are worthless? Maybe the intruder was not a murdering pervert but a thief."

Pancratius the village policeman was immediately summoned from his sick bed to investigate this possibility, admitting Bald Yannis' supposition was indeed a stroke of genius. He ordered no one to touch the bank notes on the wall until he could call in the fingerprint experts.

Fotini told the policeman she did not encourage visitors and could not imagine who knew she had been in the process of wallpapering her living room with drachma notes. "Fat Christos and Tassia knew we 'ad money, and that gormless American couple K-Went-In and Did-Rees admired it when they 'ere to eat horta."

"Well Fat Christos is in 'ospital with stomach stapling poisoning and Tassia was with 'im all night by 'is bed," Pancratius said, ruling them immediately out of his enquiries. "Maybe the gormless Americans are thieves," he suggested, though even voicing this idea seemed quite ludicrous.

"Do any others know about the money?" he pressed, only to be told by Tall Thomas that Quentin had indeed been gossiping about the eccentric decorative touch of using banks notes as wallpaper all round the village.

"So everyone knew from the village gossip vine," the policeman concluded, realising it cast suspicion on the total population of at least two villages.

"Well at least that puts the elusive underwear thief in the clear," Bald Yannis muttered under his breath in relief.

CHAPTER 107

Hospital Visiting

News of the events back in Rapanaki had of course reached the hospital beds of Fat Christos and that old fool Vasilis as the village gossip vine had many tentacles. Vasilis had been kept awake half the night by Fat Christos' incessant snoring and he was worried about Masha being alone in the house with a pervert on the prowl and only Onos the donkey for protection. He was disappointed his daughter Stavroula had not visited his bedside as yet and he hoped she would turn up soon.

Fat Christos had enjoyed an excellent night's sleep with his mother and wife both on hand to fuss over and pamper him. The two women had slept most uncomfortably in chairs by his bed. Fat Christos was now insisting Tassia return to the supermarket as he was feeling much recovered and would soon be sent home. He credited his amazing recovery to the healing properties of mail order Masha's deliciously infamous borscht. Even his doctor had approved its consumption and intended to get the recipe from mail order Masha so it could be added to the hospital kitchen's menu.

Mail order Masha breezed into the hospital in a haze of expensive perfume she had applied liberally to disguise the hospital smell. She was unsuitably dressed in lurid pink sequin hot pants and matching stilettos, and carried another large Tupperware box of her infamous borscht. Fat Christos' young doctor was quite smitten at the sight of this silicone Russian beauty flicking her long red hair extensions, and rushed to greet her, to the jealous annoyance of all the nurses.

Planting a kiss on her husband's forehead she announced she could not stay long as Evangelia at the beauty parlour had some new eyelash curlers she wanted to experiment with. She supposed she would have enough time before her appointment to have lunch with the smitten young doctor who promised to give her a 'name credit' on the hospital menu for the borscht recipe.

That old fool Vasilis was insistent his young unprotected bride move in with her new stepmother while he was in the hospital, or at least until the 'on the loose' pervert was caught. Mail order Masha 'po po-ed' her husband, telling him she would rather take her chances with the pervert than put up with Stavroula's bossy ways. Vasilis was none too pleased when the young doctor offered to stop by his house that evening and check up on Masha's safety, an offer he noticed his wife was very quick to accept.

Fotini and Nitsa had been keen to get away from the scene of last night's crime and they left that young upstart Bald Yannis soldering bars on the living room window. They thought taking the taxi out and extorting exorbitant fares from unwilling passengers would be a good way to distract themselves from the near death experience they had suffered the previous night. They had insisted Quentin and Deirdre get in the back of the old Mercedes taxi and the hapless pair reluctantly conceded, considering it was a handy form of transportation to the hospital as Quentin wanted to visit his jogging partner Fat Christos. They carried an unwrapped fish which Tall Thomas had asked them to take along to gift to the two invalids, and some grapes they had purchased.

The Pappas presumed it would make him look good in the eyes of the villagers if he went hospital calling on his two sick parishioners. Deirdre was not happy when Nitsa stopped to let the Pappas share their taxi as she considered him a revoltingly odious little weasel.

Nitsa held her three passengers hostage in the back of the cab until they paid her overpriced fare. Quentin reluctantly paid the Pappas' share as he insisted he should not be charged for performing his Holy duties for members of his congregation. "He can walk home," Deirdre told Quentin "he was doing that nasty thing with his straying foot again, which is such an inappropriate way for a married priest to act towards a happily married woman.

The two sick men were delighted to receive the grapes Quentin and Deirdre presented. "Is very goodly of yous to come K-Went-In and Did-Rees, you bigly friends," Fat Christos said, warmed to the core by their thoughtful consideration. "Would be bigly 'elp if yous can give Tassia a lift 'ome."

He could sense his wife wanted to escape the presence of the Pappas who had upset her greatly on the day of their wedding by accusing her of being a thief.

"What we supposed to do with a dead fish in our 'ospital beds?" that old fool Vasilis questioned.

"Give it to the nurse," Fat Christos told him "she looked fit to spit daggers when she saw the way the smitten young doctor looked at yours wife silicone chest."

It dawned on the Pappas it would have looked better if

he had not arrived empty handed. He rummaged through his pockets and presented Fat Christos with a condom he had found on the church collection plate, acknowledging to himself it was really an inappropriate hospital visiting gift.

"A bit late for that," Fat Christos scoffed in derision "Tassia is already pregnant."

Snatching the condom back the Pappas presented it to Vasilis who announced "get rid of the filthy thing, Masha wants to get pregnant," remembering he must ask the young smitten doctor to write him a new prescription for Viagra. The Pappas would have liked to respond with a well chosen Biblical quote on the evils of procreation but his lack of preparedness with a suitable quote meant he could not turn on his God bothering act like a tap.

Mrs Koloktronis shooed the Pappas out of the hospital room, telling him her son needed his rest and that old fool Vasilis was in pain. Nitsa refused to let the Pappas back in the waiting taxi as she now knew he was too mean to pay her fare and told him firmly "we ain't a charity taxi."

When Quentin, Deirdre and Tassia climbed into the waiting taxi they were quite amused to see Nitsa deliberately drive through a large muddy puddle, completely soaking the Pappas who was sulkily standing at the bus stop.

CHAPTER 108

Old Lady Makeovers

The young smitten doctor had not only treated mail order Masha to lunch but had also neglected his patients in order to drive her back to the village so she wouldn't be late for her beauty parlour appointment. She envisaged a peaceful afternoon having her eyelashes professionally curled. She was most put out when Fotini and Nitsa noisily arrived, demanding Evangelia give them makeovers with the money they had extorted with their exorbitant taxi fares.

Tempted as Evangelia was to throw the two old crones out she was mindful they had been through a traumatic experience the night before and her beauty treatments would be most therapeutic under the circumstances. "I've not been in a beauty parlour for years," Fotini announced to no one's surprise. She usually cut her own hair by shearing round a pudding bowl on her head.

Evangelia suggested several treatments she considered would improve the two old ladies' appearance and take years off them. She proposed bleaching their prominent black moustaches and plucking the long hairs that grew from their chins. "'Ow about hair extensions too," mail order Masha suggested, but the two crones po po-ed her idea by nodding vigorously and declaring a simple cut would suffice.

"I quite fancy a chest wax," Nitsa whispered to Evangelia "as I thinks that young fellows at the 'ardware shop 'as 'is eye on me."

"Plenty of life in yous yet," Fotini agreed, adding "but yous an attractive woman what can do better than 'im."

"Buts I likes my men to 'ave full 'eads of air and the 'ardware man 'as a lovely rug I could run my fingers through," Nitsa confided.

"He bald as a coot and 'is 'air is a terrible toupee," Fotini told her, to which Evangelia countered "but it is super glued on well and won't come off easy."

"I tells you he 'as 'is eye on me. I won't be slapping 'is face if he wants to lure me into an overgrown olive grove," Nitsa said emphatically, having no idea she was completely deluded and Bald Yannis considered she was a horrendous old bag.

Stavroula had spotted her new step-mother going into the beauty parlour and followed her in, demanding she come over to the taverna for a cookery lesson on how to prepare an octopus. Mail order Masha defied her new step-daughter, telling her she had no time to be giving cookery lessons as her rightful place was in the hospital by the bedside of her new father.

"Why yous not there then?" Stavroula questioned.

"I 'ad to come 'ome to look after the donkey and cooks more borscht. Doctor at 'ospital say my borscht so goodly it bring miraculous cure to patients, even though you sneers at my cooking," Masha boasted.

Stavroula conceded she supposed she ought to visit that

old fool Vasilis in hospital and went off to demand Slick Socrates drive her there. She was jealous of the hospital doctor's praise for mail order Masha's infamous borscht and decided to take a pan of her far superior snail and tomato stew along to impress him.

Evangelia worked miracles on the two old ladies, transforming their appearance no end. Evangelia praised Nitsa for making far less fuss over her chest wax than Bald Yannis had done over his back wax. His wimpish screams had nearly deterred her from offering anymore waxing treatments. His anguished screams had led to Mr Mandelis at the next door jewellery shop to accuse Evangelia of operating a torture chamber out of her beauty parlour.

Fotini and Nitsa's moustaches were bleached away and their newly plucked chins were left as soft as Bald Yannis' sub-par sandpaper. Fotini declined Evangelia's suggestion of false eyelashes, but Nitsa was all for them as she planned to flutter them at Bald Yannis in a 'come hither' fashion. Both women's makeovers were completed with a heavy application of blue eye shadow, blusher and bright red lipstick, and they had finally allowed Evangelia to give them each a blue hair rinse.

"Oh my, 'ave they any idea 'ow ridiculous they looks?" mail order Masha asked as the two elderly women took their leave, with Nitsa excitedly proclaiming she needed to go and try on some more old lady dresses at the hardware store.

CHAPTER 109

Fond Feelings

By the time Gorgeous Yiorgos got round to asking Thea out on another date he was too late and he discovered she had been snapped by up Toothless Tasos. He laughed as she attempted to flash off her new engagement ring. It was too miniscule to notice and confirmed the village opinion of Toothless Tasos as a skinflint tightwad.

Gorgeous Yiorgos realised he had let the lovely Thea slip through his fingers, but admitted his mind was most preoccupied with Petula. He had tried to ignore the growing romantic feelings he could feel blossoming towards her as Petula was the wife of another man, if the Pappas could be described as such.

He cheered himself up by remembering the tourist season was due to start soon. Each new season brought a fresh crop of loose foreign hussies he could try his luck with, even if most of his efforts were unsuccessful. In recent years he seemed to have lost his touch in the art of 'kamaki' and he wondered again if he wouldn't be better settling down rather than trying to play the field at his age. He thought fondly of

Petula and decided to stop by to ask if she would like to go out for a driving lesson. Perhaps they could drive to the hospital and visit his good friend Fat Christos before he was discharged.

At that very moment Stavroula was seated beside the hospital bed of that old fool Vasilis, feeling somewhat guilty she had not visited him earlier. She had been prepared to rush instantly to the hospital when she heard he had been involved in a major traffic accident, feeling distraught at the thought he may die before she got the chance to know him properly and develop a real father-daughter bond.

However when mail order Masha relayed Vasilis had suffered no more than a broken arm after falling off the donkey during a five kilometre an hour collision with Nitsa's taxi, Stavroula had not bothered to rush to the hospital. A broken arm was nothing she pondered, when she had lived her own life under the mistaken belief the old butcher Gregoris was her father. She was finding it hard to come to terms with the fact that old fool Vasilis was her true father and felt cheated by her mother keeping the truth from her.

On top of the shock of discovering the identity of her real father Stavroula had been forced to contend with the horror of realising mail order Masha was her step-mother. The situation was quite ridiculous and she did not want it becoming common knowledge in case she became a laughing stock. Now as she sat by her father's bedside it touched her to hear him speak so fondly of her mother as he obviously held special memories of their long ago romantic interlude.

In turn that old fool Vasilis was really trying to warm to Stavroula, but his initial impression of her as a cold and calculating woman was hard to dismiss. However her obvious love for Slick Socrates convinced Vasilis she must have a heart hidden somewhere within her ample bosom, and he was mightily pleased when Slick Socrates offered his lawyerly services to slap a restraining order on that ghastly old woman Nitsa.

Stavroula raised an eyebrow when Gorgeous Yiorgos arrived at the hospital with Petula. Before the Pappas' black mailing scam she would have been the first to run to him with the gossip his wife was out with another man, but after his sly scheme was revealed she rather hoped he would be cuckolded. She had banned him from her taverna and refused to set foot in the church while he remained as the village Pappas.

The smitten young doctor arrived and pronounced Fat Christos fit to return home, cautioning him once again to avoid any liquidised food prepared by his mother. Stavroula was very jealous when the doctor recommended plenty of mail order Masha's infamous borscht in his liquidised diet.

In a fit of pique she told Vasilis she had specially cooked him the snail and tomato stew she had brought along to impress the doctor, who she now considered undeserving of her efforts. The doctor was not worth impressing as he had been far too free with his praise for Masha's disgusting red brew, and was thus obviously lacking in good taste.

Fat Christos and his mother were happy to accept a lift back to the village with Gorgeous Yiorgos if he promised to take the wheel. Mrs Kolokotronis was far too nervous a passenger to suffer a learner driver behind the wheel.

CHAPTER 110

Eyeing Up

A ve you got something up with yours eyes?" Bald
Yannis asked Nitsa as she stood at his counter flut-
tering her new false eyelashes at him in a ludi-
crously provocative manner.

"Her eyes is fine," Fotini said in her friend's defence, adding "'ave you got something up with that bit of nasty old car-
pet stuck on your 'ead?"

Bald Yannis told the two women he had secured the metal
bars on their living room window and asked if they had heard
anything further from the police enquiry. "We 'ave been busy
making beautiful," Nitsa told him while surreptitiously trying to unbutton the top button on her old lady dress, hoping
to give Bald Yannis an enticing flash of her now hair free
chest.

Bald Yannis was frustrated to be kept out of the loop of
the police enquiry as he was keen to hear the elusive underwear thief had been replaced by an actual burglar thief as the
prime suspect. He didn't see why the elusive underwear thief
should get a bad name for something he had not done, but he

knew he was in no position to sue for defamation of character.

"See, he keeps giving me the eye," Nitsa whispered to Fotini. Fotini had to agree it certainly seemed Bald Yannis was staring intently at her friend. He was actually transfixed by the revolting sight of Nitsa over-done up in copious amounts of blue eye shadow she had managed to smudge all over her cheeks, with one displaced false eyelash giving her a lopsided moustache. Her blue hair rinse had an eerie glow as it reflected the light from his flickering fluorescent strip.

"'Ave you 'eard from any more women wanting to meet me?" Moronic Mitsos asked, walking into the hardware shop. "Malaka what is that horror?" he exclaimed as he caught sight of Nitsa. "I thought the local council voted down the idea of importing that there foreign Halloween custom."

"Ave some respect for your elders," Nitsa advised him, clipping him round the head with her handbag. Turing her attention back to Bald Yannis she said "young Yanni, go in the stock room and make sure there are no perverts lurking, as we want try on more of your lovely dresses."

Nitsa desperately fluttered her single remaining false eyelash in what she thought was a seductive fashion, telling Bald Yannis "no peeking," as she went in the stockroom.

"She's off her trolley, utterly bonkers!" Bald Yannis exclaimed, feeling there had to be more to life than putting up with deranged old women and moronic ex-police chiefs.

His hardware shop was a magnet for nutters who were too thick to realise when he insulted them. He wondered if it was too late for a change of career. It wasn't the shop he really minded, he mused, it was the place. Or perhaps it wasn't the place, but the people in it. He considered he had no friends apart from Moronic Mitsos, he had no woman, and he was banned from the taverna. Looking on the bright side he considered himself quite popular in comparison to the Pappas.

As he ruminated on his lot in life Bald Yannis decided to invest in a goat as a pet as he had heard the Pappas enthusiastically extolling the virtues of his new and loyal friend. He decided he would see if he could come to an arrangement with Fat Christos to take one of his newly inherited herd; after all Fat Christos owed him big time for vomiting all over his shoes.

It was getting late and Bald Yannis agreed to lock up the shop and meet Moronic Mitsos at the kafenion. Turning off the lights and locking the door he completely he forgot he had left Nitsa and Fotini trying hideous old lady dresses on in his filthy back stockroom.

CHAPTER 111

Hells Gates and Goat Ramblings

P roving true to his word the smitten young hospital doctor had called round at mail order Masha's house to check she was safe from the 'on the loose pervert'. He insisted on taking her out to dinner at 'Mono Ellinka Trofima' as the only food she had in the house was her disgusting borscht and some donkey treats. He considered it was all right for his patients to eat the borscht because if it made them sick they were already in the right place to have their stomachs pumped, but he had no intention of consuming the noxious brew.

Eyebrows were raised in the taverna at the entrance of mail order Masha with her newly curled eyelashes. There was a mutter of disapproval at the presumption she was out cavorting with another man while her husband was stuck in his hospital bed with a painfully broken arm. Everyone soon realised mail order Masha appeared as completely indifferent to the avid attention of the smitten young doctor as she did to anything not related to her own vain appearance.

"'Ave you all seen 'ow ridiculous those two old women

with the taxi look after beauty parlour treatments?" mail order Masha asked the taverna goers. She was surprised no one had seen them in their garish make-up as they had planned to go out on the town showing off their new makeovers.

"I called by the 'ouse and no one was at 'ome and the taxi was gone," Prosperous Pedros said. "But I couldn't climb in through the window to check as the new iron bars work goodly."

"Old taxi parked up by harbour," Tall Thomas volunteered as the taverna customers began to worry about the whereabouts of the two elderly ladies. The police appeared no closer to arresting the person who had broken into Fotini's house with possible rape and murder in mind, meaning last night's pervert intruder was still on the loose.

Quentin and Deirdre shared the news their stay in Astakos would sadly very soon come to an end. They had to rush back to Idaho sooner than expected to attend Quentin's widowed mother's engagement party. They reassured their new village friends they planned to return to Astakos very soon. Achilles the borrowed builder had promised to get on with all the necessary renovations to make their new falling down house in Rapanaki habitable for their return.

"Well I 'ave the goodly news K-Went-In and Did-Rees. Adonis my cousin the mechanic 'ave fixed your car an' you can leave in it," Adonis promised. Once his commission had reached his pocket he had told his cousin to get on with repairing their car as his charm offensive had been most successful. "He bring car tomorrow."

"It was a blessing in disguise our car breaking down," Quentin confessed "otherwise we would have driven right by Astakos and never discovered our new falling down house and made all these wonderful new friends."

"I 'ope you say the same thing tomorrow when yous see size of mechanic bill," Adonis muttered. "We should 'ave party in garden of new 'ouse 'fore you leaves," he suggested, and his idea was warmly received by everyone.

"I bring my infamous borscht," mail order Masha volunteered, to the delight of Deirdre who was yet to sample this Russian delicacy she had heard so much about.

"'Opefully we 'ave a bit of road-kill goat too," Gorgeous Yiorgos piped up, remembering how much everyone had enjoyed the tasty delight of the Pappas' first pet goat Krasi.

"If you gets one I will scrub off tyre marks and Takis cook it," Yiota volunteered, eager to make a contribution to the party of these new excellent customers.

Gorgeous Yiorgos asked the American couple if they got much opportunity to feast on 'road kill' goat in Idaho and Quentin advised sadly not. He volunteered the information the patriotic state animal of Idaho is the Appaloosa horse.

"Po-po we not eatin 'orses 'ere," Gorgeous Yiorgos scowled "'orse meat not traditional Greek cooking."

"Is funny you 'ave an Hells Canyon in Idaho K-Went-In as we 'ave the Hells Gates near 'ere," Prosperous Pedros said, showing off his book learning from his dead father's collection of historical books.

"Yes indeed, and we also have the Craters of the Moon Monument" Quentin said.

"I thinks thats moon landing just bigly conspiracy theory," Prosperous Pedros declared, having given much consideration to the matter. His words left everyone open mouthed at the strange tangent his mind had taken in response to Quentin's geographical information.

"Yous 'ave the olive oil?" Adonis questioned, to which Deirdre replied "unfortunately not, but we have lots of potatoes."

Prosperous Pedros kindly offered to give them a tin of his most excellent extra virgin olive oil to take back to Idaho. Deirdre expressed her thanks and hoped they would have room in their suitcases for the big tin of oil along with the patriotic shower curtains and the glow in the dark plastic Parthenon she had promised Fat Christos she would buy from his new supermarket.

"I suppose we best go looking for your mother and Aunty Nitsa," Tall Thomas said to Prosperous Pedros. "They did 'ave a terrifying experience last night and the pervert thief 'as not been caught."

Prosperous Pedros reluctantly conceded the decent thing to do would be to make sure Fotini and Nitsa were safe and instructed Yiota to cancel his second order of vegetarian chicken.

CHAPTER 112

Locked in the Hardware Shop

That malaka Bald Yannis 'as locked us in," Fotini declared, fumbling her way out of the filthy back stockroom into the pitch dark hardware shop.

"Don't be rude about my new boyfriend," Nitsa scolded. "What we goin' to do now?" she asked as they groped around in the dark, bruising their frail old limbs on obtrusive shelving and bulky stock items.

"'Ere, this is one of them new-fangled torch things," Fotini cried, delighted in her discovery, and even more so when she worked out how to use it.

"Careful with that fire hazard," Nitsa warned, voicing a sudden suspicion Bald Yannis had a torch in his shop and so did last night's intruder.

"The malaka sells 'em," Fotini explained, ruling Bald Yannis out as the new prime suspect pervert.

Fotini and Nitsa moved slowly around the shop in the light from the torch. Feeling suddenly hungry they decided to see if Bald Yannis had any food stashed away and started rummaging round beneath his shop counter.

"This pie 'as got moukla," Fotini said in disgust, holding out an old spinach pie with a mouldy green crust "that Bald Yannis he got no standards. Where's that skinflint 'ide 'is emergency supply of brandy?"

Their search for food uncovered nothing more interesting than a tub of yoghurt and another manky old pie, so they were forced to imbibe Bald Yannis' supply of emergency brandy on empty stomachs.

Nitsa was pleased to find Bald Yannis' stash of under-wear catalogues. She placed a large and expensive order for sexy bras, knickers and pop socks, using the shop telephone and Bald Yannis' plastic payment card which she discovered by prising his cash register open. "I'll 'ave these undies deliv-ered to your address Fotini," she said "you be wanting any too?"

"Get me some new bloomers," Fotini ordered "mine was all stolen off the washing line."

It never occurred to either old lady in their now sozzled state they could use the telephone to summon help and be rescued from the locked-in confines of the hardware shop. However they did have the sudden brainwave of telephoning 'Mono Ellinka Trofima' and requesting Takis deliver them a take away of souvlaki and salad.

"But 'ows he going to get it through the locked door?" Fotini questioned after she had placed the order.

CHAPTER 113

Bald Yannis is Dragged out of Bed

C razy sozzled old ladies is locked in 'ardware shop and want food delivered," Takis exclaimed to his taverna customers. Gorgeous Yiorgos volunteered to run after Prosperous Pedros and Tall Thomas to alert them to the whereabouts of their mother and aunt, leaving Takis stood at the grill asking "should I cook this souvlaki or not?"

"'Ows we going to get them out?" Prosperous Pedros pondered, vigorously rattling the securely locked hardware shop door.

"Is that our food?" Fotini called from behind the locked door, before falling drunkenly into the wheelbarrow Bald Yannis had left by the side of the door.

"We either break door down or get keys off Bald Yannis," Tall Thomas said "but if we breaks door down that bald malaka may 'ave us arrested for breaking and entering."

"Best get the keys then," Prosperous Pedros concluded, telephoning Bald Yannis, only to receive a furious reaction he was expected to get out of his bed to come to the aid of those two old nuisances. Bald Yannis suffered a pang of horror he had inadvertently locked them in his hardware shop where they were no doubt creating havoc and possible breakages. He hoped they were not the snooping type as he didn't want anyone discovering his secret stash of underwear catalogues.

"Yous is bald again," Gorgeous Yiorgos noted in surprise when Bald Yannis arrived. He had spent the last hour before bed painstakingly unsticking the super glued terrible toupee from his head. The egg-like protrusion which identified him as Stavroula's strangling attacker had receded completely so he considered it safe to uncover his follicly challenged dome once more. Large patches of dried on glue marred the smoothness of his scalp, but he decided now he was at the shop he would pick up a bottle of turpentine to remove them.

"Yous looks 'orrid without 'air young Yanni," Nitsa bluntly told him as she staggered drunkenly through the now unlocked hardware shop door, hurriedly buttoning her top button so Bald Yannis could not get a quick glimpse of her now hairless chest. She didn't want this ugly man giving her the eye any longer she decided, wondering how she could ever have imagined him attractive. "Now where did we park taxi?" she asked, rattling the keys.

Prosperous Pedros insisted Nitsa was in no fit state to drive home and bundled the two old ladies brusquely into his pick-up van. The Pappas was passing by the harbour, enjoying a late evening stroll dragging the reluctant goat behind him. He noted the state of Fotini and Nitsa and decided to share with them the wisdom of one of his Biblical quotes. "Woe to him who makes his neighbours drink, you make them drunk in order to gaze at their nakedness."

"I not make them drinks brandy, they stole it," Bald Yannis responded crossly, "and I never want to see them old crones naked." With that he went angrily into the shop to find some turpentine, threatening to send Prosperous Pedros the bill for any damages in the shop.

CHAPTER 114

Debt Collectors at the Door

Toothless Tasos was far out at sea on his fishing boat before sunrise when he received a hysterical phone call from his new fiancée Thea on his new-fangled mobile phone, demanding he get back to dry land double quick.

"The debt collectors are banging at the door," his hysterical fiancée screeched. "Those 'orrible people at 'ome shopping channel 'ave sent them round."

"Don't let 'em in," Toothless Tasos instructed, promising to get back to dry land as quickly as the boat allowed. Instead of turning the engine on he sat fiddling with his fishing nets and staring out across the sea, contemplating if he really wanted to take on Thea and her many debt laden problems. He realised her spendthrift ways were not to his taste and wondered if she would be willing to change.

He sat transfixed until his attention was caught by the stately beauty of a single dolphin dancing in the water. As the dolphin was joined in its dance by a second dolphin Toothless Tasos considered a coupled existence would be far preferable to his own lonely solitary state. Whatever Thea's faults she was the goddess of his dreams and he had to admit she made his heart leap, just as the dolphins leapt gracefully in the water.

The realisation hit him whatever her faults he could no more cut Thea from his life than he could fish for dolphins. "Oh my, my Thea needs me and 'ere I sit idling," he proclaimed, turning on the engine and pointing the fishing boat back to shore.

Thea had barricaded herself in the harbour-side house, refusing to allow entry to the two ominous looking bulky debt collectors banging on her front door. She was mortified at the thought her fellow villagers would soon be roused by the noise they were making as it was quite enough to wake the sleeping village.

"What you want to goes away?" she hissed out of her upstairs window, hoping she could enter into negotiations which would not involve a cash payment as her coffers were empty. Even if Toothless Tasos turned up quickly with some money the other villagers were bound to spot the debt collectors unless she could get rid of them immediately.

The debt collectors turned out to be not unreasonable types and they agreed to go away if Thea returned some of the unpaid for tat she had acquired from the home shopping channel on credit. As she hurriedly looked through her boxes of tat she realised she had sold the unpaid for pans to Stavroula and the unpaid for jewellery to Mr Mandelis at the jewellery shop, during the house clearance sale.

The debt collectors hurriedly loaded their van up with an assorted collection of boxes of tat and Thea bid them goodbye with a loud fake "thank you so much for calling, hope to see you again soon," as she did not want the passing Pappas to come to the correct conclusion regarding the identity of her early morning visitors.

It never once occurred to the Pappas Thea's early morning callers were debt collectors as he had instead come to the instant and wrong conclusion her early morning callers were unsuitable gentlemen and Thea was running some kind of brothel out of her harbour-side house.

The Pappas gave Thea a filthy look as she was now marked as a loose woman in his eyes. He supposed this bit of juicy gossip would help get him back in the good graces of his congregation and he looked forward to improving his standing by spreading it quickly.

By the time Toothless Tasos turned up at Thea's house the debt collection crisis had been temporarily averted. Thea told him she had managed to get rid of them by returning some of the unpaid for boxes of tat, but they had threatened to return for cash if she did not settle the outstanding bills soon.

Having determined to protect his beloved from any worry Toothless Tasos suggested Thea move into his house to avoid any future encounters with the debt collectors. He had one proviso he insisted on though, telling Thea "but you 'ave to promise to stop yous spendthrift ways."

CHAPTER 115

His Darling Agapimeni

I want attractive goat," Bald Yannis told Fat Christos, who immediately asked what size he would like, pointing out if it was too big it may be difficult to cook inside a domestic oven.

"I not eat it, I not cannibal," Bald Yannis exclaimed, before hastily correcting his malapropism and saying, "I means I not carnivore, I is vegetarian."

Unlike Prosperous Pedros the 'sometime vegetarian' Bald Yannis was a fully vocal member of the 'not eating meat' club. In fact it was his vociferous assertion it was because Yiota had included chicken in her version of vegetarian meat free vegetable pie that had led to his lifetime ban from the taverna after he insisted the feather he found in his piece of pie had not come from an aubergine as she claimed.

"I want a goat more beautiful than the one the Pappas 'as," Bald Yannis stated. "I want a pleasant goat as goodly companion." The two men were looking out over Fat Christos' newly inherited herd of goats, considering the individual merits of the animals they surveyed.

GOAT IN THE MEZE

Fat Christos had at first been reluctant to do business with Bald Yannis, recalling how he had stepped over his suffering body when he was stricken down with liquidised food poisoning. Bald Yannis pointed out he'd had to throw a perfectly good pair of expensive shoes away after the stricken Fat Christos had vomited all over them, hoping Fat Christos would not recognise the shoes he was wearing as the ones in question, now hose piped clean.

His argument finally wore Fat Christos down and he agreed to sell the hardware man a goat. When he realised Bald Yannis intended to keep the goat as a companion pet he agreed to pick out a choice one, providing Bald Yannis swore he would not use it to demonstrate chain saw hair cuts on.

Finally Bald Yannis chose a particularly pretty goat he instantly named "Agapimeni" as he declared she looked so utterly darling. Scratching his head in a perplexed fashion Fat Christos watched Bald Yannis lead the goat gently away and considered the foibles of human nature never ceased to amaze him.

Returning to his new supermarket Fat Christos was excited to unpack his new stock of tourist tat, remembering to put two 'glow in the dark' plastic Parthenons to one side for Deirdre. "'Ave them goat calendars come in yet?" he asked Tassia "as I suspect they is going to be a hot cake best seller this year."

"They 'ave indeed," Tassia told him "and a thousand goat postcards too."

The newlyweds shared a delighted smile as Fat Christos guessed his prediction goats would prove to be popular this summer was off to a fine start, as evidenced by the sudden rush of villagers acquiring goats as pets.

CHAPTER 116

Squashed Gossip

Fortunately for Thea's good reputation the Pappas' scurrilous and presumptive accusations she was operating a house of ill repute from her harbour-side house were revealed as nothing more than the ramblings of his feverish imagination. As he attempted to plant the seeds to malign Thea's good name he was exposed as a malicious meddling liar by Petros the postman who had witnessed the arrival of the debt collectors, before sunrise, at Thea's front door.

"Men arrived at crack of dawn as I was delivering the mail," Petros asserted to everyone listening in the kafenion, "and is not my business what business they 'ave with 'er and is none of yous business neither. But Thea goodly woman and refuse to open 'er door at first, most likely in case someones like yous gets wrong idea about 'er morals."

With the Pappas put firmly in his place his intentions to add some malicious tittle-tattle to the local gossip vine were firmly squashed. Thanks to the astute observations of the still half-asleep postman Thea's reputation remained intact. The

Pappas announced he was going home as he knew at least the goat Nero would have no choice but to listen to what he had to say if he dragged her out for a reluctant walk.

Back at her harbour-side house Thea had no idea she was the object of village discussion. She was busy packing her suitcases for the move to Toothless Tasos' house in order to avoid a repeat of the morning's worrying encounter with the debt collectors. She assured Tasos "'I 'ave stopped buying all tat from 'ome shopping channel and will try to be less spend-thrift."

Toothless Tasos voiced his concerns that once she moved in with him she would once again have access to the tempting home shopping channel as he had a television.

"I promise yous I only watch it to keep up with gripping soap opera 'Seven Deadly Mothers-in-Law' and we watch that together," Thea promised. "Never again I buy anything from the 'ome shopping channel, yous must trusts me Taso if yous want me move in."

Thea had eagerly embraced Toothless Tasos' suggestion she put her house up for rent and use the subsequent rental income to reduce her substantial debts. The estate agent was due round later to take photographs for prospective tenants.

"Yous sure yous can live with my cat?" Thea asked Tasos for the hundredth time as they started to carry her suitcases back to his house. He reassured her he would not let her cat become an obstacle to their true love and he would learn to live with it. He was very grateful Thea had not heard anything about his selling her cat. It amused him to think the cat itself had no way of letting the cat out of the bag regarding that unfortunate blunder.

"What's that malaka doing with a goat?" he asked as Bald Yannis passed by gently tugging a ribbon clad goat on a lead.

He was surprised when the usually surly Bald Yannis stopped in his tracks to introduce his new pet, saying "meet my Agapimeni."

"That man get more crazy every day," Thea observed, adding "yous notice how he called the goat my darling. I thinks that man needs a woman." Toothless Tasos agreed as he personally found life was infinitely better since he had manned up and voiced his feelings of love to Thea.

CHAPTER 117

Is Not What Yous Think

Q uentin and Deirdre paid Adonis the mechanics car repair bill with barely a murmur. They were pleased to once again have access to their own wheels and drove straight to the neighbouring village of Rapanaki to take yet another look at their new falling down old ruined house. It was pleasant to view the property without Adonis in tow and without Achilles the borrowed builder making endlessly bizarre renovation suggestions.

"I think we will be very happy here Did-Rees," Quentin said "it is so peaceful and the views are gorgeous."

Their peace was instantly shattered by the arrival of Fotini and Nitsa who had scrambled over the garden wall and were busy gesticulating towards Quentin's car and pointing to the road. "I think they want us to drive them somewhere," Quentin said, observing the old Mercedes taxi was not in its usual parking place.

"Astakos, Astakos," the two old ladies demanded in unison, vigorously shaking their heads to indicate Quentin's guess they wanted a ride was quite correct. Before he had time to object the two old ladies had climbed into the car and showed no sign of budging.

"I suppose we'd better take them or we'll get no peace," Deirdre said, whispering to Quentin he should definitely hold them hostage in the car until they coughed up some cab fare.

Quentin dropped the two old dears off next to the old Mercedes taxi parked on the side of the harbour, and then whisked Deirdre off to lunch. Toothless Tasos had recommended a cheap taverna in the village of Marouli which had an excellent reputation for serving the very freshest lettuce.

The American pair was surprised to see mail order Masha, tarted up to the nines, already seated in the taverna, dining on lettuce and keftedes with the smitten young hospital doctor. "Is not what yous think," mail order Masha told them blushing bright red "the doctor just giving me ride to hospital to see Vasilis."

Quentin considered it was an out of the way detour to drive via Marouli to get to the hospital as it was in completely the opposite direction. Telling himself he shouldn't jump to conclusions he imagined the doctor may have been called out on an emergency en route and then Masha may have been almost fainting from hunger and needed lunch urgently. Even to his own mind his excuses for Masha sounded lame and when Deirdre piped up "it looks like Masha found someone nearer her own age," Quentin had to agree.

Their food had just arrived and was closely followed by Gorgeous Yiorgos accompanied by Petula. "Is not what yous think," Gorgeous Yiorgos quickly explained "we is out on a driving lesson and Petula was suddenly overcome with the hungers."

Deirdre was happy to see Petula's bruises had started to fade and thought she and Gorgeous Yiorgos made a lovely couple, with Petula doing far better with the fisherman than with the odious Pappas with his obtrusively straying foot.

Each couple tried their best to ignore the presence of the others, with two of the couples hoping the other two pairs were not inclined to gossip. The tranquil peace of the taverna was shattered by the sudden noisy arrival of the old Mercedes taxi.

Fotini and Nitsa cared not a whit for discretion. As they sat down Fotini loudly announced "so this is where womens goes when don't want peoples seeing them out with men not their 'usbands. Nitsa, this is goodly place for yous to come with Bald Yannis."

"Is not what yous think," said mail order Masha, the smitten young doctor, Gorgeous Yiorgos and Petula in perfect unison. As the two old crones started to cackle manically the taverna suddenly emptied, leaving Quentin and Deirdre alone with their new neighbours.

CHAPTER 118

Shop Wars Brewing

I tell yous selling these 'ere shower curtains will antagonise Bald Yannis," Tassia said to Fat Christos, unpack-
ing a box full of lobster adorned shower curtains which
she thought he had agreed not to order.

"Is 'ealthy competition," Fat Christos asserted "and these
very popular items as patriotic with many 'undreds of uses."

"I'm not sure it is worth starting shop war with Bald Yannis over this, he's a vindictive man," Tassia mused.

"I think new darling goat makes 'im changed man," Fat
Christos opined, "he asked me to order 'im some nice goat
clothes for it, but they not easy to find. Only nut jobs dress
their goats up in clothes like foreign dogs."

"I knits something for 'is darling pet goat," Mrs Kolokotronis piped up "it will be another string in my knitted goods
line."

Fat Christos was delighted to see his mother putting so
much effort into her business idea of a knitted clothes line.
The more time she spent turning into a knitting mogul the less
time she would have to create havoc with the liquidiser he

considered.

"Tell Bald Yannis to get over 'ere with 'is goat so I can measure it up for a nice knitted coat," Mrs Kolokotronis instructed Fat Christos, who dutifully jogged over to the hardware shop to relay her message.

Bald Yannis was sat at his hardware shop counter writing an itemized list of all the damage Fotini and Nitsa had caused during their drunken lock-in, as he intended to send a hefty bill to Prosperous Pedros. His bald scalp had suffered an allergic reaction to the turpentine used to remove the superglue and now featured lurid green patches on either side of his ear-to-ear transplanted strip of weed-like wiry hair.

He had discovered his credit card had been removed from the prised open cash register and at first presumed the old ladies had stolen it, until he found it wedged between the pages of one of his underwear catalogues.

A very disturbing telephone conversation with his bank manager ensued as he insisted he was the victim of fraud and had not placed a large order for bloomers, bras and pop socks. The bank manager was not inclined to believe him and Bald Yannis got stroppy, shouting "I is bald man with no man boobs to put in bras and I not wears bloomers. Cancels order for underwear and give money back."

The bank manager flatly refused to credit a refund and abruptly hung up on Bald Yannis after telling he was offended by his inappropriate language.

Bald Yannis considered it quite ridiculous the amount of his money the two old ladies had spent on underwear when they could have had their pick from the local washing lines. He was still fuming when Fat Christos arrived and told him "I think Fotini is the elusive underwear thief as she is obsessed with bloomers, she use my credit card to order two dozen pairs. Bank manager refuse refund as he thinking I is wearing the women's knickers."

Fat Christos pondered the idea it was not so absurd to imagine a man who was demanding pretty clothes for his goat would also be inclined to wear women's underwear. However he had to dismiss the idea when he remembered it was Fotini who had actually made free with the credit card and ordered the underwear.

The two men returned to the new supermarket with Agapimeni the goat in tow. As Mrs Kolokotronis took the goat's vital statistics with her tape measure Bald Yannis noticed the newly unpacked pile of patriotic shower curtains, priced at one Euro per curtain less than his own, and hit the roof.

"You goes too far Fat Christo, this loutish not gentlemanly behaviour of yous will start the shops wars. Yous think yous rivals me but yous nothing but fisherman upstart playing at keeping shop. Yous sells those patriotic shower curtains an' I starts selling goat postcards and glow in dark plastic Parthenons."

With that Bald Yannis flounced out, only to return shame faced as he had forgotten his darling goat. "This war," he screamed at Fat Christos, while pulling Mrs Kolokotronis outside to ask if she could use just the right shade of pink wool for Agapemini's new coat.

CHAPTER 119

Vasilis has a Rival

That old fool Vasilis was waiting for the smitten young doctor to discharge him from his hospital bed. He had expected him hours ago and was very disgruntled at the inordinately long wait. Mail order Masha was late too he fumed; she was supposed to be here at his bedside ready to take him home.

Mail order Masha breezed into the hospital with suspicious bits of olive twigs sticking out of her hair extensions, and the smitten young doctor following fast on her heels. "About time," Vasilis complained. "I want to get 'ome as I'm missing the donkey."

The smitten young doctor barely glanced at Vasilis' plaster encased arm as he attempted to sign the discharge papers with an olive twig stuck in his top pocket. He was gazing with besotted eyes at mail order Masha as he offered to stop by the house that evening to check up on the patient.

"You does 'ouse calls on all your patients or just ones with stunning young wives?" Vasilis questioned, to which the doctor blushed and blustered he would just happen to be passing that evening.

"Don't bother," Vasilis snapped at the doctor, "if I needs medical attention I goes to Vangelis the chemist. Now 'ows we getting 'ome Masha, who did you get ride 'ere from?"

Mail order Masha looked totally indifferent when she explained the smitten young doctor had driven her to the hospital and she hadn't considered how they would get home. "I'm on duty now," the doctor said "but I spotted a taxi waiting outside."

Mail order Masha threatened to leave her husband behind at the hospital when he refused to get into the old Mercedes taxi, driven by Nitsa, with her. "There no bus for hours and no other taxi," Masha rationalised as Vasilis procrastinated, still holding Nitsa responsible for knocking him off the donkey and breaking his arm. With no other transport option available Vasilis finally joined Masha in the taxi.

"Was accident yous knows, I is old woman and my feet not reach pedals," Nitsa cackled, reversing into a stretcher and knocking the bandaged patient onto the floor of the hospital car park. "And don't yous goes tattling to police as it yous who is breaking the restraining order by getting into my taxi. I know you 'ave yous eye on me an' should be ashamed of yourself."

Nitsa spent the rest of the drive back to Astakos confiding in mail order Masha what a terrible time she had of it as so many men had their eye on her. "I 'ave always been magnet for men who think me sexy," the deluded old crone rambled. "Even at age of eighty-two I 'ave to fight off that young Yannis at hardware shop."

"Po po, that's nasty," mail order Masha sympathised, thinking Bald Yannis must have terrible taste in women and wondering how she could sneak away later for her rendezvous with the smitten young doctor.

"Watch out," Vasilis screamed at Nitsa as she deliberately swerved to hit an innocently passing goat.

"Is okay I got it," Nitsa cackled in delight, jumping down from her pile of magazines and tossing the 'road-kill' goat into the back seat on top of her passengers.

"I been looking for a goat to road-kill because them gormless American neighbours fancy one for their leaving party. I drive it to Yiota for scrubbing. Good job Fotini is at 'ome as she 'as a dreadful fear of goats."

"Yous is mad," Vasilis exclaimed, staring down in horror as the goat's blood seeped into his plaster cast, turning it bright red.

Mail order Masha had been so intent on gazing at her fake nail extensions she hadn't even noticed the bump. Turning to Vasilis she caught sight of his plaster cast and cheered up, commenting "oh look 'usband, yous cast fashionably matches my 'air extensions."

CHAPTER 120

Invitations

Toothless Tasos headed his fishing boat back to shore, pleased with the morning's catch. He was eager to sell his fish on to Tall Thomas so he could rush home to his beloved. It was nice to have someone waiting for him at home he reflected. Thea had brought with her one of those new-fangled electric kettles and prepared him fresh coffee in one of those foreign cafetieres, rather than brewing up Greek coffee in a brik on top of the camping gas stove. He liked having someone to fuss over him and make his coffee.

When he arrived home he noticed Thea had been adding some of her womanly decorative touches to his living room. His newly acquired nailed up shower curtain had been pulled down from the window and replaced with a posh velvet curtain. Thea denounced the shower curtain as "'ideous nasty thing." The strategically placed pot used to catch drips had been polished up and put on the stove where it was being used to boil up some horta, and Achilles the borrowed builder was up a ladder patching up the leaking roof.

"Po po, he make so much dust," Thea complained "we

goes to Stavroulas for our morning coffee."

Toothless Tasos acquiesced, calculating his excellent catch would well cover the extravagant cost of two taverna bought coffees, while reminding Thea thriftiness is a virtue.

Stavroula was busy nagging Slick Socrates about the necessity of him putting in more lawyerly hours at his practice. She rather fancied opening a tourist tat shop in competition with Fat Christos' burgeoning new supermarket empire and this aspirational new venture would require a lot of his money. "Maybe new father like to contribute too," she voiced, deciding she would seek out the company of that old fool Vasilis.

Stavroula's nagging transported Toothless Tasos back to the days of their marriage when she had constantly chivvied him to bring home more money. He had hated her endless demands to improve their lot, yet conceded Stavroula had invested his and the missing Kostas' money wisely by building a modern new house and a taverna. He considered perhaps he and Thea should come up with some business venture. If Thea had something meaningful to occupy her time it may stop her from being such a wasteful spendthrift. He decided it was something to definitely sleep on.

Adonis stopped by to persuade Stavroula to cater the traditional meze of small delicious Greek dishes for the leaving party he was organising in the garden of the 'Lemoni Spiti' for Quentin and Deirdre. "Yous know no one makes meze as goodly as yous," he charmed Stavroula "and if you don't make it there will be nothing to eats but goat and mail order Masha's infamous disgusting borscht."

Spotting that old fool Vasilis making his way into the taverna Stavroula decided to impress him by praising his wife, saying "the borscht very colourful and is now recommended as 'ealthy eatin' in 'ospital." She hoped to butter the old fool up enough to consider investing in her tourist tat shop. When Adonis pressed her on the subject of the meze she reeled off a list of delicious dishes she would prepare, promising to cook courgette balls, tzatziki dip, and spinach pies at the very least.

"Why the Pappas taking 'is goat Nero in supermarket? I 'ope he not thinking to sell it back to Fat Christos as my cousin Petula loves it," Adonis asked.

"I goes find out," Stavroula volunteered as she loved to be the first one with any gossip to spread.

"I 'ear everything now," she declared on her return "it turns out Tassia is talented with the pen and the Pappas' goat is posing for its portrait."

"The Pappas he addled in 'ead," Vasilis declared, sharing a sombre look with his new daughter as they both remembered his blackmailing scam and how he had maliciously kept the truth from them until he could find a way to monetise his secret.

"At least he not spoil party as no one invite him," Adonis said, adding "yous all invited," extending an open invitation.

The impending party was also the topic of conversation in the hardware shop as Bald Yannis complained to Moronic Mitsos he was so unpopular he hadn't received an invitation. "Even those strange American tourists 'ave been invited," he moaned, only to be told by Moronic Mitsos the party was for them so of course they were going to be in attendance. Moronic Mitsos was not invited either, but he wasn't bothered as he had much more exciting plans.

Bald Yannis had read him the latest fake billet-doux which he had penned himself from the middle-aged English woman Shirley Valentine. He wrote she was planning to arrive in Greece and would definitely like to meet him. "You'd best get you yacht ready to impress her," Bald Yannis advised in amusement, watching Moronic Mitsos' brain working overtime considering how he was going to pass his leaky smelly old rowing boat off as a yacht.

"I best make appointment at beauty parlour quick," Moronic Mitsos said, remembering he had described himself as very handsome. He had no idea the imaginary Shirley Valentine planned on standing him up.

"'Ave you met my darling new pet goat Agapimeni?" Bald Yannis called out from the hardware shop doorway to a passing Quentin and Deirdre. "Come close she not bite, does not yous thinks she is a beauty?"

"Quite attractive I am sure," Quentin responded, being completely unable to distinguish one goat from another.

"She feeling a bit sad today as not invited to party," Bald Yannis told them, openly fishing for an invitation.

"Well I'm sure we'd be delighted to have her along if you'd like to bring her," Quentin offered, receiving a daggers drawn look from Deirdre. "Now darling, it would have been churlish not to invite him, he's obviously lonely," Quentin said.

CHAPTER 121

Time to Party

Deirdre was having a hard time getting the suitcases to close as they were chock to the brim with all the tourist tat she was taking back to Idaho. In addition to buying lots of lobster adorned patriotic shower curtains as special gifts for everyone back home she had to contend with forcing a glow in the dark plastic Parthenon and a life size bust of Aristotle into the bags, not to mention copious jars of home prepared olives the locals had forced on her as they knew how she favoured them.

"I am so sad to be leaving," she confided in Quentin. "I feel the people here have welcomed us and made us feel so at home."

"I feel the same darling, but it really is quite pressing we rush home. My mother's romance with this odd sounding fellow she met on the internet does sound rather dodgy and from what I gather she appears to have been wiring him money from her savings account. It is best I am on hand to find out exactly what is going on and make sure she doesn't give all her savings away to some sort of shady gigolo intent on marrying her for her money," Quentin said, whilst sitting on the suitcase to assist his wife's zipping and wearing a traditional Greek fisherman's hat Deirdre had bought him.

"Put the cases in the car Quentin," Deirdre instructed "and then we can say our goodbyes at the party and be straight on our way. It will be our last chance to see the 'Lemoni Spiti' until we return. Just imagine how different it will look the next time we see it when Achilles the borrowed builder has completed all the renovations."

It was a bit of a squeeze in the car. Along with the suitcases Quentin had agreed to give a lift to Yiota and the road kill dead goat that had been roasted on the spit for the party. Evangelia from the beauty parlour needed a ride and they had agreed to stop and pick up mail order Masha as she did not want to balance her Tupperware box of borscht on the donkey after the seeping soup disaster of the last time.

When they arrived at the 'Lemoni Spiti' they were greeted by Stavroula who was busy placing her many tempting dishes of meze on a folding trestle table in the garden. Yiota eyed the meze dishes with suspicion; certain she would have supplied a far superior selection.

Mail order Masha was dressed in her green velvet strapless evening gown covered in donkey hairs, despite it only being the middle of the afternoon. She was busy moving some of the meze dishes to one side to ensure her infamous borscht had pride of place in the centre, leaving the spit roasted road kill goat balancing precariously on the side of the table.

"Time to party," Stavroula declared, showing off the new English phrase she had painstakingly mastered especially for the occasion, impressing Quentin and Deirdre no end with her new linguistic skill.

CHAPTER 122

Goat in the Meze

Bald Yannis was so delighted to have wangled an invitation to the party he closed the hardware shop early. He was not used to receiving social invitations as he was so unpopular. He was still incensed the bank manager was refusing to give him a refund for all the underwear the two old crones had put on his credit card, but was mightily relieved the inept police enquiry had not revealed his identity as Stavroula's strangling attacker nor as the elusive underwear thief. Dressing his goat Agapimeni in the beautiful knitted pink coat Mrs Kolokotronis had finished with remarkable speed he made his way to the party.

The Pappas was skulking in the church in a furious mood he had been excluded from the party, as it showed despite all his efforts his important status in the village still went unrecognised. Nevertheless he was mightily pleased the inept police enquiry had not revealed his identity as the pervert 'on the loose' wallpaper money stealing thief who had illicitly entered the house of Fotini, nearly burning it down.

Mrs Kolokotronis had been left in charge of the supermarket as Fat Christos was taking his new wife to the party. She had a large knitting order to fulfil as Bald Yannis wanted a whole new wardrobe for his darling pet goat. She was apprehensive about her son's pending operation to have his excess skin cut off but was mightily relieved she had caused him no lasting harm with her reckless sabotage of his liquidised diet.

Achilles the borrowed builder was once again keen to promise Quentin and Deirdre by the time they returned their new falling down old house would be restored to glory. He was delighted to hear they would be recommending his imaginative use of shower curtains as a home decorative touch to all their friends back in Idaho. Adonis promised his new friends he would try to get over to Idaho for a visit, telling them "I stays in yous 'ouse and brings wife Penelope for yous to meet as she needs 'oliday."

Gorgeous Yiorgos had spruced himself up for the party by having an actual bath and a shave, and applying some aftershave, as he wanted to look his best for Petula. They arrived together, accompanied by Nero the goat who was quite happy to travel by car as long as its head was stuck out of the sunroof. Tassia was pleased to spot Petula as she had brought along the excellent and most lifelike portrait she had drawn of the goat Nero. "You have captured the goat's good looks perfectly," Petula exclaimed in delight.

Tassia explained the Pappas had commissioned her to do the portrait as a surprise gift for his wife, but she couldn't resist showing it off before he had a chance to give it to Petula. "Don't tell the Pappas I show yous as it spoil 'is surprise," she instructed.

Petula was racked with sudden guilt at the thought that here she was gadding about at a party with another man who was obviously growing fond of her, while her husband was thinking up thoughtful ways to win his way back into her good graces. His surprise gift was the most thoughtful gesture he had ever displayed, leaving Petula horribly conflicted. Bursting into tears she dropped the goat's lead and fled behind an olive tree to weep in private.

Fotini and Nitsa arrived at the party by climbing up the three-legged olive tree ladder and then scrambling over the wall. Fotini made a scene by falling off the wall and landing in a heap with her skirts in the air. Screaming loudly she had broken her leg again she was delighted to be lifted up by her son Prosperous Pedros who she thought was actually beginning to show some filial concern since the night she had almost been burnt to death by the 'on the loose' pervert.

Toothless Tasos arrived with his beloved goddess Thea. He was happy to escort her to the party as it didn't involve spending any of his money. They were closely followed by that old fool Vasilis arriving on his donkey Onos. Vasilis was furious when he spied the smitten young doctor following his wife around, and challenged him to a one-armed fist fight.

Mail order Masha hissed at the doctor to leave and told that old fool Vasilis "stop yous jealousy, yous in no condition to go round beating up doctor, I needs yous in one piece as I is ovulating. Now goes talk to Stavroula as she 'as business opportunity to discuss and then we goes 'ome to make baby."

Adonis was called over to translate for Quentin. He wanted him to tell Nitsa they would very much miss her on their next visit as he imagined her visit to Fotini would have ended by then. The words were said out of nothing more than politeness as he and Deirdre actually hoped very much the bonkers old crone would be long gone by the time they returned.

"Nitsa say to tell yous she going nowhere," Adonis relayed "she thinkin' of making permanent 'ome with Fotini as loves her cousin an' they 'ave great times together. Driving taxi 'ere is goodly way to supplement 'er meagre pension 'an she plan to make fortune in tourist season."

Nitsa was most amused to spot the look of horror the gormless Quentin and Deirdre tried to hide at this unfortunate piece of news.

Bald Yannis arrived with his darling pet goat Agapimeni. Everyone made fun of him behind his back for dressing the animal in a pink knitted jacket. Seeking out Deirdre he addressed her in perfect English, saying "I have a leaving gift for you. It is a postcard of a goat. I recall the very first time you came into my hardware shop you requested a postcard but I had none in stock, but have now rectified the matter. When you return to Astakos you will be able to buy as many postcards as you like in my hardware shop and you will be delighted to hear they are cheaper than the ones in the supermarket."

Deirdre was lost for words at the sudden change in Bald Yannis' manner, certain he had a chainsaw secreted somewhere on his person he would whip out at any moment. She thanked him for his generous gift of one free postcard but whispered to Quentin "I still don't trust him."

Before anyone had a chance to partake of the delicious food, disaster struck. The Pappas' goat Nero had wandered off and guzzled the big pan of mail order Masha's infamous borscht and was now being violently sick all over Stavroula's carefully prepared meze.

Sensing the presence of the other goat, Bald Yannis' darling pet Agapameni broke free of his hold and rushed to head butt the spit- cooked goat into the long weeds. "Don't eat goat," Bald Yannis screeched running after his pet "yous is not cannibal."

Agapimeni reacted in shock to Bald Yannis' severe tone as she was only used to the softest of words from her new owner. She gambolled away from the now ruined food table and rushed over to head butt Nitsa violently in her bottom, throwing her back over the garden wall into Fotini's garden. At the sight of the goat Fotini screamed in terror and fainted, and that old fool Vasilis was sent off on his donkey to drag the smitten young doctor back to revive her.

"I think we should slip away quietly now with no fuss Did-Rees," Quentin suggested, "it would be a pity to spoil everyone's fun by making them sad at our departure."

"I agree, let's get out of here quickly before anymore disasters unfold," Deirdre replied, as the two Americans hot-footed it to their car where they collapsed with laughter.

CHAPTER 123

Quentin and Deirdre Fancy Greek Food

D eirdre was hanging out of the car window trying to photograph as many goats as she could for posterity as Quentin negotiated the dangerous hairpin bends taking them away from Astakos.

"I didn't think we would leave our party hungry when so much food had been prepared," Quentin complained as his stomach rumbled loudly.

"I never even got to sample mail order Masha's infamous borscht," Deirdre said in dismay "but I look forward to trying it on our next visit."

"Do you want to see if you can find a McDonalds in the guide book?" Quentin asked his wife.

"Oh no, I don't fancy that at all," Deirdre replied "but I could really kill a bit of spit-roast goat served up with some horta."

Accepting an olive Deirdre passed him from the jar she had secreted in her ample bra Quentin agreed, saying "goat and horta sounds perfect darling, keep your eyes peeled for a rustic taverna."

A TASTE OF RAMPAGING ROOSTERS
Book 2 in the Greek Meze Series

"Slow down, these hairpin bends are hazardous and you'll likely get us all killed Quentin," his mother Hattie instructed from the back seat.

Quentin slowed the car down to a ludicrous five kilometres an hour, sighing inwardly at the sight of the long tail back of cars he could see in the rear view mirror, with their Greek drivers gesticulating rudely at him for holding them up.

"Watch out for that goat," Hattie shouted, spying a goat quite a distance away up a hill, minding its own business eating some olive cuttings. Hattie's endless back seat driving was causing Quentin to curse the fact they had brought his bossy and over anxious mother all the way to Greece with them. It was the first time in her life she had ever left Idaho and the transition to foreign parts was sending his blood pressure haywire.

"Oh I don't know," Deirdre piped up; trying to lighten the mood "a bit of road-kill goat would be well received where we are heading."

Her words cheered Quentin and the two shared fond smiles as they recollected how their previous encounter with a goat on this very road had led to their meeting with Adonis and their discovery of their new holiday home they were heading to now in Rapanaki. They couldn't wait to see all the renovations Achilles the borrowed builder had made to the 'Lemoni Spiti.'

"Oh no, I will kill that borrowed builder Achilles when I get my hands on him," Quentin exclaimed several hours later when he pulled the car up outside the completely untouched and still falling down 'Lemoni Spiti.'

I Hope You Enjoyed "Goat in the Meze."

If you enjoyed this book please post a glowing review on Amazon and/or Goodreads and tell all your friends who love Greece and humour. Indie authors rely on reviews to help spread the word.

Thank you!

If you would like to be notified when the next book in the Greek Meze series is available please feel free to contact me on katerinanikolas@outlook.com

~ Katerina Nikolas

Printed in Great Britain
by Amazon